AF173986

Praise for *A Simple Justice*

"Melanie Goan's pioneering, accessible, and engaging account of Kentucky suffrage is meticulously researched. She unearthed a mix of traditional and progressive women whose relentless pursuit of the vote overcame personal and societal obstacles including those exacerbated by racism and discrimination, controversy, and ridicule. Though the Nineteenth Amendment was ratified in 1920, Goan's final sentence is a charge still relevant today: to identify injustice, to resist apathy, and to correct it.
—Eugenia K. Potter, former executive director of the Kentucky Commission on Women and editor of *Kentucky Women: Two Centuries of Indomitable Spirit and Vision*

"Finally, the little-known true story of how Kentucky women won the vote is written! Not only is it extremely entertaining but it also inspires readers to continue to fight for equality for women today."
—Marsha Weinstein, former executive director for the Kentucky Commission on Women

"This book is literally years in the making. For a century, the story of women's struggle to earn the franchise in Kentucky has awaited a comprehensive and objective telling. In Melanie Beals Goan, the movement has finally found its chronicler. *A Simple Justice* is indispensable reading."
—Thomas H. Appleton Jr., Foundation Professor of History at Eastern Kentucky University and coeditor of *Kentucky Women: Their Lives and Times*

"*A Simple Justice: Kentucky Women Fight for the Vote* is a welcome contribution to the literature on the women's suffrage movement in Kentucky and in the United States. Thoroughly researched and very readable, it is a study of the growth of suffrage sentiment and organizations in a state crucial to the development of a southern suffrage movement and the success of the Nineteenth Amendment. Goan includes new material on well-known Kentucky suffragists—the 'Big Three' comprised of Josephine Henry, Laura Clay, and Madeline McDowell Breckinridge—and on lesser-known women in the suffrage struggle including African American women."
—Marjorie J. Spruill, author of *Divided We Stand: The Battle Over Women's Rights and Family Values That Polarized American Politics*

A Simple Justice

A Simple Justice

Kentucky Women Fight for the Vote

Melanie Beals Goan

UNIVERSITY PRESS OF KENTUCKY

Copyright © 2020 by The University Press of Kentucky

Scholarly publisher for the Commonwealth,
serving Bellarmine University, Berea College, Centre
College of Kentucky, Eastern Kentucky University,
The Filson Historical Society, Georgetown College,
Kentucky Historical Society, Kentucky State University,
Morehead State University, Murray State University,
Northern Kentucky University, Transylvania University,
University of Kentucky, University of Louisville,
and Western Kentucky University.
All rights reserved.

Editorial and Sales Offices: The University Press of Kentucky
663 South Limestone Street, Lexington, Kentucky 40508-4008
www.kentuckypress.com

Library of Congress Cataloging-in-Publication Data

Names: Goan, Melanie Beals, 1972– author.
Title: A simple justice : Kentucky women fight for the vote / Melanie Beals Goan.
Other titles: Kentucky women fight for the vote
Description: Lexington, Kentucky : University Press of Kentucky, 2020. |
    Includes index.
Identifiers: LCCN 2020032965 | ISBN 9780813180175 (hardcover) |
    ISBN 9780813180199 (pdf) | ISBN 9780813180205 (epub)
Subjects: LCSH: Clay, Laura, 1849-1941. | Breckinridge, Madeline McDowell,
    1872-1920. | Kentucky Equal Rights Association. | Suffragists—Kentucky—
    History—20th century. | Women—Suffrage—United States—History—
    20th century. | Suffrage—United States—History—20th century.
Classification: LCC JK1911.K4 G63 2020 | DDC 324.6/230922769—dc23
LC record available at https://lccn.loc.gov/2020032965

This book is printed on acid-free paper meeting
the requirements of the American National Standard
for Permanence in Paper for Printed Library Materials.

Manufactured in the United States of America.

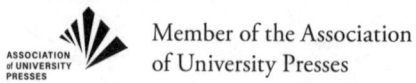

Member of the Association
of University Presses

For all the Kentucky women who cast their first ballots in 1920

And for my daughter, Addison, who will become
one of the country's newest voters in 2020

Contents

Introduction

Laura Clay, one of the South's most famous suffragists, packed a small leather suitcase on August 8, 1920, as she had so many times before. The next morning, she planned to catch a train because important suffrage business called. Unlike many of her travels that had taken her far from home and kept her away for months at a time, this would be a short trip. This trip would also be different in another important regard: it just might be her last.

Laura Clay was headed to Nashville to see whether Tennessee would become the thirty-sixth and final state needed to ratify the Nineteenth Amendment, granting women across the country the right to vote. She had been a suffragist for four decades. She had invested more energy in the work than a full-time career would normally demand. She established the Kentucky Equal Rights Association (KERA) in 1888 and served for a quarter century as its president. Even after she turned the state organization over to her hand-picked successor in 1912, she continued to be an abiding presence both behind the scenes and in the public eye. Miss Clay and the Kentucky suffrage movement were synonymous.

Over those long years, her hair had grown gray, she had become stouter, and wrinkles had formed at the corner of her eyes as she waited for the day that she would become a citizen with full rights. She had taken the podium hundreds of times to sway skeptical audiences, including governors and US senators. She had written thousands of letters to make the wheels of change begin to turn. Her name appeared so often in the newspaper that she had long ago stopped clipping all the columns.

She had spent years patiently working for one goal, and finally the end was in sight.

Of course, not everyone wanted to see women enfranchised. Plenty of opponents—women included—lined up to see the amendment defeated. Clay would join a rancorous mix of "Suffs" and "Antis" who were converging on Nashville that weekend, each hoping to convince lawmakers to vote their way. They were locked in a zero-sum game, and both needed a win in Tennessee to continue the fight.

Suffragists were running out of states that could ratify. They needed thirty-six, which meant that only twelve could say no. Southern Antis predicted that their region would stand together united against what they deemed a weapon of northern aggression. The South controlled enough votes to cut the effort off at its knees, and so far, except for Arkansas and Texas, they had managed to hold the line. Success even seemed unlikely in the border states, although Clay's own Kentucky had given a big win to suffrage forces back in January. When Delaware failed to ratify in June 1920, the Nineteenth Amendment's chances appeared slim indeed.

Suffragists needed a big win to finally get them out of their "purgatorial ordeal," which ratification had turned out to be. Plus, a well-timed win now would give them an immediate payoff: the 1920 presidential election was only three months away.[1]

For anti-suffragists, Tennessee mattered even more. If it chose to ratify, their battle would end. The Constitution would be rewritten, and women's role forever changed. Suffragists—women of the "low-neck and high skirt variety" who endorsed anarchy and black rule—would have their way, Tennessee lawmaker Hershel Candler warned. For anti-suffragists, it was do or die and they came ready to fight.[2]

Nashville's grand Hermitage Hotel, located a stone's throw from the legislative plaza, served as ground zero for the unfolding battle. Its lobbies and meeting rooms bustled with action day and night as each side recruited supporters and then tried to keep them from backsliding. Men in linen suits mingled with ladies in long dresses and fancy hats, all trying to stay cool in the stifling August heat. Representatives from both the National American Woman Suffrage Association (NAWSA), the nation's foremost suffrage organization, and the newer, more militant National Woman's Party (NWP) were on hand, each following its own careful battle plan. Their rivals, the Southern Women's League for the Rejection of the Susan B. Anthony Amendment and the National Association Opposed to Women's Suffrage, also set up headquarters at the Hermitage. Nashville became, according to one reporter intent on maximizing the drama, "the boiling point of the suffrage cauldron."[3]

For days, newspapers had been announcing that suffrage pioneer Laura Clay was expected shortly. She finally arrived at Union Station on Monday morning. She went from there to the Hermitage, taking a room on the seventh floor. Perhaps being on a higher floor would mean a better breeze. She did not choose her room with that goal in mind, but one could hope. She arrived just in time for the start of the session, and she had work to do.

There were rallies and receptions to organize, handbills to distribute, and legislators to persuade. She quickly shook off the dust of the trip and presented herself, ready to assist.

When she had freshened up, she did not join her NAWSA colleagues on the third floor, nor did she link up with militant members of the NWP. Clay bypassed the suffrage forces. She steeled herself and rode the elevator down to the first floor, where she slipped quietly into anti-ratification headquarters. She pinned a red rose to her bosom, the emblem of the Antis, grabbed one of the palm-leaf fans that were so abundant around the steamy hotel, and asked for her marching orders.[4]

Miss Clay did not come to Nashville to work for passage of the Nineteenth Amendment. She came to see it go down in defeat.

Clay had wavered on whether to come at all. Having failed to defeat ratification in her own state seven months earlier, she wondered what help she could possibly provide now. But when her close associate, Kate Gordon of Louisiana, a fellow "states' rights suffragist," asked for her help, she grimly agreed. She would do everything she could to defend her principles, even if it meant allying with her long-standing enemies, the anti-suffragists.

The Antis gleefully welcomed Clay and Gordon's assistance and proceeded to squeeze as much promotional value out of their defections as possible. Clay and Gordon insisted that their reservations concerning the amendment were very different than those of other Antis—the so-called Home, Heaven, and Mother crowd—but the distinction eluded many observers. The "centripetal force of fear" brought these strange bedfellows together. Clay likely bristled at the personal attacks the anti-ratification forces launched against her friends and at the cause she held so dear. Handbills accused suffrage forces and specifically NAWSA president Carrie Chapman Catt of everything from repudiating the Bible to defaming Robert E. Lee to jeopardizing the nation's most sacred principles. When Clay passed her former NAWSA colleagues in the halls of the hotel or in its dining room, she pretended not to see them, and they mercifully extended the same courtesy.[5]

How could a woman who had worked her entire life to gain the vote suddenly stand in the way when victory was so close? What drove her into the arms of the opposition? Clay wanted very badly to vote. She believed women were men's equal in the eyes of God and that it was time for America to live up to its promises of liberty and justice. But just as "Votes for Women"

Anti-suffrage leaders gathered in August 1920 on the eve of ratification at the home of Mrs. George A. Washington, the vice president of the Tennessee Anti-Ratification League. Laura Clay is standing toward the center of the third row, wearing a large flowered hat. (Carrie Chapman Catt albums, Bryn Mawr College Libraries, Special Collections)

was almost in hand, Clay, one of its oldest and most dedicated champions, stepped away.

This is a story of how American women got the vote and of Kentucky's role in that fight. It is a story of creative approaches, competing priorities, and severed relationships. It is the story of leaders like Laura Clay and Madeline McDowell Breckinridge who determined the course of the movement in Kentucky and of the thousands of women who supported their vision—either by contributing their time, their money, or in many cases just their names. It is also the story of women who were excluded from the Kentucky movement due to the color of their skin or their lack of wealth and status.

Suffragists predicted that it was only a matter of time before the utter absurdity of their disfranchised condition would be recognized and remedied, but it took longer than they ever dreamed: their fight stretched over seven long decades. The right to vote did not just magically materialize. It was not a gift willingly bestowed. Nor was it a natural step in the steady march of progress. As Elaine Weiss explains, while we like to think that women "staged a few picturesque marches, hoisted a few picket signs, and without much drama, 'Votes for women' was achieved . . . that's not how it happened." Rather, the suffrage movement involved a tangled web of stakeholders, entrenched interest groups, unyielding constitutional barriers, and women with competing strategies. It was, in short, a messy process.[6]

For Americans—male and female—the idea of requiring men to share political power with women seemed revolutionary and downright dangerous. Women, the movement's intended beneficiaries, were often the very people who opposed it most vehemently. Woman suffrage (although it sounds funny to a modern ear, Americans in the nineteenth century consistently referred to it as such) foreshadowed the culture wars that followed decades later. To demand that women should vote seemed to demand a complete restructuring of American society, in both the public and private realms. The Nineteenth Amendment was not welcomed by all women; many feared that it would strip them of their femininity. In a politically and religiously conservative state like Kentucky, these fears were especially potent.[7]

Woman suffrage's potential to mandate racial equality was even more terrifying to many white Kentuckians. While it seems like such a simple thing to say that all people deserve a voice in their government, the fight to achieve that high standard was anything but simple, and it remains to this day unfinished. "We were a nation torn by often vicious prejudices," historian Ann D. Gordon explains, "and a people armed with powerful tools of exclusion. Women brought those problems into their movement and did little better than anyone else in the country at resolving those conflicts." One cannot understand the fight for the vote without acknowledging that the pursuit of democracy has too often been an undemocratic endeavor.[8]

To understand the suffrage movement, we must get down in the trenches. We must follow the women and men who endured public embarrassment, who sacrificed their precious leisure time, and in some cases, gave decades of their lives to see the battle won. We must look beyond Susan B. Anthony and Elizabeth Cady Stanton, and we must travel outside of New York and

Washington, DC, to meet Americans whose names have been lost to history. Laura Clay and Madeline McDowell Breckinridge led the Kentucky movement, but they did not do it alone. While this book is largely their story, along the way you will meet many other individuals—men and women, black and white—across the Commonwealth who, while not entirely successful, did their part to move the nation closer to achieving its ideals.

1

The He-Women Come

To get to Kentucky from the North, one must cross the Ohio River. At its widest point near downtown Louisville, the Ohio River spans but a mile. A good swimmer could easily traverse it in less than an hour. But what it represents is much greater. In the antebellum period, it was a transportation lifeline for a developing frontier. When the Northwest Territory banned slavery, it became the escape route to freedom; slaves risked their lives and those of their children to cross. Coming out of the Civil War, the Ohio River resembled a scar, cutting through a wounded nation.

Even though Kentucky never seceded from the Union, Americans saw the Ohio River as the place where the North ended, and the Southland began—and for good reason. In its frontier days, Kentucky started out more west than south, but that, like so much, changed with the War. It has famously been said that Kentucky waited until after the Civil War to secede. Many of its white citizens, who signed on to defend the Union at the outset, grew bitter as the War turned into a fight to end slavery. They felt deceived, as their postwar choices indicate. In the years to follow, they celebrated the Lost Cause, they embraced the Democratic Party, and they went on a crusade to build Confederate monuments.[1]

When it came down to it, Kentuckians by and large whistled Dixie. They respected southern values, particularly the region's commitment to patriarchy and white supremacy. Like their neighbors further south, many bristled as calls for black voting rights and woman's rights challenged the patriarchal order that they viewed as natural and sacred. Upholding patriarchy was "not just an isolated, idiosyncratic whim of nostalgic Southerners," historian Marjorie Spruill Wheeler reminds, it was "part of an intense, conscious, quasi-religious drive to protect the South against the 'ravages' of Northern culture during a period of massive and often unwelcome political, social, and economic change." Woman's rights would be a tough sell in a region turned upside down by the War and its aftermath.[2]

In 1926, in his classic history of Kentucky during the Civil War and "Readjustment" (the border state equivalent of Reconstruction), E. Merton

Coulter acknowledged the woman's rights movement's difficult start. It is unclear who believed the concept more ridiculous, Coulter, or his nineteenth-century subjects. Suffrage was imported by "dissatisfied Yankee women . . . whose names were forgotten when marriage licenses were being issued," he scoffed. These interlopers were only able to attract attention, he claimed, because they sold woman suffrage on its ability to counteract "negro suffrage." Dismissive though he was, he was astute enough to recognize that woman suffrage was never just a gender issue, it was always a race issue too.[3]

Writing just six years after the American electorate expanded to include women, Coulter still saw the movement as a bit absurd. Radical, unwomanly, and imported, suffrage did not mesh well with Kentucky's conservative values. "The seeds were being sown, but nothing but rocky ground awaited them in Kentucky," Coulter reported.[4]

Woman suffrage would not be an easy sell in Kentucky by any means, but some of these seeds were destined to take root. The Commonwealth was not an infertile field as Coulter claimed, but rather became active ground for northern suffrage organizers both before and after the Civil War. Crossing the Ohio River was a key step in their plan to make suffrage into a truly national, and they hoped a winning, movement.

Lucy Stone, known for having a voice like a silver bell, was one of the first northerners to cross into Kentucky to sow woman's rights seeds in 1853. Stone was used to going against the grain, and she was undaunted by the challenges her visit to Louisville was sure to bring. Tackling the South was like carrying the "war into Africa," one of her suffrage colleagues later noted. Stone was up for the challenge.[5]

Stone attended the Oberlin Collegiate Institute, one of the nation's first interracial and coeducational institutions, but even a progressive college like Oberlin was not prepared to take on the likes of young Lucy, who suffered through a stormy career there. She studied to be a schoolteacher, but she could not bear it that male teachers earned higher salaries than equally qualified women. She decided instead to become a public orator. The meeting hall would be her classroom, the nation her students.[6]

The Massachusetts Anti-Slavery Society hired Stone as a lecturer in 1848. When she began mixing women's rights with abolition, however, her sponsors balked. Stone reminded leaders of the society that she had been a woman before she became an abolitionist and continued to do as she pleased. By the 1850s, she was recognized as one of the most famous women in

America, a distinction that did not make her embarrassed family any happier about her career choice.[7]

It was not easy work. She became accustomed to hostile crowds. Some audience members signaled their displeasure by throwing rotten fruits and vegetables. Others pelted her with "coarse and ribald speech."[8]

Stone expected to witness the same hostility or worse from southern audiences. Her message was sure to rub white southerners wrong in two directions: an abolitionist and a proponent of women's rights would face an uphill battle here, she assumed. Kentuckians had heard that some women were complaining about the limitations of their sex, but they had yet to see these complaints delivered in person.

Louisville was abuzz weeks before Stone arrived in November 1853. If her subject matter was not intriguing enough, her clothing choices guaranteed that she would get plenty of attention. Newspapers announced that she would be sporting the Reform Dress, also known as the "Bloomer costume" in honor of its popularizer Amelia Bloomer, or the "Turkish Trousers" in reference to its construction. The Bloomer looked normal from the waist up, but below that point, it was thoroughly unconventional, with its short full skirt, layered over a long set of pantaloons. Less about fashion and more about freedom of movement and healthy living, bloomers allowed the wearer to shed her "spine destroying" dresses, corsets, and layers of petticoats. The *Louisville Daily Courier* first took note of the trend in May 1852, noting that women, including "seven ladies of respectable appearance," had been spotted wearing Bloomer dresses in Philadelphia. The following spring, Bloomers were available for sale in Louisville, but whether they found wearers is anyone's guess.[9]

The thirty-five-year old Stone not only donned the Bloomer costume (and continued to do so for four long years, even after her beleaguered colleagues went back to long skirts), she kept her hair cut short, clipped at the chin, and tucked behind her ears, giving her a startling boyish look. Nineteenth-century white women rarely wore short hair unless they lost it to illness or were inmates of the poorhouse and fending off lice. Short hair made a bold statement.[10]

Louisville residents bubbled with curiosity. What would Stone look like and what would she say? George D. Prentice, editor of the *Louisville Daily Courier* and one of the first to greet the city's guest, provided his readers a sneak peek. He praised "Miss Lucy" for her "beauty" as well as her "force" and her "eloquence." His compliments came, not by accident, in that order since a southern gentleman was conditioned to measure women according to appearance. Prentice had expected a manly, irrational "Abolition agitator," but instead he encountered an attractive woman who presented a subject "chock full of common sense."[11]

When planning her Louisville stop, Stone questioned whether any listeners would show up, but with the *Daily Courier*'s ample coverage, she had no need to worry. Three talks were scheduled over four nights in Masonic Hall. All were astonished, even Miss Stone, by the size of the first night's audience, Prentice reported. The weather was terrible—rainy, sloppy, and muddy, a challenge especially for "long skirted ladies," who one suspects may have wished they too had embraced the Bloomer fad—but they came anyhow.[12]

In her first two talks, Stone chose to cover topics that were close to the hearts of conservative southerners: the Bible and marriage. She titled her last talk "The Social and Educational Disabilities of Woman," gently nudging her listeners out of their comfort zones. When the ladies of Louisville requested that Miss Stone "favor them with an afternoon lecture," a reprise of her Bible exegesis, she happily complied. The press gave "full and friendly reports" after each talk, allowing many more than the thousands that filled the lecture hall to hear her message.[13]

In late November, Stone moved on to Indianapolis, satisfied with a job well done. The South had not been so scary after all. The *Daily Courier* sent her off with a jaunty but dismissive couplet, suggesting that while he remained a paragon of hospitality and chivalry, Prentice had no intention of accepting the cause Stone peddled: "Her dress is somewhat scanty / But her tongue is somewhat long; Her heart is right they tell us / But we know her head is wrong."[14]

Stone's work in Louisville was part of a one-two punch delivered to Kentucky that year. The month before, upriver in Maysville, Lucretia Mott similarly introduced the idea of women's rights when she spoke on "Human Freedom" at the courthouse. A cordial though skeptical observer noted that though a "Radical," she was an "old girl of talent." Kentuckians were willing to hear women's rights advocates out, but their messages would be slow to sink in.[15]

Having heard the Declaration of Independence recited so often, modern observers forget how truly revolutionary its words were and are. When the US founders proclaimed, "We hold these truths to be self-evident, that all men are created equal, that they are endowed by their Creator with certain unalienable

Rights, that among these are Life, Liberty, and the pursuit of Happiness," they turned existing worldviews completely on their heads. In the eighteenth century, most Europeans assumed that some individuals were chosen to rule, and all others were destined to be ruled. Hereditary monarchy was the prevailing form of government. The American Revolution and the Enlightenment that fueled it led to a political reimagining of spectacular proportions.

The birth of American democracy transformed the world, but it also raised troubling inconsistencies and quickly revealed its imperfections. Historian Anna-Lisa Cox concedes "While the men that signed the Declaration may not have had the imagination or courage to envision a nation where all men were truly free and equal, others around them were acting on these ideals, their imaginations sparked by a new way of thinking about people and societies."[16] Inspired poor white men, African Americans, and even women took the promises at face value and set out to claim the blessings of liberty that the new nation so boldly promised. They quickly discovered, however, that the promises of equality had limits.

The great American experiment—and that is exactly what it was, a risky venture in no way predestined for success—was bold on paper but more restricted in practice. It was hard to tamp down the fear that the whole thing would implode. After all, ancient Athens was the model of democracy and look how it had ended. Throwing off British control through military action was just the first step. The gritty work of putting revolutionary ideals into practice would take much longer. The real revolution would be written in ink, not blood.[17]

What kind of government would be created and who would have a say in it? Much was at stake.

Many today might be surprised to learn that the US Constitution, so thoughtfully framed—some would say divinely inspired—does not grant anyone the right to vote. The Constitution and even the Bill of Rights are silent on the topic, only vaguely guaranteeing to every state "a Republican Form of Government." State suffrage laws, rather than federal standards, determine the franchise, even in national elections.

The omission, political historian Allan J. Lichtman argues, was a "consequential mistake." Only through constitutional amendment could the federal government protect voting rights. These amendments—the Fifteenth Amendment dealing with race, the Nineteenth Amendment concerning sex, and the Twenty-Sixth Amendment addressing age—are all framed negatively, stipulating what states cannot do, not what they must do.[18]

In part, the failure to identify who could and could not vote reflected a respect for established procedure. Largely built on imported British common law, American voting traditions predated the Constitution. Requirements varied from state to state, but most typically only enfranchised propertied white males. Owning property signaled that a voter had a stake in society and could exhibit independent judgment without fear of manipulation. And in a period when most Americans earned their living off the land, this requirement made sense. But in the wake of the Revolution new states began to drop property requirements and to rethink who deserved a voice.

During the heady days after the Revolution, with high-minded rhetoric still echoing in Americans' ears, states rewrote their constitutions. More white men gained voting rights, and in some cases, states even added women and black men to the voting rolls. The frontier especially identified itself as a progressive place that nurtured freedom. For example, when Kentucky became the fifteenth state added to the Union in 1792, it allowed all males over the age of twenty-one, property owners or not, to vote. Freed black men could even cast ballots at first, but they lost that right when the state rewrote its constitution seven years later. In 1800, only five out of sixteen states specified white-only voting; by 1860, almost all did.[19]

Women too had caught the Revolutionary spirit and were demanding a greater voice in public affairs. They argued that their wartime contributions —helping to feed and shelter troops, raising money, even occasionally serving as spies and soldiers—had earned them a say. "Remember the Ladies," Abigail Adams sharply and famously reminded her husband.

As the nation moved away from the Revolution, however, its commitment to liberty and justice dwindled. New Jersey became the first state to allow women to vote when it revised its constitution in 1776, but it revoked this right in 1807 in a partisan move. A Democratic-Republican–leaning legislature "reinterpreted" the state's voting clause, driving out women who in large measure supported the Federalist party. Calls to expand the electorate were heard less often the further the nation moved from the Revolution.[20]

Despite Abigail Adams's insistent reminders, the ladies were largely forgotten in the new republic. They were citizens by birth, assuming they had white skin, but citizenship did not automatically confer political rights. They continued to hold dependent status, classified with children, the mentally ill, and slaves, none of whom leaders trusted to think for themselves. Coverture— the legal tradition that made a woman's property the domain of her husband after marriage—remained in place. Women could not write a will, nor could they testify in court. They were publicly invisible.[21]

However, the war had brought too many changes and the revolutionary spirit was too strong to leave traditional gender roles completely untouched. Woman's public role remained limited, but her private role became redefined and politicized in the early nineteenth century, as the run-of-the-mill mother transformed into the superior "Republican Mother." A new nation needed virtuous citizens, and who better to produce them than righteous, educated, politically astute mothers?[22]

More and more, as the nation industrialized, men's and women's spaces were being precisely defined and segregated as they settled into separate spheres. Men went out to work, where they confronted the rough-and-tumble world of American commerce. Women provided a welcoming sanctuary for them when they returned home at night. In the early nineteenth century, the "cult of true womanhood" took hold, telling white women that they should strive to be pure, pious, self-sacrificing, and thoroughly domestic. They must serve as the antidote to the clawing, competitive, self-interested men that a modern industrial economy demanded.[23]

White women's exalted status as the moral guardians of the home elevated them, but it also tied their hands and left them politically neutered. To engage in politics would be to sully themselves and to give up their place on a pedestal. Women were above politics, men insisted. Their minds were focused on higher and purer matters.

The "true woman" was supposed to be home focused, but her work as society's moral guardian could not be so easily contained within its walls. Women's efforts to nurture the weak and to uplift the fallen spilled into the public sphere. Swept up by the Second Great Awakening, white women created voluntary associations and applied their special womanly touch to troubled communities.[24]

As mothers, women had a natural interest in issues involving children, and here also their efforts blurred the line between public and private, as when the Kentucky legislature created a common school system in 1838. Kentucky was certainly not the first state to prioritize public education, but its tardy attempt to catch up was pathbreaking in one important respect: Kentucky legislators quietly granted some women the right to vote on school matters, without them even asking for the privilege, it seems.[25]

Only a few women were enfranchised in limited situations, and likely few took advantage of the privilege, especially since it took at least a decade for most counties in the state to organize public schools. Still, Kentucky's school suffrage provision was unprecedented. Widows and single women ("femes sole") over the age of twenty-one who paid school taxes could vote, either in person or by proxy, on tax levies and to elect school trustees. The statute did not mention race, but presumably only white women would qualify; the promise of a common school education did not extend to black children. Women living in Lexington, Louisville, and Maysville were not covered since those communities had already created separate school systems.[26]

Although women would later use school suffrage as an opening wedge to push for full enfranchisement, this 1838 act appears less about empowering women and more about taxpayer rights. Large sums of money would flow through the school fund, and the monies could easily be misappropriated, legislators feared. Taxpayers, women included, needed to protect themselves from getting fleeced. The provision did not just give women a vote; it also allowed guardians to cast ballots on behalf of landowning minors, suggesting that property rights were its main concern.[27]

Regardless of the motive, Kentucky's unprecedented decision to give women a voice in school matters would be remembered for years to come. It was a small victory—"one little star of light," reformer Wendell Phillips proclaimed—but it was a starting point and it made Kentucky an example for the nation.[28]

During the antebellum period, no issue proved more effective at pulling women into the public sphere and at setting the stage for the developing woman's rights movement than abolition. Women, alongside men, decried the evil that slavery represented; as they did, they could not help but notice the limitations that sex placed on them. The Garrisonian wing of the antislavery movement welcomed women as full participants. They did so, partly because their Quaker background made them more open-minded, but also because women had a reputation for being excellent fundraisers. Women would get out and hustle, William Lloyd Garrison knew. He wanted them on his team.[29]

If Garrison had done a cost-benefit analysis, he may have wondered whether women were worth the trouble. They were not always content to follow instructions. In the 1830s, Angelina and Sarah Grimké, South Carolina sisters from a slave-owning family, began addressing northern audiences. It was not so much their words—although southerners certainly found their message threatening—but rather their simple act of moving out of the parlor and onto a public stage that Americans, including their abolitionist colleagues, found shocking. When critics insisted that they follow the Bible's instruction to keep silent, the Grimkés refused and instead began to advocate for woman's rights.[30]

Male abolitionists tried to shush the sisters. Discussing women's rights would jeopardize their antislavery work, they pragmatically argued. Woman's rights was associated with flamboyant, controversial foreign figures like Frances Wright, and with off-the-wall utopian schemes like Robert Owens's New Harmony community. To most Americans these ideas seemed ludicrous and dangerous. Abolition had enough obstacles to overcome without marrying itself to another provocative issue.[31]

But just as the civil rights movement of the 1960s helped to spark the women's liberation movement, the abolition movement a century earlier inspired and positioned women to recognize and resist their own bondage. Male abolitionists were all for freedom on southern plantations, but not at their own firesides. The hypocrisy of sexist abolitionists soon became too obvious for women to overlook.[32]

Most Americans today, if they know anything about the history of women's rights, identify a meeting in Seneca Falls, New York, in 1848 as the movement's beginning. The story could start in other places, but suffrage pioneers Elizabeth Cady Stanton and Susan B. Anthony chose to open their massive six-volume *History of Woman Suffrage* here. Stanton and Anthony understood the power of history, and they very consciously created what historian Lisa Tetrault calls the "Myth of Seneca Falls" in order to solidify their legacy as leaders of what was really a diffuse and at times sharply divided movement.[33]

Stanton and Anthony memorialized Seneca Falls. However, they emphasized that this historic meeting would not have taken place if women had been more kindly received at the World Anti Slavery Convention in London in 1840.[34]

Anthony was not in London (nor was she at Seneca Falls, for that matter). It was Stanton, there on her honeymoon, who suffered the abuse. Elizabeth Cady and her new husband, Henry Stanton, both claimed strong abolition credentials, so they figured the convention would be the perfect place to consecrate their union. Their romantic plan fell apart, however, when convention delegates voted to seat only men (Henry, for the record, voted against this proposal). The new bride would spend her days in the gallery while her husband went to work inside.

Left with plenty of time to ponder the injustice of her situation, Stanton made friends, including Lucretia Mott, a well-known Quaker minister in her fifties, who became Stanton's mentor. Before they left London, the two women, hot with embarrassment and seething with anger, pledged to hold a woman's rights convention as an act of protest when they returned to "the land of the free and the home of the brave."[35]

But good intentions were interrupted by the demands of domestic life. The new Mrs. Stanton had a lot on her plate with a husband who traveled frequently and a house full of active and needy children (all boys and prone to mischief). Her wealth and status meant that she had assistance from servants, but they tended to come and go, while the housework was never-ending. Mrs. Stanton read a lot, in between cooking, baking, washing, and nursing, and she worked to win property rights for married New York women, but it was not enough to satisfy her intellectual urges. She was restless.[36]

News that Lucretia Mott would be traveling through the Finger Lakes region in 1848 surely cheered her up. She looked forward to seeing an old, dear friend. The two women had not forgotten their promise to hold a woman's rights convention, made while walking arm in arm down the streets of London years before. Now reunited, they decided the time was finally right. They would hold a meeting to discuss the social, civil, and religious condition and rights of women.[37]

Three hundred people, drawn from communities surrounding Seneca Falls, turned up ten days later, arriving in buggies and wagons, on horseback and on foot. Never had women gathered publicly to state their own griev-ances. They were not there to champion the needs of the poor or widows or orphans; they were not there to promote temperance or to end slavery. They were there to demand woman's equality, and it was a first. Mott, a nationally known speaker, was the drawing card of the event, but Stanton was its intel-lectual force.

Leaning on the revolutionary power and sacred authority of the Declaration of Independence, Stanton drafted her own "Declaration of Sentiments," which she laid before the assembly. The document, "every bit as outrageous in her time as Mr. Jefferson's had been in his," stressed the ways that society violated natural law by preventing women from living up to their potential. Women lacked education and control over their own property. Stanton dropped a bombshell by insisting that women be given "immediate admission to all the rights and privileges which belong to them as citizens of these United States," including the elective franchise.[38]

Stanton knew how shocking that last demand would be. She ran the resolution by family and friends in advance, and they urged her to cut it. Mott warned, "Lizzie, thee will make us ridiculous." Henry Stanton likewise urged his wife to show restraint. Asking for educational opportunities, property rights, and divorce laws was one thing, but enfranchising women? Remove the part about the vote, he warned, or he would boycott the convention.[39]

Many people were on hand to witness Elizabeth Stanton make history that hot July day when she stated clearly and loudly that women must vote, but her husband was not one of them. He left town, just as he had threatened.

Though her husband failed to stand with her, others did. Committing themselves to "the final triumph of the Right and the True," sixty-eight women and thirty men signed the document. It took a persuasive speech by former slave, Frederick Douglass, to win support for the controversial franchise resolution, but in the end, even it passed.[40]

Sparks of interest in woman's rights flashed in the 1840s, but they would need to smolder a while before igniting. Finally, the fire started to crackle at the end of the Civil War. Reconstruction brought new hope to both former slaves and women. Ratification of the Thirteenth Amendment, redeeming the sin-stained nation and at last breaking slavery's tenacious hold, suggested momentous change was possible.

Proponents of women's rights felt the wind in their sails, especially as the frontier set an example for the rest of the nation. Wyoming Territory gave women the vote in 1869 and Utah followed in 1870. Elizabeth Cady Stanton and Susan B. Anthony believed nationwide universal suffrage would soon follow.[41]

But just when success seemed at hand, the resources necessary to accomplish this feat dried up. Male abolitionist leaders like Wendell Phillips controlled the purse strings, and they believed it best to fight one battle at a time. This must be the "Negro's hour." It would have been so easy to slip an extra word into the Fifteenth Amendment, ensuring that the right to vote could not be denied on account of "race, color, sex, or previous condition of servitude." But the fight for women's rights would wait.[42]

The Reconstruction amendments—the Thirteenth, Fourteenth, and Fifteenth Amendments—drove a wedge in the woman's rights movement for the next two decades and led to the creation of two competing organizations.

Lucy Stone, along with her husband, Henry Blackwell, and moderate feminists like Julia Ward Howe, formed the American Woman Suffrage Association (AWSA). They supported black suffrage, the Fifteenth Amendment, and the pursuit of woman suffrage through state action. Susan B. Anthony and Elizabeth Cady Stanton, unwilling to take a backseat to black men, formed the National Woman Suffrage Association (NWSA) and set their sights on a Sixteenth Amendment guaranteeing women's right to vote.[43]

Both groups agreed on the need to spread their message to new regions. They also agreed that Kentucky—that "one little star of light"—was the place to begin. It had been one of the first places in the country to allow women to vote, and national speakers had received a cordial welcome there. Lincoln had noted famously during the war that he hoped to have God on his side but that he must have Kentucky. Suffragists said the same.

With railroad tracks running through its quaint, some might say sleepy downtown, Glendale, Kentucky, today offers antique shopping and a nice, quiet spot (unless the train picks that moment to come through) to grab lunch.[44] Strolling down its main street, it is hard to imagine that this town, an hour south of Louisville, was home to the first woman's rights organization in Kentucky, and quite possibly in the South, in 1868.

None of the courageous individuals who came forward to endorse woman's rights in Glendale is known by name. The only record of the short-lived organization comes from a letter published in the suffrage newspaper, the *Revolution*. At its formation on the first of October, the association had twenty members; two months later membership was up to fifty, a Glendale resident reported. They hoped to soon have "the whole of Hardin County, and . . . the whole of the state of Kentucky enlisted on the side of *Woman's Rights*."[45]

The anonymous correspondent failed to indicate why the small community suddenly found itself so taken by the issue. Likely a single individual or a nucleus of open-minded people led the effort. Perhaps, the same people who raised the suffrage question were also responsible for establishing nearby Lynnland Female Institute the year before. It certainly seems plausible that champions of white women's education might have also supported equal rights, although it was a Baptist school and Baptists were not known for challenging the status quo.[46]

Perhaps Glendale residents were influenced by the work of economist and suffragist Virginia Penny. Penny, a native of Kentucky, conducted studies of women wage earners and published her findings in *Employments of Women*. She also became the first Kentuckian to serve as an officer of a national suffrage organization when the AWSA elected her a vice president in 1867.[47]

More likely, Elizabeth Cady Stanton and Susan B. Anthony's October 1867 visit to Louisville got the conversation started. The two "celebrated ladies" shared the stage with the Greenback Party's infamous George Francis Train, who grabbed attention wherever he went. Observers at the time called him "rambling," "irrepressible," and "eccentric." Today, we might just condemn him as a white supremacist. Author Elaine Weiss describes him as a "flamboyant businessman with an appetite for unpopular causes and an unsavory reputation for unbridled racist sentiments."[48]

Stanton and Anthony chose to team up with Train after the abolition movement cut off their financial support. An alliance with Train guaranteed not only cash but also notoriety. The way Stanton saw it, they were only doing what they had to do to advance their cause. By allying with Train, however, they announced that white suffragists' commitment to universal rights was entirely negotiable.

"Why should the plantation boor—the unlettered, ignorant African . . . who has nine cubic inches less of brain inside his thick skull" vote when superior white women are prevented from doing so? Train sneered. Train firmly linked the causes of black suffrage and woman suffrage together in Americans' minds, and they would stay forever linked.[49]

We have no way of knowing whether the suffragists in Glendale were influenced by Train's words and his racist rationale. They never stated their reasons for supporting woman's rights. After a short period of growth, the group apparently lost interest. No further record of the organization appears, leaving a bit of a mystery for historians who want to know more.

The Glendale Association's formation must have come as a surprise to many Kentuckians. Chivalrous Kentucky gentlemen had a hard time imagining that the pure and virtuous women of their state—"perfect, just as they were"—could ever give a moment's thought to women's rights. If they did, outsiders must be to blame. "Yankee Girls" were the only ones who were restless, not Kentucky wives and mothers. Kentucky newspapers frequently painted unflattering portraits of northern women. They spent too much money, were unattractive, had shapeless calves, and were unskilled in the art of seduction, various critics insisted.[50]

Beautiful and charming southern belles had their northern sisters beat in every way, it seemed, but it was northern women's efforts to upend the social order, particularly their push for the vote, that made them seem most ridiculous. Newspapers had names for these agitators, a shorthand that identified their demands as outlandish and dangerous: they were "strong-minded women," "suffrage shriekers," or "female fanatics." They were inter-lopers who intentionally sought to destroy the southern way of life.[51]

One only had to look as far as Dayton, Kentucky, critics charged, to see the damage outsiders were inflicting on southern communities. A contro-versy erupted in the fall of 1871, when Dayton councilmen announced the city would take on additional bonded indebtedness. When fiscally minded citizens questioned the decision, the councilmen decided to hold a referen-dum. Since the bond issue concerned taxpayers and because there was a rec-ognition that "taxation and representation are inseparable," qualified women were invited to vote on the matter.[52]

The *Frankfort Yeoman* reported that Dayton women flagrantly went to the polls the following January to cast ballots. The fact that they voted was not in and of itself scandalous, it seems; it was how they did it that ruffled feathers. Instead of quietly submitting their votes by proxy, they marched to the polls arm in arm with their husbands and voted in person. If that was not audacious enough, they intentionally cast votes opposite those of their hus-bands just to flaunt their independence. The *Yeoman* stressed that this esca-pade was not the women's idea; they were "prevailed upon by some of their indiscreet male friends . . . probably from the other side of the Ohio River."[53]

The indiscreet male friends the reporter referenced surely included J. B. Quinby, although he claimed no responsibility in his account of the day's events that he submitted to the *Woman's Journal.* Quinby credited his wife, Ann, a taxpayer and a "zealous advocate for Woman Suffrage" for convincing her female friends and neighbors, including the wives of Dayton's mayor and its Methodist preacher, to vote. Quinby agreed that some husbands and wives cast opposing votes but believed there were no hard feelings at the end of the day.[54]

The Quinbys had a long history of fighting injustice. The couple met in New Orleans before the Civil War, brought together by their hatred of the slavocracy, which they boldly challenged. When things got too "hot" for them during the war (one suspects it was not just the humidity that both-ered the abolitionists), they relocated to Cincinnati. Mr. Quinby started sev-eral newspapers, but his ideas were too radical to get much traction. His wife also tried her hand at publishing, producing a suffrage newspaper that, according to their son, managed to attract few readers. The couple settled for good in Kentucky in the 1870s, in the town of Dayton, nestled in the bend of the Ohio River. Though they came from outside the state, as critics charged, they must have found some like-minded individuals in their new home.[55]

Mr. Quinby celebrated the events in Dayton that day. He challenged readers of the *Woman's Journal* who assumed Kentucky's history as a slave state made it resistant to change to see it in a new light. A Kentucky city had "set the suffrage ball in motion," he boasted, promising that more progress was sure to come.[56]

Worried Kentuckians, however, saw this bold act not as a step toward progress, but rather as a harbinger of impending social doom. The events in Dayton, if repeated, would expose women to "the infectious pollutions, the horrid contaminations that . . . envelope the ballot box." If civilization continued to go down this path, the *Frankfort Yeoman* warned, there would be "no more women in this country—nothing but a nation of big-bearded men and vaunting Amazons."[57]

Dayton women's cheeky public display was not an isolated event but rather part of a larger national strategy of civil disobedience in the 1870s— what suffrage leaders called the "New Departure." If read the right way, the Fourteenth and Fifteenth Amendments to the Constitution could be interpreted as already applying to women, who were after all considered citizens. Perhaps all they needed to do was simply march to the polls and claim their rights, suffragists argued.[58]

Susan B. Anthony was not the first woman to engage in this form of direct action, but she became the most famous when in the fall of 1872, she cast her ballot for president. Anthony's experiment did not turn out as well as the one the Quinbys led in Dayton. Officials felt they must make an example of the famous suffrage leader. They arrested her and charged her with illegal voting. They slapped her with a hundred dollar fine, though no one had the audacity to collect it, she recalled. Two years later, the Supreme Court ruled in *Minor v. Happersett* that the US Constitution did not confer voting rights on anyone. The New Departure proved a dead end.[59]

With no shortcut available, a tedious effort to convince Americans that women deserved the vote and that their participation would benefit society would necessarily follow. It would require new legislation—either revisions to every state constitution or a federal amendment—and it would require an exhausting national educational campaign. The NWSA and the AWSA buckled down for a long fight.

Suffrage appeared threatening because it was imported from the North, but even worse, its ties to multiple radical causes—real or imagined—upped the danger in many observers' minds. Though slaves had long ago been emancipated, the movement's roots in abolition made it an automatic nonstarter for many Kentuckians. Then, there were its supposed connections to socialism, communism, anarchy, and free love. To embrace one "ism" was to embrace them all, opponents warned.[60]

Victoria Claflin Woodhull epitomized the "Ranting Radicals," who, conservative Americans warned, were inciting bedlam with their crazy ideas. Woodhull, a multitalented newspaper editor, stockbroker, and future political candidate, shocked many with her support for free love in the 1870s. To endorse free love meant acknowledging women's sexual desire. It also meant seeing women as sexual beings who did not exist simply for the purpose of procreation. Woodhull's insistence on full sexual freedom—she would change lovers daily if she so chose, she insisted—raised eyebrows among suffragists let alone more conventional observers.[61]

These ideas certainly did not fly in the South, where evangelical religious views held sway. The Apostle Paul enjoined women to keep silent and Ephesians told women to submit, injunctions that obedient southerners took to heart. Armed with the most powerful tool possible, the inerrant word of God, critics of woman's rights argued that suffrage was not only inadvisable, it was the road to damnation.[62]

Strong-minded women violated social norms simply by speaking up. A vocal woman, no matter her tactics or specific reform goals, was unnatural in a world that expected her to be quiet, obedient, and self-sacrificing. One editorial painted a vivid picture of the "pushing woman" (another code phrase), who steamrolled everyone in her path. She demanded a seat before it was offered, poked "luckless boys" with her umbrella, and harassed waiters and ticket-sellers. And woe to "the pale, scared and meek husband" who trailed after her hoping to die but "forbidden to do so."[63]

It was easy to dismiss suffragists out of hand with caricatures, but opponents, who eventually mobilized to become known as anti-suffragists, went further. They offered a variety of specific arguments to justify women's exclusion from politics. For instance, women did not defend the nation. One Kentucky farmer asked, is it fair to expect men to "work the public

THE AGE OF BRASS.
or the triumphs of Woman's rights

Society expected the ideal nineteenth-century woman to be submissive and to focus on the needs of others. Supporters of the woman's rights movement were characterized as unnatural and unbecoming. "Suffrage shriekers" threatened the social order, as this 1869 Currier and Ives image makes clear. (Library of Virginia)

roads, and do all the fighting" and for women simply to vote and hold office? Women, he alleged, did not attend to the serious matters of life and instead would use their votes to obtain frivolous goals, like lowering the tariff on ribbons and bonnets.[64]

The most powerful argument against enfranchising women extended from fears, growing rapidly in the wake of the Fifteenth Amendment, that the quality of the electorate had already been compromised and voting women would damage it further. While some optimistic reformers argued that female voters would elevate society or at least offset the black vote, skeptics warned that adding women would just muck it up more. The ignorant and uninformed—former slaves were assumed, without evidence, to fall into this category—offered to sell their votes for a song. Good white women would not vote, leaving only the vile and debased, including black women and prostitutes, to add their voices. Better to leave matters as they were than to risk additional corruption.[65]

Besides, when men did their duty as providers and protectors, women did not need to vote, critics added. Defending the natural gender order, one Stanford, Kentucky, writer stressed that man should cherish "the mother who bore him" and love "the wife who cleaves to him" and prevent them from tarnishing themselves at the polls. A man who shifted the burden of governing to the shoulders of his wife was no better than a man who made her curry his horse or black his boots. Woman suffrage would end "in evil and evil only."[66]

Henry Watterson echoed these warnings and used his bully pulpit as editor of the *Courier-Journal* to persuade Kentuckians that giving the vote would create "he-women." Before Kentuckians knew him only as the namesake of an expressway, they knew him as "Marse Henry," promoter of railroads and the New South. Watterson urged southerners to pursue economic development, and he often harangued the region for its unwillingness to embrace change. However, he could not imagine helping woman down from her pedestal. Watterson opposed the coming of feminism "with all of his editorial might," beginning in the 1870s and continuing until the nineteen-teens when he finally, much to suffragists' relief, retired.[67]

Considering its nostalgia for the Lost Cause, its deep religious faith, and its glorification of submissive white women, the South was going to be a tough nut to crack for woman's rights, but leaders of the NWSA and the AWSA knew they must crack it. They must cultivate the South and West in order to become a national movement. "Old Kentuck"—on the border of each—would be their entry point.[68]

But national leaders understood that they could not win the South on their own. Native southerners must be the ones to introduce their neighbors, friends, and relatives to woman's rights. Suffragists' forays across the Ohio River would only succeed if they could recruit a born and bred Kentuckian to lead the effort.

They needed someone who not only was brave and trustworthy but also had name recognition. In 1875, they found the perfect agent. Mary Barr Clay, the oldest daughter of famed abolitionist Cassius Clay, stood up and publicly endorsed woman's rights. Better yet, she did not come alone. She had a mother and three sisters who also began to work on behalf of suffrage. Leaders of the AWSA and NWSA knew they had struck gold. With the Clays on their side, the suffrage movement could finally move south.

2

Jars of Clay

Had Cassius Clay been a more devoted husband, the woman's movement might not have taken off in Kentucky as it did. There is no way to know for sure, but his philandering ways undoubtedly pushed the women in his life in that direction. The Clay family suffered through the dissolution of not just one but two marriages in the 1870s, and these events inspired the Clay women to embrace equal rights. Their solidarity and Cassius Clay's indiscretions are central to Kentucky's suffrage story. The Kentucky movement *was* the Clay women in its earliest years. Their priorities set its priorities, their worldview determined its goals and constituency.[1]

The Clay family was well-known across Kentucky and throughout the nation. Its connection to cousin Henry Clay distinguished its members, but Cassius Marcellus Clay, the family's patriarch, did plenty on his own to attract attention. He was the best-known antislavery reformer in the state. Not that he thought those with dark skin were his equal. His call for ending slavery focused on the economic harm it did, not any concern for justice. Still, it was a controversial viewpoint, and "Cash" Clay thrived on controversy. He famously defended his provocative ideas with a bowie knife and often with a pistol on the dueling field. When he began publishing an emancipationist newspaper in the 1840s, he outfitted his office with a trapdoor in case he needed to make a quick escape. If worse came to worst, he could blow the office up with the two cannons he installed.

Abraham Lincoln rewarded Clay for his dedication to the Republican Party in 1861 by naming him minister to Russia. Moving halfway across the globe, however, was not enough to keep Clay's name out of the papers. Scandal followed him to his new post. To call Cassius Clay a colorful figure is an understatement.[2]

Cassius Clay found fame while his wife, Mary Jane Warfield Clay, and his children endured the hardships of his frequent absences. To his children, he was largely a stranger. He took them to Russia with him in 1861, but they returned to the States after only a few months. Supporting his family in the

25

foreign city may have proved too expensive, or Mrs. Clay may have just preferred warmer climates. She was anxious enough to get back to Kentucky that she made the journey alone with six children, traversing a nation then at war.[3]

Mrs. Clay proved over and over that she could manage any situation thrown at her. The family was wealthy, but they were often pinched by cash-flow problems. Mary Jane's careful accounting kept them afloat. She dug into her own personal trust fund to maintain her home and feed her children during lean times.

Running White Hall, the family's Madison County estate, demanded Mrs. Clay's full attention during the Civil War. She raised mules and horses and leased land to the Union Army to graze livestock. She also assisted soldiers passing through, sometimes as many as fifty in a month. After Confederates looted White Hall, burning buildings and stealing livestock, Mrs. Clay largely oversaw repairs herself. She also initiated extensive renovations that enlarged White Hall and made it more stylish.[4]

Meanwhile, Cassius Clay remained in Russia throughout both the Lincoln and Johnson administrations. Finally, he returned to Kentucky in 1869, followed by a Russian boy who bore a striking resemblance to him and who many assumed was his son. By this point, the Clays had nothing more than a marriage of convenience. She spent most of her time living with her sister in Lexington, only returning to White Hall now and then to keep up appearances. The arrival of Clay's suspected son was an indignity Mary Jane could not bear. She and her youngest children moved to Lexington permanently, purchasing a home of their own. She had invested time and her own money remodeling White Hall, but her attachment to it was not enough to make her want to stay. Cassius Clay shrugged off his wife's exit. He had thrown his wedding ring away two decades earlier, he boasted.[5]

Their oldest daughter, Mary Barr Clay, knew her parents did not have a happy marriage, but she decided to take a chance on love anyway when it struck her in 1863. She had been slow to wed, unusual in an era when marriage was woman's destiny. At age twenty-seven, many judged her an "old maid," but John F. "Frank" Herrick, an Oberlin graduate from a prominent northern Ohio family, saved her from that stigma. The two presumably met when Herrick, the commander of a company of Union cavalry soldiers, was stationed in central Kentucky. They planned an October 1866 wedding.[6]

The Clay family was known for hosting elaborate parties, and Mary's nuptials, which also served as a celebration of the war's end, exceeded expectations. Family and friends from Kentucky and Ohio—everyone except Cassius Clay, who remained at his post in Russia—jammed into White Hall, staying for days to celebrate the union.[7]

When the celebrating was done, the new Mr. and Mrs. Frank Herrick moved north to Cleveland. He formed a law partnership with his brother, and she began bearing children, three—all boys—between 1867 and 1872. Clay may have seen her marriage as an escape. Her mother likely leaned on her oldest daughter to help manage the household and possibly relied on her for emotional support. Now, she could build her own life in a new city. Then again, she may have felt homesick and pined for the support of her mother and sisters back in Kentucky. Her son, Green Clay, noted in retrospect that his mother seemed happy living in Cleveland, but he could only speculate.[8]

Cassius Clay's return to Kentucky in 1869 set off a flurry of events that jolted everyone, including his oldest daughter and her growing family. After welcoming his suspected son to Kentucky and splitting with Mary Jane, he announced that he was dividing White Hall among his children. They would pay him rent for the rest of his life, but each would receive a farm of his or her own.

Mary Clay Herrick's 386-acre parcel, partially cleared of timber and cane, offered a tempting new start. She convinced her husband to give up his law practice in Cleveland so they could become farmers. It may not have taken much persuasion. Herrick may have liked the idea of being a gentleman farmer, which offered the satisfaction of living on the land without the drudgery. Hired hands and managers would see to the hard work.

Neither Mary nor Frank Herrick had experience turning the soil, but a successful first harvest convinced them that they could make a go of it. They built a ten-room house on Mary's land, committed enough to each other and to Kentucky to put down permanent roots.

It was, however, wishful thinking. The marriage may have already been doomed, or perhaps fate interfered. They had barely settled into their new home when their oldest son suffered a terrible accident, all too common in homes heated by open hearths: he fell into the fireplace. The marriage dissolved soon after.

No one seemed surprised when the Herricks called it quits. Family members later recalled that the couple was not well matched, and that it was a wonder the union endured as long as it did. After seven long years, citing "incompatibility of temper" they divorced. It seems likely that more specific disagreements were to blame. He may have wanted to return to

Ohio, and she refused. In a later suffrage speech, she specifically denounced laws that required a woman to follow her husband or forfeit her marriage, as if she were speaking from personal experience.[9]

Mary Clay Herrick was not one to defer simply to meet society's expectations. Her son noted that "she wanted her way 100% of the time, and she generally got it." He may have read the situation correctly or his impressions may have been colored by the era in which he lived, when women were expected to be submissive and self-sacrificing. Having been at war with each other long enough, Green Clay explains, the couple agreed to settle their case out of court, avoiding "fuss and feathers," and went their separate ways.[10]

When the couple split in 1872, the two younger boys, still toddlers, stayed with their mother while the oldest son went to live with his father and the new family he built in Cleveland. At the insistence of Mary Barr, the two youngest sons legally changed their last names to Clay in the 1890s. The oldest, who would continue to go by Clay Herrick, apparently bore enough of her family's mark without taking her surname. She mercifully stopped short of insisting that he become Clay Clay.[11]

The words "What God has brought together," carried grave implications in nineteenth-century communities. Divorce was becoming more common by the 1870s but remained exceedingly rare by twenty-first-century standards. It is hard for those raised in a culture of no-fault divorces to understand the challenges of extricating oneself from a suffocating marriage. "'Til death do us part" was not only a promise, sometimes it was a sentence. Incompatibility was not enough to call it quits. Judges expected clear proof that one of the parties was at fault.[12]

Justifiable causes varied from state to state. Adultery was the one marital sin that could warrant a divorce nationwide. Other acceptable causes included, among others, drunkenness, bigamy, cruelty, abandonment, lewd and lascivious behavior, concealment of a loathsome disease, inability to perform sexually, and for men, failure to provide.[13]

It is unclear who carried the blame in the Clay–Herrick divorce. In the Warfield–Clay case settled soon after, Mary Jane Warfield took the blame. Cassius Clay initiated the suit in 1878, claiming that his wife had cruelly deserted him when she moved to Lexington nine years earlier. Her relocation was unforgivable in his mind while he dismissed his years spent in Russia as a career move. Mary Jane Warfield Clay did not contest the suit. She had had enough. He could have his divorce. Good riddance.

At least mother and daughter could cry on each other's shoulder. They could exchange examples of the ways the men in their lives had let them down. They also could comfort each other as they came face to face with a legal system that treated men and women very differently.

Mary Jane Clay and Mary Barr Herrick each had an independent income, so they fared better than many of their peers. But it was not the same as getting their fair shares. Cassius Clay refused to split the assets he held in common with his wife even though it was her management that kept them solvent during their forty-five-year marriage. She would get by on Warfield money that her father had wisely willed to her in a separate estate. Cassius had at least agreed that their youngest child, Annie, would stay with her mother. He could have taken her too. Under Kentucky law, which tilted in favor of men, fathers had absolute right to their minor children.[14]

The two divorcees differed in their levels of comfort with their new status as single women. The elder Mary Clay quietly played the hand she was dealt, while her daughter more enthusiastically embraced her independence. In 1874, either financial need or professional ambition led Mary Barr briefly to sign on as a commissioned sales agent with the Buckeye Sewing Machine Company. The venture did not last long, perhaps because she discovered that her farm income would comfortably cover her needs.[15]

The name each woman chose to take following her divorce signals how comfortable she was with her new status. Kentucky law allowed a woman to reclaim her birth name, if she so chose. Although she would have had plenty of reason to shed the name Clay, Mary Jane Warfield kept it. Mary Barr meanwhile decided she wanted the Clay name back, in part to recover her identity, but more importantly, to capitalize on the Clay name's power to open doors. By 1879 she was signing herself "Mary B. Clay."[16]

Years later, describing the Kentucky suffrage movement's roots in the late nineteenth century, Kate Trimble de Roode recalled that it took one woman who had felt the "iron teeth of the law in her own flesh" through some "sudden turn of the wheel of fortune" to demand a change and to wake up her "slumbering sisters." Mary Barr Clay felt those iron teeth intensely and directly, and she vowed to keep other women from feeling them too. It just so happened that she had a contingent of "slumbering sisters" (and a committed mother) at the ready within her own family.[17]

Mary Warfield Clay saw that her daughter was ready to endorse woman's rights in the late 1870s, and she offered her full support. The earliest record of

Mary Barr Clay, the oldest of the "Clay girls," took the first steps toward organizing Kentucky suffragists. She, along with her sisters and her mother, would be the driving force behind the Kentucky movement in its earliest years. (*History of Woman Suffrage*)

Mary Barr Clay making her beliefs publicly known came in the summer of 1875 when she wrote to Lucy Stone's *Woman's Journal* to announce that she was a "soldier of the cause, enlisted for the war." The "dawn of freedom" had begun, and Kentucky women were committed to throwing off the "Lords of Creation," she reported. Young women in the state were restless and thirsty for meaningful lifework. They wanted to "make something of themselves," just as their brothers could do. Married women did not want to depend on a man but were in fact demanding a stipend from their husbands to acknowledge their financial contributions, Clay noted.[18]

Mary Barr Clay claimed to speak for Kentucky women generally, but it is likely that she was speaking mainly for the Clay women. They were tired of domineering and misbehaving men, and they were ready to let the world know it.

The eldest Clay daughter was willing to endorse suffrage individually in 1875 but was not yet ready to mobilize others. Sometimes before you can lead a revolution, you need to live one. Clay was newly divorced and pondering how to use her newfound freedom. She felt torn between seeking higher education, becoming a better farmer, and being a good mother. Suffrage work would have to squeeze in among her many other priorities.

At first, Mary Barr Clay demonstrated her support for suffrage by making small monetary donations to support the work in other states. Soon, she was attending national conventions. When the NWSA met in St. Louis in the spring of 1879, she went as a self-appointed delegate from Kentucky, one of nineteen states represented. There, she learned about a proposed Sixteenth Amendment to the US constitution, which would give every American woman voting rights.[19]

Clay returned home excited to do more to support the cause. A national speaker, she decided, would be just the thing to get the ball rolling. She humbly wrote to Susan B. Anthony, sure that the suffrage pioneer would not remember her.[20]

Instead, she received a warm letter in return. Not only did Anthony remember her well, she addressed her as "My Dear Friend." Unfortunately, she noted, she would not be able to visit Kentucky that fall, but she wished Clay, who had shared her plan to attend medical school in Michigan, well. Anthony, with some naïveté, signed off her letter by offering her regards to Clay's "dear noble Father."[21]

The opportunity to come to Kentucky as the guest of the famous Cassius Clay's daughter, however, proved too valuable to pass up. It may have taken some serious juggling, but Anthony reworked her schedule to make an October trip possible. Anthony's visit, which included stops in Owensboro, Bowling Green, and Richmond, cemented the Clay women's commitment to woman's rights. It also gave Anthony a few thrills—getting to meet the infamous Cassius Clay at the "proud old mansion" and drinking Kentucky coffee (which she requested in place of the state's better-known drink, bourbon). For years to come Anthony would remember fondly the hospitality that the Clays and Kentuckians showed her.[22]

She was well entertained, but more importantly Anthony's visit kicked off a period of intense suffrage work in the Bluegrass State. During the fall of 1879, with the Clay women (except Laura who was away at school) all congregated in Richmond for the harvest season, the first permanent local suffrage organization in Kentucky, the Madison County Equal Rights Association, held its first meeting.

Mary Jane Warfield Clay returned to Lexington to spend the winter, and suffrage energy followed her, permeating the parlor of her Gratz Park home. She, along with daughter Annie and a few close friends, established the Fayette Equal Suffrage Association. They began pressing newspaper editors to print suffrage articles, and they circulated literature.

Determined to show measurable proof that their efforts were winning converts, they organized a petition drive. Each of the 146 signatures they collected was hard-won, but especially the 44 female signatures. Some women never agreed to sign because they feared upsetting their husbands. The tepid response led Mrs. Clay to conclude that "many masters were standing in the way of the enlightenment of their slaves [their wives]. Aren't you glad we have no masters?" the former emancipationist asked her daughter, Laura.[23]

Mary Barr Clay was not part of the force stationed that winter in her mother's parlor. She spent the 1880s bouncing between Michigan and Kentucky, seeking education for her boys and considering it for herself as well (first medical school, then law). She did not stay in one place long, leading an exasperated Lucy Stone to wonder where to send her letters.[24]

Clay did her part for suffrage wherever she happened to be. When in Kentucky she worked with the Madison County E.R.A. From Ann Arbor, she did state organizing and edited a local newspaper column.[25]

Perhaps to avoid the geographical tug-of-war in which she found herself, she focused increasingly on national work. Clay's profile was on the rise in the early 1880s, and it's hard to imagine that her increasing prominence did not give her at least a little thrill. While her father's name opened doors, and she readily relied on it to do so, some part of her resented the need to capitalize on his fame. At the 1880 NWSA convention when she was introduced as the daughter of Cassius Clay, she quickly and proudly corrected the record: "I am also the daughter of Mary J. Warfield Clay."[26]

The AWSA viewed Mary Jane Warfield Clay's daughter as especially useful to its work. In 1881, looking to extend "its outposts," the organization decided to hold its annual convention in Louisville. Kentuckians were a little skeptical of the effort, and attendance at the opening sessions was light, smaller than the audience that gathered to hear Lucy Stone speak back in 1853. Perhaps remembering Stone's bloomer costume, locals expected that the 1881 convention would be filled with "strong minded women in ill-fitting petticoats," yelling for their rights. Instead, as the *Courier-Journal* reported, attendees found "a plain business meeting of cultured ladies," 90 percent of whom were married and all "dressed as ladies dress." News reports provided detailed descriptions of delegates' fashionable outfits for good measure. Black brocaded satin, lace cuffs, diamond ornaments, typical ladies' attire.[27]

With younger sister, Laura, looking on, Mary Barr Clay made her speaking debut on the last (and best attended) day of the convention. The previous year, her sister Sallie had been scheduled to speak before the NWSA convention in Chicago, but when the time came for her to take the platform she could not be found. Mary may have worried that a similar fate would befall her, but she made it to the platform. She proceeded to offer a long and winding account of the ways American religion and the Kentucky legal system, both directed by men, denied women their natural and God-given rights. "We are not assembled here to abuse the other half of mankind," she threw in as a half-hearted attempt to lighten the mood, but that is exactly what she proceeded to do.[28]

Women were held in slavish bondage by laws made by their brothers, fathers, and sons, she concluded, delivering a charge that carried a particular sting in a former slave state. From there, she launched into a litany of wrongs done to women: they were more severely punished for murder than men, husbands could bruise and mangle them at will, and their children could be taken from them and given to "their bitterest enemy." It did not matter how smart a woman was. She could not be a lawyer, a juror, or an officeholder. The audience may have expected Clay, as a southern lady, to show more restraint. She did not offer any "bless your hearts," southern women's snide way of softening criticism. She told it like she saw it.[29]

Mary's speech lived up to the promise of her famous name. She quickly became a rising star in the national suffrage movement. She was elected a vice-president of the AWSA in 1881. In 1883 she became its president. While attending the NWSA convention in Washington, DC, the following year, Clay was one of several women selected to address the US House Judiciary Committee in favor of a federal amendment giving women the vote.[30]

The Louisville convention increased Mary Barr Clay's stature in the movement, and it also led to the creation of a state equal rights organization for Kentucky, the first ever in the South. Determined to strike while the iron was hot, interested individuals convened on the morning after the convention. For too long their efforts had been scattered; they needed to be organized, efficient, and deliberate. Louisville attorney Colonel John Ward moved that they establish a Kentucky Woman Suffrage Association (KWSA) with Laura Clay as president. He would be vice-president. They adopted the constitution and by-laws of the AWSA and named existing Fayette County, Madison County, and Louisville groups as official chapters. One day, they hoped to have auxiliaries in every county in the state. All present were invited to come forward and sign their names in what resembled a solemn profession of faith. Around a hundred people, mostly women, enrolled and paid their required one-dollar dues. Some of the same women met later in the day to form an organization to promote women's education.[31]

Mary Barr Clay would have been an obvious choice to help lead the KWSA; and in fact, national reports mistakenly announced that she had been named president, when actually her name is conspicuously missing from its first constitution. She likely understood that being gone so much from the state prevented her from serving, and she may have wanted to focus on national work. Or she may have just been realistic. A divorced mother could only take on so much, after all. Her single, younger sister would lead instead.[32]

Laura Clay's biographer Paul Fuller notes that ironically even though her name would become the one most associated with Kentucky suffrage (its equivalent of Susan B. Anthony, according to one admirer), she was "eclipsed by her sisters" in these early years. Reporting on work done in Kentucky in 1884, Mary Barr Clay called her youngest sister, Annie, the "driving spirit" behind suffrage work in Lexington while sister Sallie oversaw the action in Richmond. Each wrote a weekly column for local newspapers. Mary's contributions were assumed since she was the one to provide the state update. Laura, despite her position as state president, gets no mention.[33]

Laura Clay may have had good intentions when she accepted the KWSA presidency in 1881, but she was not ready to assume active leadership. The organization only had a "paper existence" until 1888. Representatives of the organization—a few Clays assisted by John Ward, the Louisville attorney— would swing into action each spring when the legislature was in session to advocate for woman's rights bills, but with no success. Lawmakers gave them "due and proper respect," but nothing more. Laura later blamed the organization's narrow focus on the vote—a far too radical proposition—as the

National suffrage leaders immediately recognized Laura Clay's potential, but she hesitated to get involved. Finally, in 1888, she made suffrage work a priority. It would become her life's main focus. (White Hall Historic Site)

reason the group languished, but the more likely factor is that suffrage had not yet become her focus. She had failed to lead.[34]

In their haste to recruit Laura Clay for their cause, national leaders may have jumped the gun. They saw that she had a sharp intellect and a gift for public speaking. All the "Clay girls" were similarly blessed. Laura offered one thing her sisters could not though: she was single and had no family obligations to interfere with her work. Sallie was a married mother of five. Annie would marry in 1886 and move to Virginia.

National leaders carefully groomed Laura, asking about her often in their correspondence with her sisters. Susan B. Anthony inquired about Laura's plans in 1880: "Will she be a lawyer, or will she devote herself to our cause?" Four years later, Lucy Stone similarly expressed hope that Laura could be convinced "to take Kentucky in hand, hold meetings, organize societies, and push it to activity." In short, she hoped that Laura would assume the role she had accepted but was clearly not fulfilling.[35]

Much like her older sister Mary, Laura Clay spent the 1880s on the move and searching for a sense of direction. She thought about completing a degree in teaching or law perhaps. She took a year of courses at the University of Michigan (brother Brutus was a graduate) in 1879–1880, rooming with her sister Mary and her nephews. Then, she enrolled at Agricultural and Mechanical College of Kentucky soon after it began admitting women in 1880, but she only stayed for one semester.[36]

Her desire to succeed as a "practical farmer" may have lured her back to Kentucky. Mary and Laura both "personally superintended" their inherited acres, studying hard to learn the business. They began without know-how or equipment, but through "observation and experience, prudence and industry," they mastered the craft. The *Stanford Interior Journal* reported in 1884 that Mary had sold thirty-one head of hogs, averaging 165 pounds, in Cincinnati. Laura had sold thirty-six newly weaned pigs as well. The sisters also grew wheat, but they struggled to turn a profit. When selling prices were low and overhead costs were high in the late 1880s, Mary went to work organizing a wheat pool that included about forty Madison County farmers. Farming required both women periodically to put their suffrage work on hold. The effort proved a good investment. Later, Laura's farm income would allow her to commit significant time and money to the cause.[37]

During these years—the decade of her thirties—strong religious faith also drove Laura Clay's decisions. As a young girl she chose to be baptized into the Episcopal church. Laura and Sallie, much more than the other Clay sisters, felt strongly that their first duty was to serve God. Religion and women's rights did not seem immediately compatible. Over time, however, with careful scriptural study and much prayer, Laura would come to see them as intersecting.[38]

Like many women of her generation who struggled to find their paths in a world that offered limited avenues, Laura Clay wondered how to combine her many interests and obligations—religion, education, farm responsibilities, and woman's rights. She eventually hit on the right combination, but only after some wandering.

Laura Clay joined her mother and sisters in the suffrage movement, but she got there later and in her own way. Frances Willard, president of the Woman's Christian Temperance Union, encouraged Laura to join the Association for the Advancement of Women in 1877. The AAW was committed to developing women's minds, but it steered a more conservative course than most suffragists. Throughout the 1880s, Laura faithfully attended the AAW's Woman's Congresses. She often shared papers she had written, but her big breakout moment came when she presented a paper titled, "A Practical View of Woman Suffrage" in 1886. National leaders had been trying for many years to get the last of the Clay sisters to embrace the cause, and now they had finally succeeded.[39]

Laura Clay's childhood was enough to make almost anyone into a feminist, but she was slow to grow into the role. Why did her interest suddenly sprout in 1886? The timing of her political awakening likely had something to do with her father, who began doling out a new batch of irritations sure to prickle the women in his life. Cassius Clay released his memoirs that year, and they were filled with editorial asides that belittled women. In a speech delivered at Yale to his reunion classmates the following year, he denounced female suffrage in no uncertain terms. Enfranchising women, he warned, was likely to destroy civilization. Citing ancient Rome, perhaps with a nod to his namesake, the old abolitionist warned that bold experiments rarely turned out well.[40]

A new chapter of the Kentucky suffrage movement was set to begin, and Laura Clay committed to lead it, this time for real. In May 1888, she organized a speaking tour for Lucy Stone and husband, Henry Blackwell. Later that year, with assistance from her friend Henrietta Chenault, Clay reorganized the Lexington club and reincarnated the state organization, assigning it a new name—the Kentucky Equal Rights Association. Six locals became its first auxiliaries: Richmond, Laurel County, Fayette County, Glasgow, Kenton County, and Louisville. Clay would serve as president.[41]

Unlike the KWSA, the Kentucky Equal Rights Association from day one served as an active, continuous force for reform. No longer would the

Kentucky suffrage movement be an almost exclusively Clay family enterprise. It would, however, forever bear their indelible stamp.

2 Corinthians 4:7 refers to Christians as "jars of clay," repositories for treasure and God's all-surpassing power. Laura Clay, a devoted student of scripture, could have quoted this passage, chapter and verse. She may have considered her role, both as an evangelist and a suffragist, in these terms. She held something that was precious and that needed to be shared. But even though jars of clay can be useful and hardened through fire, they are still breakable. The good news 2 Corinthians speaks of is carried by frail and fragile messengers, and similarly the suffrage message would be carried in fallible vessels.[42]

Laura Clay's social standing helped make suffrage a respectable cause, but it also blinded her to other women's challenges. Clay set the Kentucky suffrage movement on a course that prioritized the rights of some women, rather than those of all women. It would focus on white, educated, Christian, financially comfortable women—women who looked a lot like herself. Clay's steady and dedicated leadership would provide useful continuity that allowed Kentucky to stand out among its southern neighbors for its suffrage activity, but that continuity would come at the cost of multiple perspectives and inclusivity.

3

To Frankfort

For most of the lawmakers headed to Frankfort right after Christmas in 1889, the trip to the capitol and the work that awaited them when they arrived was old hat. They kissed their wives and babies, hopped on trains or in carriages, and settled in for the trip.

The session promised to be routine. Several legislators were fixated on cigarettes and the moral threat they represented to the children of the Commonwealth, and there was talk of disbanding Harlan and Perry Counties due to lawlessness. Calls to expand Kentucky's public road system and to more carefully regulate its railroads were heard, but otherwise, few big issues loomed.[1]

Heavy fog and a demoralizing pall settled over Frankfort as the 1890 session sputtered to life. Members of the general assembly oversaw the minutiae of governing the Commonwealth, approving so-called special legislation that applied only to specific communities, organizations, or individuals. For example, it took an act of the legislature to incorporate the Butler Deposit Bank, another to establish a new voting place in Muhlenberg County, and another to regulate the sale of vinegar. Those were the most pressing matters lawmakers considered some days.[2]

For the women headed to the session as representatives of the new Kentucky Equal Rights Association—boarding trains and kissing husbands—this trip would be anything but routine. They were not going as seasoned elected officials, but rather as interested citizen-activists in training. The wives and daughters of elected officials sometimes appeared in the lobby of the legislative chambers, but rarely did women enter its inner sanctum. Now, they were coming as players, rather than as spectators. They planned to insert women into the governing process, and they knew that a new adventure awaited. This was the moment for which KERA's Petitions and Legislative Work Department, led by Mrs. Josephine Henry, had been carefully preparing.

Weighing in at only eighty-five pounds, Josephine Henry was pound for pound the most powerful Kentucky suffragist in the smallest package.

No one could deliver "pure and unadulterated suffrage" like Josephine Henry, one admirer noted. (University of Kentucky Special Collections)

"Though she be but little, she is fierce," Shakespeare would have said about her. Tiny spectacles emphasized her small, dark eyes and gave her a seriousness of purpose, if somewhat of a pinched look. Listeners did not expect a speaker with such a "slender, almost frail physique" to be so potent. Henry electrified audiences; the "Woman Henry Clay," some called her.[3]

Henry's life up to this point—forty-three years spent as a daughter, wife, and mother—had informally prepared her for the important role she would play in advancing women's rights. Her parents, Euclid and Mary Williamson, deeply valued independent thought and championed reform, including abolition, in their Newport community. Henry spent her adult life in Versailles following her marriage to Captain William Henry, headmaster of the Henry

Academy for Boys. The couple had one son, but now he was grown and her nest was empty. Facing the end of active, hands-on motherhood, she was left to decide what the years that remained in front of her would hold.[4]

She had a sharp legal mind that she had developed through informal study. Other women might prefer the society pages and clipping recipes that appeared in the newspaper, but not Henry. Her eye went right to columns on legal matters and politics. She had long been a suffragist, the only one in her community, she boasted. She supported the cause independently in a "feeble way," but she craved connection with others who shared her interest and looked for these fellow travelers the best way she knew how. In 1888, she sent a simple appeal addressed to a national audience through the *Woman's Journal*: "Light Wanted in Kentucky."[5]

Soon, a light blinked back. Laura Clay invited Henry to attend KERA's inaugural meeting that fall. Henry was unable to make the trip to Cincinnati, but Clay was not about to squander her interest. Henry was "astonished" to later learn that she had been appointed superintendent of one of the organization's most important departments in absentia. She had been entrusted to develop KERA's legislative plan.[6]

They made an odd pair, Laura Clay and Josephine Henry. A "massive woman," Clay cut a very different profile than the slight Henry. Clay had inherited her father's thick arched eyebrows and his distinctive stance. The round face she shared with her mother softened her look, but acquaintances described her as a commanding presence. Mrs. Henry would have beaten her in a public speaking contest—she was "the people's favorite"—but Clay could certainly hold her own. Like her father, she could easily sway a crowd with her commanding oratory.[7]

Clay and Henry, together with Eugenia Farmer, an Oberlin graduate and wife of a Covington railroad executive, formed the "big three" of Kentucky woman's rights in the 1890s. Clay, as president of KERA, Farmer, as its corresponding secretary and state organizer, and Josephine Henry, as superintendent of petitions and legislative work, made up the core of what became known as the Frankfort Committee. The women shared many similarities. They were all white women of means. Travel and education had exposed all of them to new ideas. Each was connected to powerful men and enjoyed status within the community that these connections brought. Finally, they all had the time and the will to work for change. None had pressing domestic responsibilities, and they were all inclined to support unpopular ideas.[8]

These three women made Frankfort a home away from home during each semiannual legislative session for nearly a decade. Others joined them periodically, such as Clay's sisters Mary and Sallie, long-serving KERA treasurer Isabella Shepard, Frankfort's Mrs. T. M. Goodknight, and Louisville septuagenarian Susan Look Avery; but Henry, Clay, and Farmer were the committee's most faithful "watchers." They traveled, lodged, and fought together, and they would be bonded forever by their experience.[9]

The 1890s were a heady time for Kentucky suffragists. Victory seemed just around the corner, and their excitement was palpable. Woman's role was expanding before their very eyes. Not so long ago, no one had thought to ask "the Woman Question," but now it was on everyone's minds. Women were going to college, and they were building professional careers. They had even gone "bicycle mad." Suffragists, lacking the benefit of hindsight, had no way of knowing that it would take three decades of sustained effort to win the vote. At this point, with the momentum seemingly in their favor, they could still dream of quick and easy victory.[10]

The vote was the ultimate prize, but KERA identified other, seemingly more attainable, ways to remove women's legal impediments. Clay believed that the first attempt to create a state woman's rights organization for Kentucky had failed because they had focused too narrowly on the vote. Kentucky women, she decided, were not ready to accept a cause that had long been painted as radical, unwomanly, and a threat to social harmony. She pledged to recast the movement. Dropping the words "woman suffrage" from the name of the organization was a good start. "Equal rights" sounded better. KERA valued the vote and would work for it through state and national channels, but its mission was broader, encompassing the industrial and educational rights of women as well as their legal rights.[11]

When Henry, Clay, and Farmer arrived in Frankfort in January 1890, the trio came with two specific goals. They hoped to force Kentucky leaders to hire female physicians to staff all state asylums and charitable institutions. This requirement would doubly benefit women by creating job opportunities for the small but growing pool of female physicians and by ensuring that female patients had access to better care. Second, they hoped to pass legislation protecting women's right to their property.[12]

Since the Civil War, many states had passed married women's property laws. Even the South, so vigorously resistant to change, had accepted these reforms, though not for altruistic reasons. The end of slavery had left white southern men vulnerable to creditors and eager to protect their assets. Women were the beneficiaries. Kentucky, however, lacked even basic protections. KERA leaders claimed that the state's laws were the most backward in the country, and national women's rights leaders agreed they were "medieval."[13]

Property rights attracted wide sympathy, even from those who would never support voting rights for women. A woman's personal property, unless protected in a separate estate—a costly practice that ate up much of the proceeds—became her husband's possession the minute she married. He could squander it or it could be taken to cover his debts, and she had no legal recourse. If she worked a job outside the home, her husband received her pay. Kentucky men could legally say, "What is yours is mine, and what is mine is my own."[14]

Josephine Henry, the most vocal defender of women's property rights, told shocking stories of women in her own community who had been stripped of their assets: "A man sold a cow that his wife had bought with money that it took three months to earn with her needle, and the only concession the poor woman got was that they allowed her to milk the cow before they drove it away." Worse, Henry noted, the greedy husband traded the cow for a gun, "filled up with whiskey and started on the war path."[15]

The clearest example of how Kentucky law failed married women was the tradition of curtesy and dower, better known as the "widow's thirds." A man automatically inherited a life interest in all of his wife's property when she died, while she only received one-third interest in his estate and then only so that she would not become a burden to the public. A man could leave more to his wife than the minimum required by law, but she had no such flexibility since she could not legally write a will. Even if she had a "princely fortune in real estate," she could not profit from it during her life and she could not leave it to her chosen heir, which Henry concluded was the same "*as not owning it at all.*" The right to control her own property, Henry believed, was foundational to women gaining every other right.[16]

Heading into the 1890 legislative session, KERA's representatives hoped at the very least that lawmakers would fix these backward property laws and allow Kentucky to catch up with the rest of the nation.

Henry, Clay, and Farmer's legislative work began months before the session's start. Exhaustive legal research to understand existing laws and to assess the feasibility of reforms came first. Then, they set out to educate both the public and lawmakers by publishing in newspapers across the state and by printing their own pamphlets. Lawmakers received copies of these publications and multiple personal letters from Farmer and her team—1,482 letters in total. The women identified sympathetic leaders and squeezed out promises that they would submit KERA's bills when the time came. Lawmakers would likely question how much support there was for women's property rights, so they circulated petitions across the state to prove the issue's popularity.[17]

Once the session began, the Frankfort Committee members were on hand to grease the wheels. They had much to learn. They needed to understand the political process and how to draft bills. They had to become comfortable speaking in public to men who were not always welcoming. They had to learn to deliver logical summaries of their arguments and to do so efficiently in committee hearings, using the language of lawmakers. They might be quickly shown the door, so it was important to be succinct.

Their experiences as wives, mothers, daughters, sisters, and friends of public officials provided them some informal training, but they largely learned by doing. It was often trial by fire, such as when Clay, Henry, and Farmer addressed about fifty members of the legislature early in the 1890 session. The *Courier-Journal* offered begrudging praise: the women were "fair arguers."[18]

Lawmakers had expected to finish their work in the 1890 session by mid-April, but as May dragged on, they were still at their desks, which meant suffragists were still on alert. The days were getting longer and hotter, and the Louisville paper reported that the men were dreaming of "blackberries, bass fishing, and mosquitos." Little was being accomplished and the session finally, reluctantly expired. It was time to go home.[19]

Clay, Henry, and Farmer could point to the experience they had gained over the long session and the close bonds they had formed, but they had little else to show for their months of work. The senate considered a bill that would have required all state institutions to have a woman on staff, but it did not make it out of committee. With seven bills related to women's property proposed, the women had reason to be hopeful, but they came up largely empty-handed. They did manage to secure legislation that allowed employers to pay a woman's wages directly to her instead of to a male custodian. It was a small improvement. Other changes related to dower rights passed in the Senate but died in the House, which Henry blamed on political chicanery.[20]

Kentucky men celebrated chivalry. They claimed to be women's defenders and protectors, but when offered the chance to honor them they failed to do so. Very soon, however, they would have another chance to make it right. KERA representatives promised to continue the fight, and they wouldn't have long to wait.

KERA started small with only about sixty members spread across the Commonwealth. Not all of them could travel to Frankfort like Farmer, Clay, and Henry. Most, even if they lived nearby, were tied down by domestic responsibilities. Still, they found ways to assist the cause from afar. Many KERA members poured their time in these early years into expanding women's educational opportunities through writing letters and meeting personally with local college administrators. Suffragists tended to be educated women, and they wanted to make sure the opportunities they had enjoyed were available to other members of their sex.

State College (today the University of Kentucky) opened its doors to white women in the 1880s, greedy for the tuition revenue they could bring. But just because women became eligible for admission, that does not mean that many enrolled or that the school threw out the welcome mat. In the late nineteenth century, Americans still assumed that females were too weak to endure the rigors of study. Some even feared that intellectual pursuits would cause women's reproductive organs to "wander" or dry up. When the first female student earned a normal school certificate at State College in 1884, the *Louisville Times* reassured skeptical readers that she was leaving school "a happy, wholesome, appetizing creature." Her training had not ruined her health apparently, nor had it made her less attractive.[21]

Society was slowly coming to accept the idea of college-educated women, but that did not make it any easier to be a co-ed. Originally called Kentucky A&M, State College was a land-grant institution designed to serve the public good. It was also a decidedly male place. Students dressed in cadet uniforms and participated in daily military drills. Administrators had many rules to keep unruly young men in line, but hijinks still went on (in one case, students painted the president's horse flesh-colored as a prank). No women's dormitories existed and the university's restrictions on where female students could live made it impossible for them to enroll unless they had family nearby. If they did enroll, they could only take classes in certain departments.[22]

KERA representatives pledged to make State College more welcoming for women and to press other institutions across the state to admit female students. In 1889, they formed a committee to convince Kentucky University (now Transylvania University) to follow State College's example. They started with this institution because they knew its president, C. L. Loos, to be an ally, and they were not disappointed. By the end of the year Kentucky University began serving women. Male students seemed to like the idea of having females on campus. They offered an enthusiastic welcome and promised to behave like gentlemen.[23]

Sometimes gentle persuasion worked and sometimes strong-arm tactics were necessary. KERA encouraged women to restrict their philanthropic dollars to institutions that admitted women. By 1892, KERA had helped to make Georgetown College, Wesleyan College at Winchester, and Homeopathic Medical College in Louisville coeducational. Central University in Richmond (now Eastern Kentucky University) followed the next year. Centre College proved more resistant. It finally created a woman's department in the 1920s, but women did not move to its main campus until the 1960s.[24]

After it got women on campus, KERA turned its attention to ensuring that they were well served. Throughout the 1890s, KERA kept a steady eye on plans to build a women's dormitory at State College. The project had stalled due to lack of funding (or at least funds the trustees did not prefer to use for other purposes), but a $30,000 state appropriation that KERA and the Women's Christian Temperance Union (WCTU) jointly secured in 1900 allowed the project finally to start moving forward. KERA members celebrated when Patterson Hall, "a College Home for Women," finally opened in 1904, though they would have preferred that the building be named for someone who supported woman's rights instead of their crotchety adversary, president James Patterson. Their work to make higher education more equitable was not finished. They continued to push State College to add women to its board of trustees, to create a domestic science department, and to hire a dean of women, but these goals would take nearly a decade of struggle.[25]

Goals such as adding female trustees were viewed as long-term objectives for KERA. If they were not accomplished this year, there was always next. In 1890, suffragists faced a very different opportunity—a now or never chance to secure far-reaching change. In 1890, Kentucky was living under an outdated frame of government, what some called an "old slavery constitution," in place since 1850. Progressive Kentuckians had argued for two decades that new circumstances required a new governing structure. And now, finally enough voters (a majority had to sign off on a new constitution not once, but twice) agreed. On September 8, 1890, one hundred elected delegates—as "motley a delegation of constitutionalists as had ever been seen in a convention hall," historian Thomas Clark noted—got to work.[26]

It was an auspicious moment for Kentucky suffragists, newly organized and raring to go. They could write women's equality into the very fabric of the Commonwealth. Property rights, voting rights, the wrongs of society could all be fixed in a flash of reform brilliance. Constitutional framers, many of them elected as representatives of the Farmer's Alliance, were promising sweeping change: "Equal Rights to all, exclusive privileges to none." The words were a sweet song to suffragists' ears.[27]

They did not intend to squander this golden opportunity. Suffragists rejoiced when Laura Clay's cousin, Cassius M. Clay Jr., was elected president of the convention; having an in would ensure they got a careful hearing. They arranged to have representatives on the ground throughout the convention, each wearing a yellow ribbon, the national suffrage movement's symbolic color. The Frankfort Committee, along with a handful of other supporters, were there when the convention opened. They did not stay continuously during the 226 days of political tug-of-war (it took twice as long to write this document as it had taken to write the US Constitution), but they were ready at a minute's notice to head to the capital and promised to stay as long as necessary.[28]

Kentucky suffragists came to the convention full of hope, but they quickly realized that their view of "Equal Rights for All" did not square with that of the convention delegates. Women were one-half of the adult population, they were citizens, and many were taxpayers, but they did not have the right to self-government. Keeping their expectations reasonable, Josephine Henry and her team did not ask the convention to enfranchise women directly. They simply hoped that the constitution would untie the hands of the General Assembly, inserting an open clause that would allow legislators to give women the vote when they saw fit without future constitutional change.

When the convention finally wrapped up, KERA representatives let out a sigh of disappointment; their work had been entirely in vain. The vote was still specifically limited to male citizens over the age of twenty-one, excluding the incarcerated and "idiots and insane persons." Property rights hit a dead end, never coming up for a vote. The new constitution did not even include the word *woman*, the even-tempered Eugenia Farmer fumed.[29]

The constitution's amendment provision, however, proved the biggest disappointment. The document, unlike the three previous versions, at least could be amended—a good thing since this was their only hope to vote—

but voters could only consider two amendments during each election cycle. Women's issues, suffragists accurately predicted, would likely get elbowed out by other matters. If they did finally manage through pluck and luck to get a suffrage amendment on the ballot and it went down in defeat, they would have to wait five years before proposing it again.[30]

When male voters ratified the new constitution in August 1891, suffragists knew that they had lost their easiest path to victory. Kentucky's constitution would not establish justice and ensure liberty with a single stroke. Change would come slowly and only with exhausting effort. The legislature was set to convene again in three short months. The small but mighty Mrs. Henry pledged that she and the other members of the Frankfort Committee would be "on the ground" when it did. Until then, they would unpack their suitcases, catch their breath, and strategize.[31]

KERA leaders could have called their annual convention, held each fall, a revival meeting, for in many ways, that was what it was. It offered a welcome chance to gather with fellow believers and restore their weary souls. In 1891, after a year of almost continuous legislative work, they were beyond weary. But the title fit in other more obvious ways, too, highlighting the evangelical tone and spirit that pervaded KERA gatherings and publications. Prayers, Bible lessons, hymns, and free-will offerings could make attendees think they were at Sunday services rather than at a suffrage meeting.[32]

Henry considered KERA's legislative work its main priority, but Clay thought otherwise, calling the Bible department its "first and strongest" division. Woman's rights were God's cause, Clay stressed. Led by Sarah H. Sawyer, representative of the Conference of the Southern Methodist Church and officer in the Laurel County Equal Rights Association, the Bible department's purpose was to "set forth the true position of Woman." KERA adopted as its motto a passage from John: "If you abide in my word, ye shall know the truth, and the truth shall make you free." The Bible and women's careful reading of it would lead them to the truth, KERA leaders argued. They proposed that each local chapter devote time to studying scriptures that their enemies might use against them to "find their true meaning."[33]

Unlike many Christians who believed the Bible instructed women to keep silent and to submit themselves to men, Laura Clay embraced the liberating power of scripture. Equality had always been the Creator's plan for men and women. Adam had thwarted this plan, however, by subjugating woman instead of making her his true helpmeet. Rather than seeing

Christianity as a roadblock, Clay saw it as the solution. Once one believed that men and women were equal before God, it was impossible to reject political equality of the sexes, she concluded.

Clay's influence over the organization is impossible to miss, but she could not have stamped KERA so strongly with her personal faith if others did not share it.[34]

Members of KERA saw parallels between their circumstances and those of early Christians. They stood for truth despite the persecution that might follow. Though a small band of believers—still fewer than three hundred spread thinly across the state, and not all of them active—they believed in the power of conversion to increase their numbers. Employing Jesus's words in Matthew, the Plan of Work committee instructed that "where two women can be found," a new chapter could form. Every member was encouraged to choose one woman to proselytize during the coming year.[35]

Annual conventions, like the one held in Louisville over three days in early December 1891, provided an opportunity for the faithful to commune and to gather strength from one another. Representatives from the six existing local auxiliaries (Lexington, Covington, London, Louisville, Newport, and Richmond) provided reports of the previous year's work. Department superintendents recapped their successes and outlined goals for the coming year. Many prayers were said. This was only the fourth year to meet, but already a routine was established and rituals were in place.[36]

One member was conspicuously absent, however, at the 1891 convention. The minutes cryptically note that Mrs. Henry's "deep affliction" had kept her away. Two months before, when the constitutional convention had barely wrapped up, her only son, Fred, a "brilliant . . . highly educated, but erratic" boy had been killed in a tragic railroad accident. Hoping to make it as a journalist, he had volunteered to write a story involving a lightning overnight train. He had been doing research when the crash occurred. His mother was so overcome, reports stated, that she could not even attend his funeral.[37]

Henry's grief elicited an outpouring of support from her suffrage colleagues. Convention delegates offered a resolution sending greetings, prayers, and loving sympathy to Henry and stating their fervent hope that she would soon be able to take up her work once again "for suffering humanity." The selection of Psalm 23, referencing the "valley of the shadow of death," for the convention's opening devotion was likely chosen in her honor.[38]

Clay and Farmer wrote Henry long and tender letters of condolence following the convention. Farmer could easily empathize; she too had buried her only son. Clay admitted that being childless, it was difficult to imagine that she could offer any effective words of comfort to her "dear, dear, friend," but she tried. Clay reminded herself of the important work to be done, she admitted, when it came home to her that she did not have "a woman's nearest and dearest ties." "Life is not all desolate," she stressed. There was plenty left to occupy all the energies of Henry's heart, "now torn and emptied of its treasure."[39]

The core members of KERA were a tight-knit group. The sorrows that affected one of them, affected them all. The outpouring of love they showed helped Henry prepare for the work that lay ahead. She would not allow herself the luxury of grieving too long. The 1892 legislative session would get under way soon, and it was her duty to be there.

When Henry, Clay, and Farmer returned to the capital in February 1892, their goals were largely the same as before. They hoped to equalize property rights and to place female doctors in state institutions. This time though, they came with a third priority that would dominate KERA's agenda for the next two decades: school suffrage.

The new constitution had done almost nothing for women. Women could not vote in statewide races without a constitutional amendment. Legislators, however, could award women partial suffrage (school, municipal, or presidential) through statutory law. Eugenia Farmer saw this as a window of opportunity, and she intended to crawl through it. Second-class cities were scheduled to have their charters renewed. Originally, charters had been renewed individually through special legislation, but the new constitution had taken steps to instill uniformity, assigning each city a class based on its size (Louisville was the state's only first-class city; sixth-class cities included its smallest villages). By 1895, the charters for every class of city would come up for renewal. Farmer recognized that school suffrage could efficiently be written into revised city charters, and she made this her mission.[40]

Select Kentucky women could already vote in limited situations in school elections, depending on their marital status, their race, and where they lived in the state, but most were excluded, at least officially. Kentucky had been the first state in the nation to extend limited school suffrage to women in 1838, but since then it had failed to keep pace with progress elsewhere. By 1890, more than twenty states had approved school suffrage for women. Legislators saw this as a low-stakes way to soothe women's rights forces. It did not involve real politics, they figured, and it would get women off their backs.[41]

KERA wanted all adult Kentucky women to vote on educational matters. Giving women, even black women, a say in their local schools just made good sense. Women cared for children at home, and they understood the challenges of running schools because so many worked as teachers. Proponents also argued that women had more time to attend to school matters and were less likely than men to use schools as party spoils. Woman's rights advocates saw school suffrage as a step toward achieving broader rights, an entering wedge you might say. School suffrage would allow women to prove they were worthy of the public's trust.[42]

Besides, they pointed out, women were already leading the state's schools. A growing number of women were serving as school superintendents across Kentucky. Women were breaking down important barriers, and KERA cheered each time one fell.[43]

Amanda T. Million's election as the first county superintendent of schools in Kentucky was certainly a victory worth celebrating. Something of an accidental hero, Million came to her post through tragedy in 1886. Her husband, Jackson Million, had served a term as Madison County superintendent and was up for reelection. He did not have to run very hard; he was running unopposed. But when election day arrived, uncertainty prevailed. Jackson Million was on his deathbed, ill with typhoid fever. Voters insisted that he would recover, but they were wrong. Jackson Million expired just as his second term began.[44]

Madison County residents endorsed the old adage "behind every good man, there is a good woman." They had lost an upstanding male public official—"one of the noblest and most generous hearted of her young men"—but his wife, Amanda, remained to carry on his work. She passed a certification examination and Judge J. C. Chenault, with consent from the state attorney general, appointed her to act temporarily in her husband's stead. Based on her performance, voters approved her bid to serve out the rest of the term in a special election the following year. Kentucky had its first "Lady School Commissioner." Inspired by Million's example, four more Kentucky women won election in their counties in 1889. By the end of the century, the Commonwealth had eighteen female county superintendents, including Million who remained the head of Madison County schools until she retired in 1901.[45]

Josephine Henry applauded the success of Million and others. She felt strongly, however, that women belonged in *all* public offices, not just those related to school management. Women needed to break down barriers, and she saw herself as just the one to do it. In 1890, she threw her hat in the ring to become clerk of Kentucky's court of appeals, a plum position by all estimates. The clerk of the appeals court raked in between ten thousand and fifteen thousand dollars annually in fees. If you were going to make a statement, you might as well make a big statement and seek the most lucrative office in the state, Henry figured. It may have been her own idea to run, or the Prohibition Party—the party of "high morals and cold water"—may have solicited her to do so. Either way, she became its candidate.[46]

Henry took her candidacy very seriously. A statewide race required extensive travel—Louisville, Hartford, Maysville, Richmond, a new town each day, sometimes two speeches a day. Henry did not flinch. Speaking was her gift, and she was in her element. But it was grueling. When Henry got up to speak at a picnic hosted by the Good Templars in Spottsville (Henderson County) on the Fourth of July, the strain she was under revealed itself. Perhaps it was the heat. Maybe she had skipped lunch. "THE LADY FAINTED," the Owensboro paper announced. Critics assumed women were too delicate for the rigors of politics and now they had their proof. Five hundred people watched her swoon and then remain out cold for thirty minutes until the doctor arrived and applied necessary restoratives. Henry must have been mortified, both by the collapse and by being misidentified in the news coverage yet again as Cassius Clay's daughter.[47]

She followed doctors' orders and rested a few weeks but soon returned to what the *Stanford Interior Journal* called her "wild goose chase." She finished out the campaign strong. When the votes were tallied, reported totals varied significantly. Some sources claimed she had received only 1,200 votes, fewer than the last Prohibition candidate to run for the post. Henry maintained that she received 5,000 votes, all from men, of course. Either way, she was soundly defeated, losing by about 150,000 votes. An editorial in the *Louisville Post* credited Henry for being a "sincere and talented lady," but concluded that it was a "cranky idea" for the Prohibition Party to run a female candidate.[48]

Women were swooping in on politics, establishing a presence in Frankfort, buttonholing lawmakers, influencing party platforms, and even running for office as the nineteenth century wound to a close. Woman's rights continued to be a bit avant-garde, a little "cranky," but they were on people's minds. KERA was starting to see victories, too.

Its first big wins came during the 1894 legislative session. After several failed attempts, Eugenia Farmer steered through a bill giving school suffrage to women—white and black—in Kentucky's second-class cities (Lexington, Newport, and Covington). Josephine Henry's efforts to win property rights also saw success. Women had won the right to make a will in 1892. In 1894, curtesy and dower were equalized when the "Husband and Wife Bill" passed. This law "practically made every married woman a *feme sole* (woman without a husband)," the *Owensboro Twice-a-Week Messenger* explained.[49]

These were sweet victories and hard fought. While Clay praised the men of Kentucky for their generosity and cited lawmakers by name who had championed their cause, Henry dwelled on what remained to be done. These reforms were a start, but the ballot was really what they needed. They could have obtained these crumbs of justice with far less effort if only they could vote for their own representatives, she grumbled.[50]

A few brave women had opened their eyes to the way society silenced them and they pledged to be silent no more. Their collective voice, however, was little more than a whisper in the early 1890s. It would take thousands, not just dozens, of concerned women to stand up. An awakening was on the horizon, and when it finally came, misbehaving men would have themselves to blame.

4

Woman Triumphant

Sometimes, when looking back over a lifetime, one moment stands out as a turning point. For Mrs. A. M. Harrison, a tall fashionable woman with a long, patrician nose, that moment came during a routine business meeting of the Confederate Veterans Association in 1894 as she helped to plan the upcoming Decoration Day festivities.

There were few things as sacred to southerners who worshipped at the altar of the Lost Cause as the grave of a Confederate soldier and few days as solemnly honored as Decoration Day. Decoration Day—later it would be known as Memorial Day—was a time to remember the fallen, to grieve collectively, and to encourage sectional reconciliation. The day was filled with bands, "tottering" old soldiers, rousing speeches, flags and fresh flowers, and of course, pretty women. No tribute to the Confederate dead would be complete without them. In the civic religion that developed around the Lost Cause, Decoration Day was the holiest day of the year and white women were its sacred keepers.[1]

Planning began early each year. In 1894, the Lexington Confederate Veterans' Association along with its women's auxiliary group gathered the week before to finalize the schedule for the day. Everyone assembled had a strong Confederate pedigree. Ida Withers Harrison certainly could claim her bona fides.

Ida Withers had grown up at Fairlawn Stock Farm in Lexington, the daughter of a very successful trotting horse breeder. William T. Withers's success in this business was a consolation prize in some ways, the product of a life rebuilt in the wake of the war's tragedy. Before the conflict, the Withers family, to hear Ida tell it, "lived handsomely," growing cotton in Louisiana and Mississippi on land that eventually would become stingy in its bounty but that started out fresh, fertile, and profitable. With the assistance of a large enslaved labor force, the family claimed its place in the southern aristocracy.[2]

But the war disrupted their charmed life. William Withers, like most of his peers, joined the Confederacy. A veteran of the Mexican conflict, he was an experienced and highly respected fighter. He raised a division of soldiers from Kentucky and then led the First Regiment of the Mississippi Light Artillery at the Battle of Vicksburg. Withers rose to the rank of colonel, but in the southern tradition of inflated honorifics, he became known to his friends and family as "the General."[3]

High-ranking Confederates found themselves in a bad spot at the war's end, but hard times began even earlier for the Withers family. Colonel Withers was captured and surrendered to Grant at Vicksburg in 1863. Grant generously provided the Withers family papers guaranteeing them safe passage within Union lines, but they spent the rest of the war as refugees trying not to starve. Withers had hoped to rebuild in Mississippi, but the uncertainty of Reconstruction led him instead to start over in Lexington. He chose a profitable and growing enterprise, trotting horses, and saw success almost immediately.[4]

The war experience of her husband, Albert, further enhanced Ida Withers Harrison's Confederate credentials. Allie had almost been born too late. He was only thirteen when the war started, but instead of serving as a messenger or drummer as many boys his age did, Harrison secured an appointment to the Confederate naval academy as a midshipman. Barely a teenager, he had little chance to distinguish himself during the conflict, but that meant he had many years to serve the Lost Cause after the fighting ended. Ida and Allie made an impressive team and became prominent members of the Confederate Veterans' Association of Kentucky.[5]

The group's meeting on May 22, 1894, should have been routine. Besides the fact that the veterans grew a little grayer each year, few details of the annual Decoration Day celebration changed. This year, however, the planning meeting took a sharp turn. Angry women issued ultimatums and the meeting finally adjourned with no resolution. It was "quite a sensation," the press reported.[6]

The firestorm began when Ida Harrison stood up and announced that the women's auxiliary of the Confederate Veterans' Association would not place "a flower on the grave of a single Confederate" unless the men dismissed one of their own, Colonel W. C. P. Breckinridge, from their membership. A few women, including her sister-in-law, Miss Mary Harrison, bravely nodded in agreement. If the men failed to act, the women would boycott the festivities. It was a bold announcement, and with it, Harrison demonstrated that she was no longer willing to remain silent. That 1894 meeting marked a political awakening—an awakening shared by other Lexington

Ida Withers Harrison's Confederate pedigree and her standing in the Lexington community positioned her to lead a variety of women's causes, including suffrage. (*Kentucky Woman's Journal*)

women. It was the beginning of an impressive reform career and the making of a suffragist.[7]

The year before, Colonel Breckinridge had been the featured speaker at Lexington's Decoration Day events, but much had changed since then. Breckinridge was an esteemed veteran, the son of a leading Kentucky family, and a Democratic US congressman from the seventh district. But now the "silver-tongued orator" was mired in scandal, and central Kentucky was feeling the strain.[8]

Breckinridge's troubles began ten years earlier on a train, following a chance encounter with a young woman named Madeline Pollard. The congressman, a forty-seven-year-old married man, had met the seventeen-year-old schoolgirl when he was traveling from Lexington to Frankfort. As Pollard explained it, the encounter turned into a more "confidential" meeting in a closed carriage (his choice, the evening air supposedly irritated his throat) on a hot summer night. Another man was pressing Pollard to marry him, and she had called upon the congressman to help her free herself from his demands; but the interaction turned into more. By August, "Willy" had "completed his seduction," Pollard recalled.[9]

Pollard became his mistress and the two began a long affair. He installed her in fashionable boardinghouses in Lexington and Washington, DC, so he could see her often. He helped her secure employment at the Department of Agriculture and the US Census Bureau. When she twice became pregnant, he set her up at a "foundling asylum."[10]

When news of the affair broke in August 1893, Breckinridge did not deny that he had shared a relationship with Miss Pollard. "She was a woman of passion; I was a man of passion. We yielded ourselves to each other. That was all," he later explained. He did, however, object to Pollard's rendering of the details.[11]

And these details suddenly mattered very much when Pollard sued Breckinridge in 1893, claiming breach of promise and revealing their long affair to the world. When news of the suit broke, Pollard suddenly became the most famous woman in Kentucky. Americans could not get enough of the sordid story.

The death of Breckinridge's wife in the summer of 1892 triggered the dispute. Breckinridge promised Pollard that he would marry her after a sufficient mourning period passed. He repeated this pledge several times and in front of witnesses. Accustomed to living a secret life in the shadow of a famous man, Pollard likely thrilled at the offer of a secure and stable future, not just for herself but for her unborn child (again pregnant, she would later miscarry).

Soon after, Breckinridge remarried, but he did not marry Pollard. He secretly wed a cousin instead. When Pollard cried foul, Breckinridge tried unsuccessfully to buy her off. She rejected his offers of hush money and demanded justice in the courts instead.[12]

Pollard's legal team put a price tag of $50,000 on Breckinridge's offense but their client was not just seeking a quick fortune. By suing for breach of promise, Pollard hoped to reclaim some of her dignity. She was an innocent victim, she insisted. He was the victimizer. He had taken her chastity, left her damaged, and deserved to pay. Society agreed that lustful men must be held in check; breach of promise and seduction cases were an important way to do so. To successfully sue for breach of promise, however, one had to prove that the woman's virtue had been stolen, not squandered. The courts and a curious American audience attempted to determine whether the woman at the center of this case was an innocent schoolgirl or a calculated social climber. Pollard claimed the former, and Breckinridge insisted the latter.[13]

Breckinridge testified that he took liberties with the teenager the *first night* he met her, therefore he could not have possibly seduced her. A maiden or a virgin, she was not, Breckinridge insisted, nor was she as young as she claimed. He denied ever asking her to give up a child (though he did not deny that it could be his) and insisted that he had never proposed marriage, though he did admit to rendezvousing with Miss Pollard as often as three times a day during their long relationship.[14]

The trial began on March 8, 1894. Racing season was getting under way by the time attorneys delivered their closing arguments six weeks later. Pollard's attorney issued a call for justice: "This defendant came before a jury to vilify, traduce, and blacken the character of a woman he had destroyed. Gentlemen, what will you do?" The jury deliberated an hour before deciding Breckinridge was guilty. The court ordered him to pay his former mistress $15,000 (equivalent to three years' congressional salary). It was, the *Pittsburgh Press* reported, "The Wages of Sin."[15]

The verdict came while Breckinridge was in the middle of a reelection campaign, a campaign he now could scarcely hope to win. This would be a career-ending event, most believed. The scoundrel would slink away into an early retirement. Willy Breckinridge, however, had no plans to slink away. He had a race to run.

Even before the trial wrapped up, Breckinridge suggested that the suit would have no impact on his political plans. He claimed that letters were pouring in from all over his district, urging him to run again no matter the trial's outcome. He intended to win his primary that fall and thus win "vindication." He officially announced his campaign to seek a sixth term on May 5 in Lexington, leaving some to sarcastically ask if he would make the house of assignation where he often met Pollard his campaign headquarters.[16]

Breckinridge's decision to run again shocked and divided Lexington society. It was bad enough, many argued, that he had behaved immorally, but his refusal to step out of the public eye brought scorn to them all. Ministers led the opposition, declaring Breckinridge a "disgrace to Kentucky, a shame upon manhood, an insult to womanhood, a sinful example to youth, and a menace to both society and the home." Joined by the women of the Seventh District, who saw themselves as the protectors of public morality, the anti-Breckinridge movement was a powerful force.[17]

Although many complained that it was wrong for ministers to mix religion and politics, women's participation riled some even more. White women were supposed to lead through indirect influence. Stepping too far from home or hearth would jeopardize their virtue. A proper woman would never allow herself to be sullied by the muck of politics. That was better left for the men—they seemed to thrive in muck.[18]

Women had traditionally kept a low profile, but not always. Occasionally, Lexington women threw their weight behind a cause and stepped into the public spotlight. In fact, Colonel Breckinridge's late wife, Issa Desha, and his sister-in-law, Mary Desha, had been the instigators the last time women had loudly made their voices heard back in 1884. The sisters along with nearly two hundred women from the community worked together to culturally enlighten Lexington while taking a silent jab at its men.

Their goal: to raise the money necessary to purchase Joel T. Hart's sculpture "Woman Triumphant" and place it on display in the city's new courthouse. Carved from marble, the work was said to be Hart's best. It featured a naked female Venus towering over a chubby childlike cupid who had his bow pointed up at her. His arrows, meant to inflict her with uncontrollable desire, failed to hit their mark and lay scattered at her feet. She held his last arrow above her head and out of his reach, a move both defensive and condescending.[19]

Several Kentucky women, including Mrs. Breckinridge, had seen the statue while touring Italy. Now, they pledged to bring it home. The statue resided in a Tiffany's showroom in New York City, but the jeweler offered to sell it for $5,000 (roughly $140,000 in 2018 dollars).[20]

Both the artist himself and the subject matter of the sculpture appealed to the women. They described Hart as their beau ideal. Unlike most men who chased after wealth, power, and glory, Hart, a native Kentuckian, was content to live in poverty and pursue his art. He was a model for young men to emulate, his life filled with useful lessons, the women stressed. But they also hoped to make a larger point about women's value in society. Hart's work celebrated ideal womanhood: purity, patience, beauty, and strength.[21]

The women were unfamiliar with public activity, especially the act of "begging," they later recalled. They knew nothing about parliamentary procedure or the ins and outs of organization. They were criticized for trying to learn, but their confidence grew with each donation they received. Although they welcomed individual contributions, they looked for bigger

Lexington women mobilized in the 1880s to raise money to purchase Joel T. Hart's statue, "Woman Triumphant." Until then, Kentucky had honored its men in bronze and marble, but never its women. (*The Work Shall Praise the Master*)

pots of money. The Kentucky legislature rebuffed their request to kick in state funds, but a personal appeal to the Fayette County Court of Claims resulted in a $1,000 appropriation. To raise the remaining $1,000, they hosted a carnival in Woodland Park.[22]

The result of the women's efforts was unveiled on July 4, 1885, alongside a new statue of John C. Breckinridge (fully funded by the state of Kentucky) that would stand on the courthouse lawn for many years. "Woman Triumphant" would have a more protected spot inside the rotunda of the new building once it was completed. It moved to its new home the following month, marked by another ceremony and a speech by W. C. P. Breckinridge. The irony of his role in dedicating a work that would often be called "Triumph of Chastity" would only later become apparent.[23]

The statue sparked a public debate about Kentucky's willingness to embrace high culture. The women who sponsored it believed it would elevate the state and establish it as a place of refined tastes. Others doubted transformation would come so easily. Prudish members of society questioned the decency of the statue, and a few demanded that it be removed. Some viewers found its nakedness titillating (this was the Victorian era, after all) and made sure to visit the courthouse just to see it.[24]

The novelty wore off quickly, however, and soon reports circulated that the statue was covered in dust and tobacco spit. The *Richmond Register* predicted as much. Placing an "exquisite work of art in a public Court House where the vulgar and unrefined do most congregate" was asking for trouble, the editor moralized. Concerned about its safety, the women investigated the possibility of building an annex to the library to house it but settled instead for supplying a glass case.[25]

Issa Breckinridge and the white women of Lexington had stepped into the public sphere for the benefit of their community when they raised funds to purchase and display "Woman Triumphant." Their statue indirectly critiqued a value system built around men's priorities, but on its outward face their project seemed self-sacrificing and their motives pure. When women stepped out again ten years later to denounce Breckinridge's husband and to demand his political demise, their actions attracted more scrutiny. Once again, women would call men's values and their weaknesses into question, but this time much more brazenly.

Ida Withers Harrison had had enough in the summer of 1894, a point she sharply punctuated when she threatened to leave Confederate graves undecorated. It is unclear whether she was one of the two hundred Lexington women who had raised money to purchase the Hart statue ten years earlier. Her son, James, was only three years old then, and likely demanded her full attention. Now, however, the obligations of mothering no longer tugged at her. Jamie had died when he was just six years old, and she likely needed an escape from the numbing grief and the quiet his death left behind.[26]

Harrison's first recorded public activity, driven by her strong religious faith, came in the early 1890s. In 1892, the Kentucky Woman's Board of Missions elected her president. She would oversee a gospel-spreading division of the Christian Church that focused on caring for both the spiritual and physical needs of women and children. Missionary work, an enterprise that seemed appropriate and dignified, would become Harrison's grand passion.[27]

Harrison could have endorsed and worked for woman's equality if she had wanted. The Fayette County E.R.A. was always recruiting, but she apparently did not pursue this option, likely seeing suffrage as too radical. In the early 1890s, her activities centered on church work and celebrating her southern heritage. She also organized the Woman's Musical Club of Lexington (later to become a division of the Woman's Club of Central Kentucky), whose members shared "music of a high order" and quality literature. Like many of her peers, Harrison agreed that a woman should improve her own mind and elevate the culture and morals of society in a quiet, humble way without calling attention to herself.[28]

That all changed in the spring of 1894 when congressman Breckinridge's philandering ways became America's great obsession. Lexington women, Harrison included, held their tongues (at least publicly) at first, but when he announced that he would run again, they unleashed their fury. In a newspaper notice boldly signed "THE WOMEN OF LEXINGTON," they appealed to Democratic voters. Breckinridge must be defeated. If a man were to support him, he would "proclaim himself equally guilty," they warned.[29]

Women themselves could not vote for Breckinridge's challenger, William C. Owens. They had to trust in men to do the right thing. Traditionally, they would have relied on indirect influence—a soft whisper in a husband's or son's ear—but Breckinridge's "hideous immorality" warranted more extreme action. Working with local ministers, outraged women planned a public rally at the Lexington Opera House on May 14, 1894. Only the "women's suffrage cranks" would turn out, some critics warned, but they were wrong. The hall was packed with "beautiful and charming" women, the *Courier-Journal* reported; five or six hundred people were even turned away.[30]

The ladies gasped when a male speaker toward the end of the rally apparently forgot his manners and cursed. Women's commitment to see Breckinridge go down in defeat, however, could not be wrecked by a little salty language. News of how the women of the Bluegrass had become "thoroughly aroused" made the front page of newspapers across the country. They had declared war on Breckinridge.[31]

It was not just Breckinridge they were warring against, however. They were attacking a system that for too long had excused white men's bad behavior and endorsed a sexual double standard. Kentucky was renowned for its beautiful women, as stereotypes of the state emphasized, and many Kentucky men, it seemed, felt entitled to partake of the bounty. But now women were making themselves clear in no uncertain terms: they were tired of turning a blind eye to their husbands' indiscretions, they were sick of ignoring the knowing wink. They intended to make Breckinridge their sacrificial lamb. By punishing him, they could punish all the men in their lives who had humiliated them.

Sex and power seemed to go hand in hand. Leading bankers, lawyers, businessmen, and especially the horse set frequented the city's brothels. In her study of famed Lexington madam Belle Brezing, Maryjean Wall describes smoky rooms, exclusive clubs, and bawdy houses that featured free-flowing alcohol and high-stakes gambling. The webs of influence were spun in such environs. Young men from prominent families visited Madam Belle's at a young age for "indoctrination into the mysteries of manhood," which included an introduction to the political and professional worlds they would one day inhabit.[32]

Men acknowledged that they were prone to weakness. Friends of Breckinridge sent notes of knowing support when news of his troubles broke. "I expect you have made some mistakes," former Kentucky secretary of state G. W. Craddock wrote, "and who in the H——L has not!" He assured Breckinridge he was not the only one to stumble.[33]

Breckinridge's cronies might give him a pass, but women would not. Lacking the power to punish him at the polls, women creatively used the power that they did possess. They refused to shop at stores run by Breckinridge supporters or seek treatment from family physicians who were backing him. Young "maidens" even monitored possible suitors; when a young man wearing a Breckinridge campaign button called on a debutante, she instructed him to leave and never come back.[34]

Not all women, of course, condemned Breckinridge. A few were willing to attend his rallies, arguing that Christians had an obligation to forgive. Others, while silently condemning his hypocrisy, refused to take public action against him. Ida and Mary Harrison promised that they would not decorate Confederate graves, but their colleagues in the ladies' auxiliary did not share their resolve. When questioned about the contentious meeting, the president of the auxiliary stressed that contrary to reports their planning session had been "perfectly harmonious." When Decoration Day arrived, so did the women. They "fairly covered graves with the choicest of flowers," a special dispatch to the *Cincinnati Enquirer* reported with relief. Editorials from faraway places applauded the women's return to reason. The *Asheville Citizen Times* agreed that women should help to defeat Breckinridge, but they must not lose their hold on good sense. "Let there be no quarreling over the graves of Confederate dead," an Austin, Texas, critic directed.[35]

Ida Harrison stood her ground and resigned from the Confederate Veterans' Association over the disagreement. Throughout the summer and into the fall she remained committed to seeing Breckinridge defeated. As the election neared, Harrison and other Lexington women turned their attention from convincing men to vote the right way to praying that God would control the outcome, which looked increasingly dire. Friends and neighbors were now "at sword's points" and violence seemed likely. Women across central Kentucky met in churches on the eve of the election to pray that the man elected be a man after God's own heart and that peace prevail.[36]

The women's prayers were answered, just by a hair. Owens defeated Breckinridge by 255 votes, out of almost 19,000 votes cast. "THE SUN STILL SHINES ON THE OLD KENTUCKY HOME," the *Courier-Journal* cheered. Women gathered at the home of Mrs. Frank K. Hunt, president of the city's woman's club, on election night to celebrate. When asked to comment on the outcome, Hunt, raising white-gloved hands, noted that Kentucky was again "God's country." Finally, Breckinridge could be sent to the "wilderness of oblivion."[37]

It was not just Kentucky women who celebrated Breckinridge's defeat. Members of the Massachusetts Woman's Rescue League, which had bitterly opposed Breckinridge throughout the contest from afar, sent Kentucky women special greetings, applauding their "moral and political crusade." An editorialist in the *Caldwell (KS) News* agreed that women were responsible for Breckinridge's defeat and for preventing blood from being spilled. After all, "colonels and brigadiers were walking arsenals." But it was not public activity that made the difference, rather it was women's "gentle influence"; their electioneering was done "at the fireside" and at church in quiet supplication, as it should be, the editorialist inferred.[38]

KERA representatives recognized that the Breckinridge scandal offered them a perfect chance to build support for their cause. Josephine Henry argued emphatically that this situation was precisely why women needed the vote as it was the only way women could hope to "make or unmake congressmen," but her colleagues thought it best to emphasize other woman's rights issues, hoping to woo a broader cross section of women. In the wake of this scandal, they focused like a laser on laws to control male sexual predators.[39]

It was a good time to try to revise "age of consent" statutes with the Madeline Pollard case attracting so much attention, they agreed. In a published appeal to lawmakers in 1893, which also functioned as a call to action to Kentucky women, KERA stressed the need to throw off barbarism and to protect its maidens from the "lust of men." Kentucky declared twelve the age when a young girl could "consent to her own ruin." She had to be twenty-one to make decisions about her property, but she could squander her "crown of womanhood" when just a child. KERA's plea, though politely worded, seethed with rage. Men were too absorbed in "material progress . . . power and gain." Only women could keep the state from moral ruin. KERA urged lawmakers to unanimously vote to declare eighteen (one year older than Pollard had been when Breckinridge defiled her) the new age of consent. If the 1894 session brought no success, they would be back again, they vowed.[40]

Observers could not help but notice white Lexington women's efforts to recalibrate the moral compass of their community in 1893, but they were not the only group roused to action that year. Black women were also standing up, protesting a new state law that required trains to carry white and "colored" riders on separate cars. It was the first significant struggle by black Kentuckians to resist Jim Crow, and women were there front and center to lead it.[41]

In some ways, black Kentuckians seemed to have it better than their neighbors to the south in the years after the Civil War. The state had never made it illegal to educate black children and it was home to Berea College, the first college in the South to allow black and white students (male and female) to learn together side by side. It also became the first state to pass an antilynching law, making it illegal for a public official to turn over a prisoner to a rabid mob intent on dispensing its own vigilante justice. Unlike former Confederate states that went to great lengths to legally disfranchise black men using literacy tests, poll taxes, and grandfather clauses, Kentucky did not follow suit. Democrats employed violence and harassment to keep black men away, knowing that their votes would go to their rivals, but they largely failed. Kentucky continued to be a two-party state and black male voters remained a legitimate force.[42]

Kentucky did not need to disfranchise black men wholesale because its black population was small, largely concentrated in few cities, and shrinking all the time. By 1890, with freedom leading many to seek opportunity in places like Kansas—former slaves' new frontier—Kentucky's African American population fell to just 16.9 percent. Kentucky leaders did not fear black domination, unlike states where blacks outnumbered whites.[43]

Despite its reputation for being more progressive on race matters, Kentucky was not immune to the growing desire to legally separate the races to ensure that everyone knew "their place." Lines of segregation began to harden in the 1890s, and white Kentuckians enthusiastically embraced the policy of "separate but equal," which became the law of the land. Public institutions like schools and lunatic asylums were already segregated largely by race, and it had become custom to require blacks to enter businesses through a separate entrance. In 1892, attention turned to imposing racial segregation on the trains.[44]

Separate coach laws had already been adopted in other states by the time Kentucky began considering one. Congressmen representing poorer rural districts liked these laws because their white constituents were more likely to purchase cheaper tickets that put them on cars with African American riders. Race baiting has long been a good way to build a political career, as a lawmaker from Calloway County proved when he proposed a separate coach law during Kentucky's 1892 legislative session. It easily passed, the governor signed it, and it was scheduled to go into effect the following October (noon on the third to be precise), allowing rail companies time to retrofit their cars.[45]

African Americans sprang to action as soon as they heard that separate coaches might come to Kentucky, and they were well organized by the time it became law. They considered two opposition strategies. They could boycott the trains, a less expensive but more inconvenient approach, or they could test the constitutionality of the law through the courts. National black leaders like Ida B. Wells and Frederick Douglass urged Kentuckians to pursue the former course, arguing that the "appeal to the white man's pocket" was always the most effective. Kentucky's Anti-Separate Coach League decided instead to pursue legal action.

In October 1893, a black Baptist minister, Rev. W. H. Anderson, and his wife boarded a train in Evansville, Indiana, and calmly sat down in a white car, as Indiana state law allowed them to do. From there, everything went according to plan. When they crossed the border into Kentucky, they were told they must move. They refused, they were ejected from the car, and they proceeded to sue, arguing that Kentucky's law violated the interstate commerce clause of the US Constitution. The Andersons sought $15,000 in damages.[46]

The Anti-Separate Coach League had carefully considered every detail of this official test case. Donors from all over the state had chipped in small sums to defray the costs and talented lawyers had honed their arguments. The league intended to demonstrate that this law violated the rights of every African American who traveled into, out of, or through Kentucky and interfered with protections the federal government had promised.

But even while this official case was still in the planning stages, women acted on their own accord to challenge the law. Amanda Redd, a well-known and highly respected seamstress from Georgetown in her early fifties, was one of the first to do so. She operated a dress shop on North Broadway, and we know that she had at least one employee, as her shop was the site of a tragic murder in 1889. The estranged husband of one of Redd's employees came to the door, grabbed his wife by the neck, and slit her throat from ear to ear with a dull pocketknife. Luckily, most days were much more routine.[47]

Redd had long been a member of the Baptist Women's Educational Convention of Kentucky, a group known for opposing both race and gender discrimination. Her decision to stand up for her rights in 1893 may have come from her involvement in race work, but it was more likely spontaneous. Redd had gone to Chicago to see the World's Fair with her husband. They started back to Kentucky in early October, only days after the new separate coach law went into effect. When they arrived in Cincinnati, they were instructed to switch cars. Mrs. Redd, a light-skinned woman, was incensed and refused. She instructed her husband to return to Georgetown without her and to lease her property. She would not reenter Kentucky until she could freely travel, she vowed. She meant what she said. She posted a notice in the *Cincinnati Enquirer* that she was looking for a suitable residence and planned to make the city her home. The following year, the paper reported that she had settled at 284 West Eighth Street and was entertaining guests there. She had also filed suit against the Queen of the Crescent rail line, claiming $10,000 in damages.[48]

Redd, like many of the women who launched anti-separate coach cases, highlighted her status as a respectable woman in her suit. Leaders of the anti-separate coach movement claimed they represented the "better class of colored citizens"—what would later be known as the "talented tenth." They saw themselves as distinct from the "roughs" that the law targeted. Separate coaches might drive the better element of blacks from the state (a point Redd seemed particularly intent on driving home) and would threaten existing bonds of unity between the races. They argued that if segregation was necessary, it should occur along class lines rather than race lines. Black and white opponents of the law agreed that they would rather sit on a train car with a well-bred person of a different race than be forced to mingle with the coarser elements of their own race.[49]

Fannie Quinn similarly leveraged this claim of respectability when she filed suit against the L&N Railroad the same year. Many suits related to the separate coach law focused on its illegality and the ways it threatened African American riders' constitutional rights, but Quinn turned matters on their head, defending the law. She argued that it served a vital function by allowing her, a well-bred African American woman, to protect herself from brutal white men.

Drunk and rowdy passengers were a common problem on the trains. Conductors did not want white hoodlums to bother other well-behaved white passengers, so it became common practice to throw them on to the black car to sober up. Fannie Quinn was returning to Elizabethtown from a meeting of the Baptist Women's Educational Convention in Louisville in mid-October 1893, on "the coach assigned her and her race by the company," she stressed, when the conductor allowed three drunk white riders to board it, despite the signs that clearly read "colored only." The men did not care that a lady was present. They began to curse and to humiliate her. One offered her a drink and "perhaps laid his hand upon her," the trial transcript noted. Mrs. Quinn complained to the conductor but received no assistance.[50]

In its first hearing, the jury decided for the L&N, but the verdict was overturned on appeal. By allowing a white passenger to stay on a black car, the prosecution argued, the company became responsible for the mistreatment that occurred and made the law into a "dead letter." The appeals court ruled the conductor had failed to uphold the law and had failed to protect Mrs. Quinn. It awarded her $100 in damages.[51]

Sixty years before Rosa Parks famously opposed discrimination in public transportation, Kentucky women like Amanda Redd and Fannie Quinn took a stand. While their efforts did not have an immediate effect (the US Supreme Court ruled in 1896 in *Plessy v. Ferguson* that separate coaches were legal; Kentucky's separate coach law would not be repealed until 1966), they stood up boldly to racism and claimed their right to protection as women.[52]

Women—black and white—were opening their eyes, asking questions, and refusing to be bound by custom any longer. In 1895, Josephine Henry published an article in the national journal, the *Arena*, in which she called attention to the awakening under way. Long considered "a drowsy civilization," the South was emerging from its slumber, and the "New Woman" was responsible. When she praised women for throwing off their "social and political incarceration," it was white women she had in mind, but she could have been talking about black women just as easily. Women were no longer content to remain silent. Southern men had messed things up. They had left the region in "ruin and despair," according to Henry. Now, women would be the ones to repair the damage.[53]

Church woman and proud Confederate daughter, Ida Withers Harrison was one of those New Women rising to confront the challenges of a new age, and once she did, she never looked back. The ultimatum she issued to the Confederate Veterans' Association seemed to flip a switch in her. Church activities continued to occupy her time, but increasingly, she took up political and civic work. She became president of the Woman's Club of Central Kentucky and a trustee of the public library.[54]

Then, in 1895, she attended her first state suffrage convention. KERA delegates nominated her superintendent of political study, but she politely declined the position. Maybe she was still not completely comfortable with full female equality, but it did not take her long to shake off her lingering squeamishness. By 1897, she was serving as secretary of the Fayette County E.R.A. The following year, she agreed to chair KERA's political study department, the position she rejected two years earlier. For the rest of her life, Harrison remained a dedicated suffragist, holding leadership roles at the local and the state level and eventually becoming active in state Democratic politics once the vote was won.[55]

One imagines Hart's "Woman Triumphant" smiling from her position in the courthouse at the changes the 1890s brought in women like Harrison. White Lexington women believed Hart's statue would be an enduring tribute to their quiet and largely hidden influence. But as a new century approached women grew less content to shape their communities in indirect ways. They intended for their voices to be heard.

Sponsors claimed that Hart's statue would be immortal, but they did not account for unexpected tragedy. In 1897, the Lexington courthouse burned. Two chivalrous firefighters risked their lives to save the statue, knowing how much it meant to local women, but to no avail. As they attempted to remove it from its pedestal, big chunks of glass began to fall on them, and they had to abandon their rescue mission. The statue met its demise when a huge bell that hung over it fell and crushed it. Only bits and pieces remained for relic hunters to carry off. In the days following the fire, the women of the city pledged to recreate the artwork. However, the energy that was once there for such pursuits had been channeled in new directions. Women were no longer interested in celebrating women's value through passive and symbolic means; they were committed to demonstrating their worth to the community in new, active, and ultimately more constructive ways.[56]

In the 1890s, votes for women was still an unconventional idea, too radical for most Kentuckians to consider; but a change was under way. The first step was to convince women that their ideas mattered and that they had a responsibility to make not just their homes but also their communities cleaner, purer, and more efficient places. Only after they began to see themselves as public change agents could women start to see themselves as potential voters.

5

How Do You Spell Equality?

It was an audacious proposal that Josephine Henry made, but that is the way she tended to operate. In 1892, Henry demanded that Kentucky's state seal get a makeover. The emblem, which featured two men, was old-fashioned and failed to acknowledge women's growing importance in society. Give one of the men "his walking papers," she instructed, and put a woman in his place. After all, women were one-half of the population.[1]

When the general assembly called for the creation of an official state seal in 1792, it only specified that it should depict two friends embracing and should include the state's motto, "United We Stand Divided We Fall." In the twenty-first century, the blue and gold emblem features two men at the center, one dressed in frontiersman garb, the other sporting formal attire. This, however, is only the latest rendition of the seal. While the motto has stayed the same throughout the years, the engraved image at its center has evolved. Every so often, the men changed clothing (Roman togas in one variation); a warm hug became a polite handshake. But Henry's proposed revision caused quite a stir.[2]

Critics laughed. To put a woman on the seal would require it to be redrawn quarterly to reflect shifting female fashions, one opponent scoffed. The woman's voluminous skirt would take up the entire frame, the *Courier-Journal* warned. The man in the scene "would have to stand on the edge and hold on with his toes like a chicken holds to its humble roost." The motto would need to read, "Unsettled I stand. I am afraid I will fall." Henry's demand was dismissed as ridiculous. "It is safe to say," a St. Louis writer concluded, "that no alteration will be made in the State seal of Kentucky."[3]

Josephine Henry offered a new vision for the Commonwealth, one that demanded equality, at least gender equality. She insisted that Kentucky must live up to its stated ideals and finally pursue unity, as its motto so solemnly promised.

Her insistence on a new seal, however, while moving women out of the periphery and into the center, did not address other existing class and race hierarchies that Kentuckians, even those committed to working for woman

71

suffrage, tenaciously upheld. The nineteenth-century woman was not monolithic, but rather represented many races, ethnicities, class positions, education levels, and religious beliefs. Even women who agreed that the vote should be the goal were divided over the best way to achieve it. Equality sounded like a simple idea, but in practice it would prove complicated and contestable. The woman suffrage movement called for equality, but equality for whom?

By the late 1890s, Josephine Henry, Eugenia Farmer, and Laura Clay had grown accustomed to the annual suffrage work routine. During even years, the spring was consumed with legislative work in Frankfort. Summers slowed down a bit. It was too hot to work, at least according to Clay. But as soon as temperatures cooled, they were back up to full speed, preparing for KERA's annual convention, touring the state to build interest, and during odd years, preparing for the session to come. Each woman had her niche. Henry focused on property rights and full voting measures. Eugenia Farmer was the expert on all matters related to school suffrage. Laura Clay took care of executive details, both state and national. Divide and conquer. Together, they were a powerful force.

The close bonds that these women—the powerful triumvirate of Kentucky suffrage—shared would soon shatter, however. They would part ways, giving Laura Clay almost exclusive command of suffrage work in Kentucky from 1900 until 1912. A shared interest in gender equality was not enough in the end to compensate for other, fundamental disagreements that left the women at odds.

Summer was usually the time that suffragists took a little rest, but not the summer of 1895. That fall, for the first time, all women over the age of twenty-one in Lexington, Covington, and Newport would be eligible to cast school ballots. KERA had much to do to prepare for the important milestone. Ever since the legislature had authorized school suffrage the previous year, dire predictions had followed. Respectable women would not show up at the polls, naysayers warned. If they did show, they wouldn't know what to do once they got there. Suffrage leaders understood that the fall elections must go smoothly if their plan to expand school suffrage to all Kentucky women was to succeed.[4]

It would require more than women just showing up in November and marking a ballot. They would need to register in advance. Special polling sites were needed, away from the saloons and stables where men often voted. Women must have assurance that they could vote safely and respectably.

It just so happened that three of KERA's most active auxiliaries operated in the cities included in the school suffrage expansion. Suffragists in these communities jumped into high gear to prepare, meeting with officials in each city to discuss plans, and they were pleased by the response. In Fayette County, Judge Frank Bullock promised to make new female voters feel safe and welcome. He selected private homes, one per district, to serve as registration sites, with female registrars to staff them.[5]

Women in Fayette, Kenton, and Campbell Counties were "all in a flutter" that summer, but suffragists offered calm assistance. Right away, they conducted a census to see how many women were currently qualified to vote. They first tried to reach women through special parlor meetings and church gatherings, but the results were disappointing. Instead, they began house-to-house visitations. As KERA representatives suspected, many women did not even know they were eligible to vote, but once their rights and duties were explained, many promised to do their part.[6]

The school suffrage measure authorized women not only to vote for school board representatives but to run for these offices as well, and KERA made sure female candidates from each ward would appear on the ballots. In Lexington, the WCTU, the Woman's Club of Central Kentucky, and the E.R.A. united to nominate a "woman's ticket" that included four well-known local women, including two suffragists: the newly converted Ida Withers Harrison (having mended fences with the Confederate Veterans' Association) and Mary Creeghan Roark, the wife of a local educator. When the Republican and Democratic parties of Fayette County refused to add women's names to their slate of nominees, they joined with four male allies to form an independent ticket. The Republican Party proved more welcoming to Covington women, placing Eugenia Farmer and two other women's names on the ballot. In Newport, the Republican Party told aspiring female candidates that it was "too soon," but two women ran on the Democratic ticket.[7]

Suffragists' get-out-the-vote efforts leading up to the 1895 contest, while directed primarily at white women, acknowledged that many black women would also be voting for the first time. The school suffrage issue led the exclusively white KERA to look across race lines for the first and one of the only times. School suffrage champion Eugenia Farmer led the effort. Partly, she did so to leave no stone unturned—high turnout would prove wrong men who claimed that women did not really want to vote—but she also appears to have been a racial moderate whose liberal ideas distinguished her from most of her suffrage colleagues.

Farmer encouraged black northern Kentucky women not only to vote when the time came but also to establish their own local suffrage associations. She visited the Colored Methodist Church in Covington three times that summer to recruit interested women. And from these efforts, one club, the Covington Colored Organization, formed. Although it did not last long and little record of it remains, it stands as Kentucky's first and only black E.R.A. The club's annual report does not appear alongside those of white locals, but Mrs. Farmer read it aloud, which suggests that white suffragists were at least curious about black women's suffrage work, if not willing to see it as equivalent to their own.[8]

Fayette County school suffrage organizers did not go as far as Farmer to reach out to black women, but they, too, took some halting steps toward interracial cooperation. Acting as emissaries of the Fayette E.R.A., Louise Bemley and Mary C. Cramer met with Prof. Green Pinckney Russell, superintendent of colored schools, to ask him to instruct and recruit female voters. A house-to-house canvas would be best, they advised, but they would not conduct it themselves as they were doing in white neighborhoods. It made more sense, they argued, for black women to hear the call from "their people."[9]

Black women took their new responsibility as voters very seriously. They would use their ballots with the utmost care, they promised. For years, black men throughout the South were accused of selling their votes. The charges were in most cases unfair, an attempt to prove the Fifteenth Amendment had been a mistake, but even many black women believed them. They vowed that they would be more discerning.

Hence, when asked to show solidarity with white women and support the Independent Ticket running in Lexington, black women didn't immediately consent. They had heard a rumor that white women, if elected to the school board, would fire black teachers and replace them with white instructors. They demanded to know whether it was true. A committee of black women, led by E. Belle Jackson, a successful female businesswoman with varied interests—she could sell you a hat or embalm you when you died—met with each candidate and made them promise that they would not replace black teachers. The candidates all swore that they had no such intentions and declared that "colored people were the proper ones to teach their own race." It had been a hoax to prejudice black women against members of their own sex, Jackson's committee concluded. The Independent Ticket could count on their support.[10]

They kept their promises come November. The *Lexington Press-Transcript* reported with some disappointment that white women "did not turn out in full force . . . but the colored vote nearly all went in." The ambivalence of white women was blamed on a last-minute adjustment to the polling sites, moving them out of private homes and into spaces shared with male voters. That could not have been the problem, however, since few white women had bothered to register in advance. Still, enough voters supported the Women's Ticket in Lexington to sweep it to victory. Female candidates in Kenton and Campbell Counties did not win, but they made a respectable showing. Eugenia Farmer shrugged off her defeat. Now, she would have more time to work toward expanding school suffrage to other Kentucky women.[11]

The 1895 school elections revealed that black women in Kentucky deeply valued the vote. They had long understood its power. In the summer of 1887, a year before KERA began active suffrage work, black schoolteacher Mary Ellen Britton spoke at the Colored State Teachers' Association at the African Methodist Episcopal (AME) Church in Danville, where a half-dozen women participated in a symposium to consider the ways woman suffrage could advance their public reform agenda. Only Britton's remarks survive, published afterward in the *American Catholic Tribune*, an African American publication out of Cincinnati.[12]

Britton fearlessly defended woman suffrage, noting that the vote would allow "creation's gentle half" to improve a flawed society. Enfranchised women could push out the "bad men," who spent public money on cigars and fine drinks, and could inject valuable moral influence into public decision-making. Had Laura Clay been there to hear her speech, she likely would have added her "amen" to many of Britton's points. Britton offered examples of strong women from the Bible such as Huldah, a prophetess, and Deborah, "a warrior judge," to undercut those who claimed God intended women to be silent. She painted a picture of Jesus as protector of truth and justice. Those who believed men superior to women, she noted, invoked the words of Paul rather than Jesus, who as "risen Savior" had appeared first to a woman, after all.[13]

A commanding woman with steely eyes, Britton was born to parents who had been free before the war and who were well established within the Lexington community, giving her a useful head start in life. She was well educated at a time when many of her peers were not. She studied at a local AME missionary school before attending Berea College from 1871 to 1874.

Mary Ellen Britton gave the first recorded suffrage speech in Kentucky when she spoke at a teachers' conference in Danville in 1887. (Berea College Special Collections and Archives)

She graduated with a teaching degree, went to work in Lexington's African American schools, and became a proud member of a large and potent fighting force of black educators committed to uplifting the race.[14]

By the time she gave her speech that steamy July day in Danville, Britton had already developed a national following as a talented and prolific writer. Writing in black periodicals such as *American Citizen* and *Cincinnati Commercial* under the penname "MEB," she raged against racial injustice, intemperance, and the sexual double standard. She described herself as "an agitator." Her fellow black Kentuckians considered her "plucky," with wide-ranging interests (she studied phrenology—the idea that skull contours determine personality and intelligence—and metaphysics). All Louisville knows her, one admirer remarked in 1893, "she is our Meb."[15]

Britton was part of an extensive network of reform-minded African American women spread across the state. Many were teachers; nearly all were active in church work. Black women, just like their white counterparts, were becoming more educated by the end of the nineteenth century. Black literacy rates (male and female) rose from 5 percent in 1860 to 70 percent in 1910. One of the first black Baptist-owned colleges opened in Louisville in 1879. State Colored Baptist University, later renamed Simmons College, became a launching pad for many energetic black women, including Mamie Steward, Mary V. Cook Parrish, and Lucy Wilmot Smith, who either trained there, served on its faculty, or were mentored by its founder.[16]

Black women organized for many of the same reasons white women did, but they had added incentive: they had misconceptions to correct. White Americans assumed black women were immoral and promiscuous. These stereotypes served white men who sexually abused black women under slavery and beyond, giving them an excuse before they raped them and offering a reason to judge them afterward. Black women intended to revamp the image of the race by demonstrating moral and material improvements that lined up with white society's definition of refinement.

Women like Mary Britton carefully demonstrated respectability. Viewing themselves as part of a Female Talented Tenth, they called on members of the race to do likewise. For example, one Baptist women's organization offered instruction on proper behavior on trains. Buy your ticket early, it advised. Don't hang your head out of the car and yell. Don't buy your kids the stale snacks that vendors are hawking. At every moment prove yourself to be decent and upright. "Be a credit to your race" was the principal message.[17]

In an era when racial inequality was deepening, and the promises of Reconstruction were slipping away, black women found plenty of needs within their community to address. They assisted the poor, the young, the elderly, and the sick. They lobbied to increase school funding, fought segregation (including the Separate Coach Law), and protested lynching. They were less focused on dramatic protest and more concerned with everyday forms of resistance, standing up to a system that classified them as inferior.[18]

Their resistance extended to men of the race who attempted to mute them. Black men were the recognized leaders of the church, but black women were its muscle. They demanded that their contributions be acknowledged, developing what historian Evelyn Brooks Higginbotham calls a "feminist theology." For example, after Simmons College ran into financial troubles, women pushed to create a separate Baptist Women's Educational Convention to rescue it. Between 1883 and 1914, the group raised almost $35,000 for Simmons, which helped keep the institution afloat and even funded construction of a women's dormitory.[19]

Women's assistance was welcomed more readily in organizations that were not tied to the church, such as the State Association of Colored Teachers. Women held officer positions and participated fully in the organization's yearly conventions. These meetings were long, often lasting nearly a week, and were broad in the topics they covered. At the 1886 meeting, the year before Britton gave her suffrage speech, Lucy Wilmot Smith presented a paper on "New Employment for Our Girls." She argued that black women needed to strike out on their own, rather than expecting men to support them. Smith, a single, independent woman herself, urged listeners to think entrepreneurially and to "trust their own brains." Consider beekeeping, running a dairy, or growing fruit instead of washing and cleaning houses, she advised. Above all, "despise mediocrity."[20]

Kentucky's black female reformers often expressed views that could qualify as feminist, but there is very little evidence that they worked directly for suffrage. Other than the short-lived Covington Colored Organization that Farmer encouraged in 1895, no record exists of any black suffrage clubs in the state. Many Kentuckians affiliated with the National Association of Colored Women's Clubs, which explicitly endorsed suffrage; and a few individuals argued for the ballot, like Lucy Wilmot Smith, who was described as "an ardent supporter of suffrage" before an early death cut short a promising career. Mainly, however, black women focused their energies in other

Nannie Helen Burroughs (shown left) was highly active in Louisville African American reform networks around 1900, but she did not directly fight for the vote. Her suffrage work began after she moved to Washington, DC, in 1909 to lead the National Training School for Women and Girls under the auspices of the National Baptist Convention. (Library of Congress)

directions. Mary Britton's 1887 speech and its clear demand for the vote was extraordinary.[21]

Participating in the same 1887 symposium, Mary V. Cook gave a paper titled "Women: A Potent Factor in Public Reform." Women needed to educate and improve society through schools, journalism, and advocacy work, she argued, saying that according to woman's influence, "nations will rise or fall." Cook made her influence abundantly known. A renowned speaker and author, she became a professor at State University and a leading force in national black women's organizations, both religious and secular. Later, alongside her minister husband, Charles H. Parrish, she became one of the most recognizable African Americans in Kentucky. Cook was not "a loud clamorer for 'Rights,'" her biographer emphasized, "but nevertheless, she quietly and tenaciously demanded all that is due her." This description sums up Kentucky African American women's efforts to expand their role as they served both the race and their communities at the turn of the century.[22]

Even Mary Britton did not continue to advocate directly for suffrage after the 1887 Danville meeting. She went to medical school and became the first black female doctor in Lexington. She fought to repeal the Separate Coach law, she helped establish the Colored Orphans Industrial Home, and she became president of Lexington's Women's Improvement Club. She prioritized efforts that seemed tangible, immediate, and possible. The vote, episodic and indirect, just did not seem to offer the same return on investment.[23]

Had KERA been more welcoming, Kentucky's African American women might have shown more enthusiasm for the cause, but it is possible that even if the organization had made more overtures, black women still would have prioritized other issues. White women might not have the vote, but they enjoyed social standing and connections. Skin color alone offered them certain protections. Black men and women had to fight for basic rights and dignity, and they bore the scars of slavery.[24]

White suffragists rarely comprehended or acknowledged the extra challenges their black peers faced, but a few did. In a 1903 pamphlet, "Justice to the Negro," Louisville's Susan Look Avery expressed her sympathy for America's "colored people," abused by whites and then resented when they made progress. Eugenia Farmer understood that black women faced different challenges than white women; as she geared up for the 1895 school elections, she tailored her overtures accordingly. Similarly, Josephine Henry occasionally acknowledged black women's extra burdens. When appealing to lawmakers in 1893 to raise the age of consent, she pointed specifically to "helpless negro girls" who needed protection. In an era when most Americans viewed black women as sexual predators rather than as victims, Henry's call stands out as rare.[25]

Laura Clay meanwhile did not share her colleagues' racially progressive views, which may seem a bit surprising considering her emancipationist roots. Laura Clay represented a new, younger generation of suffragists nurtured on Lost Cause lore and stories of the dark days that followed emancipation. Though Clay paid lip service to the idea of justice, she doubted that black and white Americans would ever be equal, echoing arguments her father had made years earlier. Like many of her fellow southerners, she firmly believed in white supremacy—the idea that the United States must be preserved as a white-dominant nation. Her fierce desire to win the South over to suffrage and her fear that black women stood in the way of that happening moved her even further toward seeing them as enemies rather than allies.

By the 1890s, the suffrage movement had defined a "narrow channel" for itself, historian Sara Hunter Graham explains. Elitism, racism, and expediency eroded suffrage pioneers' idealism and undermined the movement's commitment to work for universal voting rights. Working-class women and a few rare black activists were sometimes included in the National's activities, but beneath the surface of the crusade's democratic rhetoric lurked hostile race and class prejudice. By 1900, white suffragists had thoroughly embraced the "intellectual temper of the times," tolerating virulent southern racism, and even declaring it beneficial to their larger objectives.[26]

Laura Clay was no different than so many of her late nineteenth-century peers: she attached great meaning to skin color. Clay shared the widely held belief that African Americans were a childish and irresponsible race and that skin color determined an individual's mental and physical abilities. She claimed that she did not "hate the negro," but others thought differently. In fact, Susan B. Anthony, when considering who should be the next president of NAWSA in 1904, ruled Clay out because of her "negro equality-hating." If she were to lead the organization, Anthony predicted, never again would a person of color grace the NAWSA platform.[27]

That black men could vote before she, an educated, well-bred white women, could was almost too much for Clay to bear. She accepted emancipation, but she felt that Radical Republicans like Charles Sumner had gone too far by extending political rights. The black man, she claimed, now had "the laws on his side, physical force on his side, and the bias of sex always pleading for him." Black men, facing discrimination, disfranchisement, and the dangers of lynching, surely would have laughed at her insistence that they had it so good.[28]

Early suffragists viewed the vote as an inalienable right that should be open to all—white, black, propertied, propertyless, native born, or naturalized —and they advocated for universal suffrage. But as the woman movement grew, these high ideals softened. Increasingly, Americans argued that only the intelligent element of the population should vote. The American electorate had expanded considerably, but citizens were becoming more and more distrustful of democracy. The nation looked very different by 1880 or 1900 than it had in 1840. Not only had slaves secured their freedom but immigrants were also pouring in, and the nation's economy was shifting from a rural farming base to an urban industrial model. The "march of democracy stalled," Alexander Keyssar notes, just as women were fighting to gain their place in the electorate. Property requirements traditionally had been a preferred way to limit the vote, but increasingly talk swirled around the need for literacy requirements.[29]

Laura Clay, like a growing number of suffragists, argued that adding an educational qualification to any expansion of suffrage made good sense. She insisted that white southerners did not begrudge black men the vote (which was clearly not the case considering their frantic and illegal attempts to keep them from it) but rather that they were worried that the impact of their vote was out of proportion to the intelligence and virtue they brought to the process. Clay believed the principles of true Democracy must be upheld—all should have a say—but her demands for fairness were undercut by the rest of her argument, which pointed to her real goal. She promised that an educational qualification would ensure white supremacy because white literate voters could be counted on to "snow under" the "ignorant negro vote." One group should not have undue influence over another, she insisted, unless it worked to preserve white supremacy.[30]

One might expect a white southerner born in the nineteenth century like Laura Clay to hold racist views, but her racism was fueled to an extra degree by her desire to be recognized as a national suffrage leader. In 1890, the NWSA and AWSA agreed to merge, calling themselves by the clumsy and rather unimaginative name the National American Woman Suffrage Association. Clay attended NAWSA's first joint meeting in 1890 in Washington, DC, representing Kentucky along with Eugenia Farmer. Throughout the 1890s, Kentucky suffragists, especially Josephine Henry, were visible in national suffrage work, but Laura Clay would be the one to make it into a career. Now in her early forties, never married, she had the time and the resources to commit to suffrage, and she decided to make it her life's work.[31]

In her 1890 inaugural address as president of the National American Woman Suffrage Association, veteran suffragist Elizabeth Cady Stanton called for the organization to embrace "all shades of opinion" and to accept women of all "parties, sects and races, tribes and colors." "Colored women, Indian women, Mormon women, and women from every quarter of the globe have been heard," she noted, "and I trust they always will be." It was a lovely thought as a new beginning was under way, but Stanton was naive to think that a shared desire for the vote was enough to erase the other differences that separated women.[32]

NAWSA ignored the calls from Mary Church Terrell and other black women leaders asking "sisters of the dominant race" to stand up against race as well as gender oppression. It would become a predominantly white organization, and Laura Clay would play a significant role in making it so.[33]

The older generation of suffragists, such luminaries as Stanton, Anthony, Gage, and Stone, had aged, and by the end of the century everyone could see that a changing of the guard was imminent. Plenty of younger women were ready to step into their shoes, including women like Carrie Chapman Catt. Like Clay, Catt first attracted attention at NASWA's 1890 meeting. She gave a short, enthusiastic speech, which left many asking, "Who is that woman?" Her attention-grabbing performance earned her an invitation to join a suffrage organizing tour through South Dakota. The rest was history. Catt went on to serve two terms as NAWSA's president (1900–1904 and 1915–1920) and eventually led the movement to victory by securing ratification of the Nineteenth Amendment.[34]

Laura Clay wanted to be noticed as a promising suffrage leader too. To do that she had to distinguish herself from other heirs apparent; there must be something special that she brought to the table. She decided that her southern identity was her greatest asset. The Civil War had been over for a quarter century, but Americans still viewed the South as an exotic place with a distinctive culture and spirit. NAWSA leaders hoped to expand their movement there, and Laura Clay planned to be the native expert who could help them achieve this goal.[35]

The South, Clay insisted in a sweeping prediction, was the key to unlocking the vote for women. If you could get the Solid South on board, then the North and West would follow. Her national suffrage colleagues thought she might be onto something. At the very least they hoped to organize suffrage clubs in every state, and they believed Clay could assist. In 1891, NAWSA announced that it planned "to give especial attention to suffrage work in the southern States." The following year, NAWSA created a Southern committee with Laura Clay at its head. In 1895, Clay became the first southerner to serve on the NAWSA executive committee when she was elected auditor.[36]

Clay longed to hand deliver the region to NAWSA leaders. She understood, however, what a touchy issue suffrage was for white southerners. To raise the woman suffrage question in the South was to reopen the thorny race question. Southerners had managed to create a "white man's government" by the 1890s, having effectively disfranchised black men, but they did not feel that it was entirely secure. They worried that at any time their representation in Congress could be reduced according to the terms of the Fourteenth Amendment.[37]

Clay refused to see the race issue as an impediment to woman suffrage. Instead, she decided it could advance her cause. She sympathized with southerners' fears, which had been learned from "painful experience" and were, in her mind, justified. And she knew this: the one sure thing that they desired above all else was "permanent and legal white supremacy." She intended to give them permanent white supremacy and to win the ballot for herself in the process. The "Southern Strategy," she argued, could solve multiple problems simultaneously.[38]

The Southern Strategy was the creation of veteran abolitionist and women's rights advocate Henry Blackwell. He had tried unsuccessfully in 1867 to convince southerners to empower their wives and daughters as an alternative to black suffrage, but they weren't going for it. He did not give up. Working with Laura Clay in the early 1890s, he reintroduced the concept, as a wave of state constitutional reform crested in the South.[39]

Blackwell's Southern Strategy (not to be confused with a different version employed by the Republican Party in the 1970s and 1980s) sought, in a nutshell, to ensure that white voters retained control of the electoral process. States were experimenting with any number of plans to circumvent the Fifteenth Amendment, but many feared that the Supreme Court might pull the rug out from under them by ruling poll taxes, grandfather clauses, literacy tests, and the like unconstitutional. Southerners' plans to restore whites-only democracy might be thwarted by a high court audacious enough to require the nation to live up to its ideals.

Blackwell argued there was a better way. Adding educated (mostly white) women to the electorate would "neutralize" illiterate men (mostly black) who were already voting, he explained. He used 1890 census data to underscore his point, allowing the raw numbers to speak for themselves. By adding woman suffrage with an educational qualification to state constitutions, southerners would get their much-desired white dominance; at the same time, they would also potentially solve the problem of too many illiterate immigrants, which pestered the North. Demanding that voters be able to read and write in a nation that offered free public education was not too much to ask, he insisted.[40]

It was hard to miss the irony. The South, the most conservative region in the country, could be the ticket to finally winning the vote for women if only their racism could be leveraged effectively. Laura Clay saw it as a brilliant idea and began enthusiastically to peddle its mean-spirited practicality. A writer for the *Cincinnati Enquirer* raised an eyebrow, calling the plan "Novel, to Say the Least." Speaking to a crowd of women from Newport and Cincinnati in 1893, Clay argued that enfranchising literate women would allow white women to participate in politics while guaranteeing "Anglo-Saxon Supremacy." It is not clear whether the reporter was recording Clay's remarks verbatim or paraphrasing to make a point. Regardless, the meaning was clear. Clay wanted white rule.[41]

Even after the Supreme Court upheld the constitutionality of southern methods of disfranchisement in 1898, making the Southern Strategy a dead issue, Laura Clay continued to beat the drum of states' rights and southern values into the next century. She fiercely and consistently defended the South, as she did in 1899 when the NAWSA convention considered a resolution protesting southern segregated trains. Mrs. Lottie Wilson Jackson, described in the minutes as an African American woman "so light-compexioned [*sic*] that most people would not have supposed that she had any tincture of colored blood," testified to the conditions on filthy smoking cars, where she was forced to ride. How could "respectable colored women" ever hope to morally elevate their less fortunate sisters, she asked, when they were forced to endure such conditions? She did not ask NAWSA to act; she simply wanted suffragists to acknowledge the injustice.

Laura Clay jumped to her feet to object. It was not fair to southern delegates who had traveled to Grand Rapids to attend a conference on woman suffrage to have a measure sprung on them that was completely off topic. Defending Separate Coach laws, she vigorously denied that the conditions

Mrs. Jackson described existed, certainly not in Kentucky and likely nowhere in the South. Clay wanted to play the race card both ways. She wanted race to be considered as a factor when it helped the suffrage cause in the South, but she vigorously spoke out when individuals called attention to racial injustice.

Other delegates chimed in, agreeing that they had never seen black women face discrimination or filthy conditions on the trains. Others spoke up to smooth over the tense situation. A delegate from Missouri reported that as a white woman she had often been "saturated with tobacco smoke" while riding on trains. She suggested that the word "colored" be removed from the resolution and that it be allowed to pass. Mrs. Jackson, its author, urged against amending it. It should either be adopted or defeated as it stood, she firmly held.

Susan Anthony finally stepped in to close the conversation. Surely, "no one will doubt that I am true to the colored race," she prefaced. "I am true to the races the blood of which is mingled in Mrs. Jackson's veins." She advised, however, that it was best to drop the matter, endorsing Clay's solution though for different reasons. Women "are a helpless, disfranchised class" and thus are not positioned to go passing resolutions against railroad companies or anybody else, Anthony concluded. And with that, the matter was closed. Vindicated, Laura Clay proceeded to read her auditor's report.[42]

Clay played a key role in steering NAWSA toward a narrower vision of equality. NAWSA officially embraced a states' rights policy in 1903. State chapters could decide who to admit as members (and who to reject) and could determine for themselves the arguments and strategies that would play best in their regions. In the South, this meant that E.R.A.s could keep their memberships all white, advocate for suffrage as a protection for white supremacy, and focus their work exclusively on state rather than federal means of winning the vote. In Kentucky, this meant that KERA would remain a thoroughly segregated organization throughout its history.[43]

Just as NAWSA underwent a changing of the guard in the 1890s, KERA did also. Eugenia Farmer, Josephine Henry, and Laura Clay had worked together closely for so many years, traveling to national meetings, addressing Kentucky lawmakers, and touring the state on behalf of the cause, but by 1900, their partnership ended, leaving Clay as KERA's sole guiding force. Farmer moved to Minnesota in 1898 when her husband took a job there—an "irreparable loss," Henry sadly noted—and when she did, any interest in reaching across the color line seems to have disappeared, at least on the state level.[44]

Around the same time, philosophical disagreements led Josephine Henry to break with her KERA colleagues. Temperamentally, Laura Clay and Josephine Henry had always been very different. Henry tended to dwell on what they had left to accomplish even when they celebrated victories, while Clay tended to be a glass half full kind of person. Henry was always more willing to go against the grain than Clay, who, besides her progressive calls for women's rights, was protective of the status quo in most other ways. Henry was not one to support tradition for tradition's sake, and she did not keep her thoughts to herself. Her name appeared often in the newspaper, such as when she protested the "barbaric" custom of expecting women to take their husbands' last names, or when she denounced the "brutalizing" sport of football and the colleges that encouraged it, or when she attacked the decorative arts craze that led women to fill their homes with "jim-jams."[45]

Henry dismissed much of what preoccupied other women as silly distractions. She compared society women—the "representative class"—to the New Women who were willing to look beyond "drowsy civilization" and pursue work that had real meaning. But one gets the sense that even these New Women—even Clay possibly—did not meet Henry's exacting standards. Clubwomen, she noted, seemed "never so happy as [when] voting some woman into or out of office, or some question up or down." They ignored substantive matters and instead focused on the trivial, including "dreams of ante-bellum family legends" and maintaining their social prestige.[46]

Clay and Henry likely could have agreed to disagree on some of these matters, but it was their opposing views about the Bible that doomed their relationship. Like Clay, Henry's early suffrage work had been underscored by a strong religious faith. By 1894, however, she began to rethink her deepest assumptions. Perhaps it was the death of her son that soured her on religion. In one of the first signs of her transformation, she became both a subscriber and a contributor to Free Thinkers' (later Free Thought) Magazine. Even though her first submission, a poem, was in no way outlandish (although she did reference being set free from "Orthodoxy"), the publication provided space to explore all things unconventional, and soon that is what she did. She began to write for the Blue Grass Blade, a Lexington newspaper edited by the eccentric Charles Chilton Moore, a former Versailles minister who proudly claimed he had "lost his religion." Most readers did not agree with

Moore's controversial opinions, but they kept reading just to see what crazy thing he would say next.[47]

Henry's new interests and relationships alarmed Clay. She likely worried about her friend's soul and perhaps her sanity, but she certainly worried that her growing radicalism would harm the suffrage cause. When Henry decided to participate in Elizabeth Cady Stanton's *Woman's Bible* project in 1895, Clay predicted that great damage would result. Stanton saw the project as the "crowning achievement" of her life, an exploration of the ways the church, the clergy, and the Bible had kept women in a subservient position for thousands of years. Stanton put together a "Revising Committee" that would provide commentary and new interpretations of scripture. Historian Kathi Kern notes with some understatement that "the book touched a nerve," especially among those who never read it. Preachers called it the work of Satan, and even suffragists across the country ran as far as possible from the *Woman's Bible*.[48]

Laura Clay worried that Stanton's project would impede their efforts in conservative Kentucky, and evidence suggests she was right to worry. Susan B. Anthony and Carrie Chapman Catt stopped in the Bluegrass in 1895 as part of a scheduled southern organizing swing. Of their visit in Wilmore, they reported that they "had an old-fashion pious, cold & generally comfortless time." The Methodists they encountered dismissed their message and tried to get them right with God instead.[49]

For years, Clay had railed against the ways that power-hungry men had perverted God's plan, subordinating women instead of accepting them as equal partners. Her talk "The Bible for Equal Rights," which pushed for a new interpretation of scripture, was one of her most popular. But she always returned to the same conclusion: the Bible was a perfect book and should be the guiding force in every person's life. She recoiled from Stanton's *Woman's Bible*, even though it argued many points that she herself had made. Clay did not see the Bible as an obstacle to women's empowerment, and she could not support anything remotely insulting to the Bible.[50]

Henry saw the matter very differently than her friend. The Bible, in her mind, was not a tool for women seeking equality. Clay saw the Bible as "elevating and consoling," while Henry thought it cruel and debauched. Look through its pages, Henry instructed. Look at the examples of polygamy, slavery, cannibalism, murder, robbery, ruin, and war, not to mention the curse it laid upon women. It was the "worst of all books," and she was happy to have her commentary included in Mrs. Stanton's book. Henry is not listed as a reviser in the first volume published in 1895, but she is listed in the second. Two of her commentaries appear in the later edition.[51]

Sparks flew when NAWSA delegates gathered in Washington, DC, in January 1896 for their annual convention. In one of the opening sessions, the organization's secretary, Rachel Foster Avery, slipped a denunciation of the book into her annual report. "I should be untrue to my duties," she primly noted, "if I failed to report that our work is being damaged." Though she never mentioned her by name, Avery called for a resolution denouncing Stanton and her team of revisers. Susan B. Anthony deftly managed to table the resolution, but in the convention's closing session, the resolution reappeared and refused to go away. After what the minutes call a "long and animated debate," the convention voted to censure Stanton, stating emphatically that the organization had "no official connection with the so-called 'Woman's Bible.'" Clay remained uncharacteristically silent during the debate, but everyone knew how she would vote. She had had it in for Stanton ever since the older woman had demanded that the Columbian Exposition remain open on Sundays several years before, in violation of the Sabbath. Clay saw her as a dangerous infidel. Five out of six members of the Kentucky delegation voted to support the resolution.[52]

Stanton was aware of the conservative drift that had begun to lead NAWSA away from its more radical roots. She had hoped her book could reverse that shift, but instead it mobilized a new generation of conservative suffragists like Carrie Chapman Catt and Laura Clay, who emphasized pragmatic strategy rather than bold ideological stands. A tug-of-war for power followed. Allies of Stanton like Josephine Henry found themselves losers in the struggle. She would not be among those who would lead the movement into the next century.[53]

Henry, the engineer of some of KERA's greatest legislative victories, had become too much of a liability. She needed to go. Henry later recalled that she gave Clay the chance to "get rid of her gracefully," but Clay chose to publicly eject her as "an undesirable member." The offing took place on Clay's home turf, in Richmond, which hosted KERA's tenth annual convention in December 1898.

KERA's executive committee had contemplated what to do about Mrs. Henry in advance, but they could not agree. Most officers supported Henry and hoped to see her reappointed as superintendent of legislative work. Her skills were too valuable to waste. But Clay and several others opposed her nomination. At the convention (which Henry did not attend) a majority report that favored Henry was offered, along with a minority report that recommended Louisville's Margaret A. Watts be appointed instead.[54]

At the convention, tensions surged. One delegate tried to circumvent the issue by nominating Laura Clay to fill the role. Clay declared the nomination out of order, but she took the opportunity to present her reasons for opposing Henry's reappointment. Nominating Watts would doubly benefit KERA. She had legislative experience (she had been a member of the Frankfort Committee) and she was from Louisville where the work needed to grow. Clay did not mention that she was also a devoted Christian and Sunday School teacher, who regarded the Bible as the "Magna Charta of a true Republic." Sarah Sawyer, a former chair of KERA's Bible committee who herself would later pivot to embrace free thought, moved that Josephine Henry retain her position, but the convention chose Watts. Like Henry, Sawyer would also soon cut ties with KERA. Both women were "prayed out," Henry later recalled.[55]

Henry stoically assured Clay that she was not offended by the events at the convention: "I am not made of that kind of stuff." She did not see why a difference of opinions should shatter friendships, but it did. Henry and Clay never mended fences. Eugenia Farmer, now settled in Minnesota, served as an intermediary between the two (she often passed Henry's letters on to Clay but not vice versa). Clay also heard word of her old friend through her sister, Mary Barr Clay, who, as the least religious of the sisters, kept up a correspondence with the now-declared atheist.[56]

By 1900, KERA's path was set. It was a homogenous organization—white, affluent, educated, and overtly Christian—that held rigid ideas about the limits of change. Like NAWSA, it focused narrowly on the vote instead of seeking liberation through the church, the state, and the family as Stanton and Henry preferred. Debate and disagreement would not be welcomed as healthy but would instead be severely punished. A mature KERA looked a lot like Laura Clay, and it closely reflected her values. For the next decade, after her falling-out with Henry and Farmer's move to Minnesota, only Clay's imprint remained.

6

Rescission

In January 1898, Miss Clay, Mrs. Farmer, and Mrs. Henry gathered in Frankfort for the last legislative session they would work together. It marked the close of an important chapter in KERA's history. Josephine Henry had not been ceremonially ejected from the organization—yet—but everyone who was in the know understood that she had become something of a black sheep.

Mary Barr Clay and Mary Cramer, the other members of the Frankfort Committee, could feel the tension in the air. Mary Cramer had served as an officer of the organization since 1889, sometimes as treasurer, sometimes secretary, and currently as a vice president. Henry was an old friend. It is not clear where the other Mary, Mary Clay, stood on the *Woman's Bible*, but one suspects she was more tolerant of Henry's actions than her more religious sister, Laura.

Anyway, there was no time to dwell on these personal disputes when they arrived in Frankfort. KERA's officers had sent them with an ambitious list of goals.[1]

KERA planned to sponsor four bills during the 1898 session. Two involved long-held aims: an extension of school suffrage to all Kentucky women and a requirement that all state institutions hire female physicians. These measures had come close to passing before, and their chances for success seemed high. Two other measures on their list were new and less likely to gain traction.

That year, for the first time ever KERA sought a state constitutional amendment. Later, suffragists would seek an amendment to fully enfranchise women, but they were not ready for such a bold step yet. This amendment would simply exempt women from paying taxes until they gained their rights. It was a protest move, not likely to get very far. Changing a constitution is not easy, for good reason. In Kentucky, an amendment had to be approved by both houses of the legislature before it could be sent to the voters. Then, a majority had to vote to approve the change. Even if lawmakers supported the women's amendment it would likely never make it onto the

PUBLIC SPEAKING!

AT THE

REPRESENTATIVE HALL.

MISS LAURA CLAY,

MRS. EUGENIA B. FARMER,

MRS. JOSEPHINE K. HENRY,

Will make speeches bearing on Equal Rights for Women, in Representatives' Hall,

THURSDAY EVENING,

JAN. 13, 1898.

The members of the Legislature are particularly invited, as also the public in general.

ADMISSION FREE.
8 O'CLOCK, P. M.
THURSDAY EVENING. **COME ONE, COME ALL!**

Roundabout Print, Frankfort, Ky.

Eugenia Farmer, Laura Clay, and Josephine Henry were a powerful collective force for suffrage in Kentucky. The 1898 legislative session, during which the three women addressed the Kentucky House of Representatives, was the last they would attend together. (University of Kentucky Special Collections) ballot since only two amendments could be considered during each election cycle. KERA leaders realized it was a long shot, but they had to start somewhere.[2]

A co-guardianship bill was also new but seemed more achievable. Kentucky law allowed a spiteful man to appoint anyone he chose as guardian of his children after he died—possibly even his wife's bitterest enemy. A mother's rights be damned, he could take her baby right out of her arms. Suffragists, convinced that there was nothing more sacred than a mother's love, could imagine nothing more disgraceful. The only mother who had legal claim to her child, KERA publications delicately noted, was "the woman whose offspring is the sign of her own shame." Only mothers of illegitimate children were safe from losing their custodial rights, though they faced enough of their own hardships.[3]

As they expected, the tax amendment went nowhere. They were disappointed that school suffrage and co-guardianship also received little consideration. They could claim only one victory: the women's physician bill passed, and Governor William O. Bradley signed it into law. At least, Henry consoled herself, they had "forcibly reminded lawmakers that one-half the people in the State are women."[4]

It was a victory to savor, especially since wins were about to become scarcer. Henry's break with KERA seemed to take the wind out of the organization's sails as it moved into its second decade of work. Leaders had less and less good news to share at annual conferences, though they always hoped that new legislative gains would require them to revise and enlarge their "What the Kentucky ERA Has Done" pamphlet. Instead, suffragists spent the first decade of the twentieth century fighting to maintain ground already won. Sometimes KERA members tasted victory, but too often during its thirty-two-year history they endured the agony of defeat.[5]

Instead of feeling the sense of promise that a new century usually brings, gloom settled over the state of Kentucky in 1900. For months, the nation had been following the Commonwealth's gubernatorial race, shocked by its incivility. Knowing Kentuckians' reputation for being trigger-happy, it seemed unlikely that the "hot fight" would end peacefully, observers predicted. Four years earlier, largely due to the free silver issue and well-organized tobacco farmers, the state had elected a Republican as its chief executive for the first time ever. Democrats intended to reclaim power in 1899, but when William Goebel, a controversial reform-minded candidate, secured the nomination, the party split. With the Democratic party divided, a tight race became even tighter. Few believed that a new independent election committee created by then–state senator Goebel would ensure fairness. The chance of fraud was always high in a state like Kentucky where "buying votes was as common as buying groceries," but especially now Goebel's many enemies— who dubbed him "Boss Bill"—expected the worst.[6]

Events transpired quickly after election day. With the vote too close to call, Goebel's election committee reviewed the outcome and declared Republican William S. Taylor the winner. Questioning the legitimacy of his own committee, Goebel asked the state legislature to overrule its decision. The matter was still being considered on January 30, 1900, when an unidentified shooter brazenly gunned Goebel down as he walked toward the state capitol with his bodyguards. The general assembly quickly threw enough votes to the mortally wounded man to make him the winner. Supporters knew their candidate could die at any moment and hastily swore him in. He dutifully pledged, as all Kentucky elected officials still must do, that he had never fought in a duel even though he had killed a man in one five years earlier. When Goebel succumbed to his wounds three days later, Kentucky became the only state to have a governor assassinated, forever marking it with a "vile and wicked stain."[7]

Weeks later when suffragist Mary C. Roark gave the legislative report for Kentucky at the annual NAWSA convention, she only had to say that "turbulent conditions" had hindered their work and her national colleagues gave a knowing nod. But she really could not blame their inertia on the political crisis; suffrage work had already begun to stall. Mrs. Henry's replacement as chair of legislative work did not remain in the position long; KERA's 1899 meeting minutes list the position as empty. Going into the 1900 legislative session, KERA presented a whittled-down plan of work. They hoped to convince the legislature to fund a woman's dorm at State College, they pushed again for a co-guardianship bill, and school suffrage remained a goal, but the energy that had once been behind legislative work had fizzled. KERA did not even hold a convention in 1900.[8]

They were making few forward strides, but even worse, KERA would soon take a giant step backward. Suddenly, instead of looking to expand school suffrage to all Kentucky women (women in Kentucky's third- and fourth-class cities and in Louisville were still unenfranchised), suffragists hunkered down to protect existing rights. The first inklings that school suffrage might be in jeopardy came in the fall of 1901. Women had voted in school elections in Kentucky's second-class cities since 1895, but now lawmakers began to wonder whether school suffrage had been a good idea.[9]

"Women don't really want the vote," accusers claimed. This accusation had some merit, at least among white women. White women had to be coaxed to register. As the 1899 election approached, the *Lexington Leader* cajoled the hesitant: "It is not necessary to be a woman suffragist to register . . . put on your hat and go and do it." But the nudging did not work; white women, fearing that they would have to mingle with "ward bummers and heelers," stayed away.[10]

Black women, however, were another story. No one could accuse them of apathy, especially not in 1901. They had a score to settle.

Black women in Lexington were dissatisfied with the leadership of their children's schools, and they intended to force a change. They were tired of how political schools had become, but mainly they were tired of Green Pinckney Russell. Russell had started as a teacher before becoming principal of Chilesburg elementary school. From there, he steadily consolidated power, eventually earning the title Supervisor of Negro Schools. Lexington's mayor further honored him by renaming Fourth Street School the Russell School. Russell was not promoted on his merits, and he certainly did not advance because of his winning personality. "Obnoxious," one observer called him. He built his career by conspiring with Democratic power brokers.[11]

While most African Americans faithfully supported the Republican Party, the party of Lincoln, Russell allied with Democrats, and they welcomed him with open arms. Not only could Russell deliver valuable black votes, but his curricular goals and his support of Booker T. Washington's accommodationist agenda made him popular with those who wanted to protect the status quo. Like Washington, Russell argued that African American children would benefit more from manual industrial training than liberal arts instruction.[12]

Some black voters saw Russell and his Democratic connections as an asset because he could secure greater funding for black education, including a new black (industrial) high school. Many others, including mothers who wanted more for their children, vowed to see him gone. They realized, however, that it would not be easy to push him out. The editor of the African American *Lexington Standard* noted that for years Russell had made teachers do his bidding or lose their jobs.[13]

Defeating what one critic called the "great Negro Democrat potentate" would take a united effort, and the mothers of the community were ready to do their part. Every mother, one letter to the editor instructed, must go to the polls and vote for the Republican school board ticket to show they were "free women." The author did not identify Russell by name, calling him only "a so-called leader of the colored race," but everyone knew the target of her vendetta.[14]

With the support of mobilized mothers, Republicans won the 1900 school board election in a landslide. The new board proceeded to abolish Russell's position as head of colored schools and to name a new principal for Russell School. The *Lexington Leader* called it a "severe rebuke." As the 1901 school elections approached, black women once again promised to make their voices heard to protect the gains they had won.[15]

When voting registration opened, black women came out in full force. Everyone knew that registration numbers were almost as important as the actual vote count on election day since voters tended to be exceedingly loyal to their parties. Consequently, Democrats were on high alert following the first day of registration. Black women's numbers far exceeded those of white women, giving a decided advantage to the Republicans. The Democratic press pleaded with white literate women to register before it was too late. If they didn't register, illiterate voters would be happy to make important school decisions, the paper warned.

Call it a pep talk or call it an ultimatum—the call to action also mentioned a rumor that women might be deprived of their rights moving forward if they did not do their part now—it failed to inspire white women. The *Lexington Herald* offered a careful accounting, separated out by race, gender, and party affiliation, of the final registration tally. It reported 1,883 "colored" female registrants, compared to 775 "white" women. Even if all the white women who registered showed up to vote and voted together as a bloc (Democratic, of course), they would be outvoted two to one. The *Morning Democrat* called it a "shame and a disgrace to the fair name of this city." To further highlight the travesty, the *Democrat* added that it was not just black women who had registered in large numbers but specifically prostitutes had been "hustled to the polls . . . as a farmer drives his hogs to market." Black women's high registration numbers could only be explained as part of a scheme to fix the election.[16]

Even though Republicans carried a 320-vote advantage (counting all registrants, male and female) into the election, the final tally gave Democrats a 572-vote margin of victory. They had managed to turn a deficit of registrants into a surplus of voters through all manner of fraud. Only Democrats served as election officers. Polls opened late, especially in precincts where black domestics had to report to work early. In some reported cases, black voters had to find three white men willing to vouch for them before they could vote. Some poll officers just whiled away the day talking with friends to slow the process down and then sent would-be voters home when time ran out. In total, 8,925 individuals had registered the month before, but only 4,570 votes were cast. Some "melt" is to be expected, but the nearly 50 percent loss was unprecedented. Even the Democratic-leaning *Lexington Herald* admitted that the victory had not been entirely honest.[17]

Chicanery had worked this time. But would it always? Democrats sought surer ways to win future elections. If sacrificing school suffrage would bring party advantage, no matter how small, they would take it. Immediately, rumors began to swirl that women's voting rights would be on the chopping block during the next legislative session. Writing to the *Lexington Leader*, "A Colored Citizen" predicted that if a school suffrage repeal came to pass it would be due to a backroom deal between Russell and his white supporters.[18]

The rumors that school suffrage might be rescinded proved credible. When the 1902 legislative session opened in January, William F. "Billy" Klair, state representative and "undisputed czar of Lexington," led the effort to repeal the 1894 statute, assisted by Democratic state senator and Confederate war hero J. Embry Allen. Klair, known for his bow tie, cigar, and jolly grin, was a master of patronage politics. He encouraged his constituents to just call him Billy, and they saw him as a valuable friend. To maintain these "friendships," Klair needed to provide favors such as school positions and contracts. To do that he had to control school elections.[19]

But that is not the reason he gave to justify rescission. It was necessary to rescind school suffrage, Klair argued, to prevent a repeat of scenes witnessed at Lexington polls the previous November when black women descended like an invading army. Knowing that they would have to "mix it up with the negroes in order to vote," the "best white women" would be even less likely to show up moving forward. Schools would fall under black women's sole control, the warnings went. For good measure, supporters threw in that repealing school suffrage would save cities money by ending the need for two sets of polling sites, appealing to the frugal. One observer wondered whether lawmakers' sudden interest in economy was because they were a little ashamed of their real motive: partisan gain.[20]

KERA prepared for war, organizing before lawmakers even settled in for the session. The Fayette E.R.A., the Central Kentucky Woman's Club, and the WCTU formed a joint Committee on Retention of School Suffrage for Women. Lexington's most influential women stepped up to lead. Laura Clay, the WCTU's Frances Beauchamp, school board member Ida Harrison, tireless reformer Madeline McDowell Breckinridge, educator Mary C. Roark, and Eugenia Dunlap Potts, noted Civil War historian and enthusiastic Confederate memorialist, all agreed to serve on its executive committee. But they needed even more women who were "up in arms"—the more influential and "home-loving" the better—to make up a Committee of One Hundred. As was often the case, a few select women did most of the work, but many agreed to lend their name to the cause. There were legislative committee hearings to attend, newspaper editorials to publish, and personal letters needed to go to each legislator to reinforce the impact repeal would have on white women who simply wanted to make their children's schools better.[21]

Eugenia Potts volunteered to correspond with J. Embry Allen, cosponsor of the bill, strategically leveraging their shared Confederate ties. She led by sweetly reminding Allen of everything she and other Confederate women had done to honor his fellow soldiers, and the promise he had made to return the favor. Now it was time to pay up, she insisted. Allen indeed remembered making such a promise, but he demurred, noting that it would be irresponsible to allow a personal debt to interfere with his public duty. If she was willing to put the screws into him, he was happy to return the same. He politely reminded Mrs. Potts of the work he had done to secure an appropriation for a woman's dorm at State College. Had women thanked him for his efforts? Not one had dropped him a line or stopped him in the streets, he chided. His mind was made up on the Klair matter. He must protect Kentucky public schools from black women, "this race of people, who are so easily made arrogant and overbearing." Allen was willing to play hardball, but he was deep down still a southern gentleman, or at least he played the part. He was sorry to see Mrs. Potts and her associates—the "intelligent women"—become collateral damage, he soothed. If they could suggest a way to amend the measure to protect deserving women, he would happily consider it.[22]

Suffragists jumped on Allen's invitation to revise the bill that had just passed the House. The best solution, they argued, was to preserve school suffrage but to add a literacy requirement. Laura Clay had promoted educational qualifications in the past, particularly to allay southerners' fear that woman suffrage would upset the racial order, but KERA had never suggested a literacy requirement for school suffrage, before now. Unlike lawmakers, suffragists saw the high black turnout in 1901 as a "benign aberration" instead of a cause for alarm. But if race was lawmakers' primary concern, Clay and her colleagues were ready to answer.[23]

They proposed the addition of a literacy requirement, and they did so it seems, without much second thought. White Kentucky suffragists willingly shifted their strategies and arguments to fit a national mood that increasingly emphasized racial separation. A requirement that only literate women could register spoke directly to Klair and Allen's stated reasons for repeal. An educational qualification served as shorthand terminology to imply black disfranchisement, though in reality, most black women could read and write.[24]

Suffragists immediately broadcast Allen's promise, alongside their proposed compromise, in the *Lexington Herald*. They needed to act fast while the Senate was still considering the measure. But like Confederate dollars at the end of the war, Allen's word turned out to be worthless. Within days, Allen wrote to Mrs. Potts to explain his reversal. So many people had written him to oppose school suffrage even with a literacy restriction that he could not possibly support it without angering 90 percent of his constituents, including many educated women. Surely, you would not expect me to go against the will of the people, he sanctimoniously added.[25]

The strenuous appeals and alternative proposals that the women offered had no impact on the Klair Bill. It passed both the House and the Senate by nearly a straight party vote (only one Democrat in each body opposed), and without discussion. Soon after, Governor J. C. W. Beckham signed it into law. Klair tried to placate women by reminding them that they could still run for and hold school board positions, even if they could not vote for them, but it seemed a poor consolation prize.[26]

Klair insisted that the repeal was about promoting efficiency and preventing black control of schools, but Clay and her fellow committee members believed there was more to their grievous loss. Black women had never voted in such large numbers before 1901, and the unusually large turnout did not represent a legitimate threat to white control moving forward, Clay insisted. Look at all the names of women who stood opposed to repeal. They were relatives of war heroes like John C. Breckinridge, John Hunt Morgan, and

General Withers. These women, true Confederates at heart, would not support school suffrage if they thought for a minute that it would lead to "negro domination." Black residents had not attempted to run their own slate of candidates. "The worst they could have done," Clay explained to her colleague and NAWSA historian, Ida Husted Harper, "was to elect the white Republican ticket nominated by whites." "The whole truth is our state is in a miserable political condition," Clay admitted. Democracy had been torn into two factions, each "determined not to lose one particle of partisan advantage" over the other, "even in so small a matter as electing a school board."[27]

Partisan maneuvering was to blame, according to Clay, and historian Duane Bolin agrees with her assessment. Billy Klair did not take stands on significant issues based on deeply held values, Bolin notes, but rather on how they fit into his agenda to secure power. Republicans' growing strength, bolstered significantly by black voters, threatened his political future. He had tried to secure the black vote (through methods both fair and foul) and failed. Now he looked for more foolproof ways to protect his majorities by manipulating the electorate.[28]

But black women were not Klair's only problem. If they had been, he would have been more willing to consider a literacy restriction. Bolin argues that women—black and white—did not take well to Democratic policies. Perhaps it was Republicans' commitment to reform that drew progressive women. Or maybe it was the inefficiency of the Democratic machine that turned them off. Men were more likely to toe the party line, while women tended to vote based on a candidate's individual character or positions on issues. They were wild cards, and Klair decided it was better to remove them from the deck than to have them ruin the game.[29]

Still, race had more to do with it than Clay suggested. In general, Kentucky women were less concerned about the race implications of suffrage than their peers in the Deep South, but in certain pockets of the state, this issue cut deep. The effort to repeal school suffrage originated in Lexington, home to one of the state's largest concentrations of African Americans. In 1900, Lexington's black population stood at 39 percent, making it comparable to southern cites, like Nashville (37 percent) and Birmingham (43 percent). In areas of the state where the black vote mattered, the fight for women's suffrage became more complicated.[30]

National leaders, perhaps trying to cheer their defeated colleagues, predicted that Kentucky's repeal of school suffrage would mean a growth spurt for KERA as disgruntled women signed on to recover their lost rights. Clay and her associates, however, found that it hurt the cause as much as it helped, especially in areas of the state where the race issue mattered most. Anna Miller, KERA's corresponding secretary, discovered as much when she attempted to recruit Mary Atkinson Cunningham to assist their cause in western Kentucky in the spring of 1902. Cunningham was well connected, and she had recently been appointed Kentucky regent for the Daughters of the American Revolution. If properly cultivated, she could help draw in more women from her area of the state, where suffrage work had always lagged. Miller wrote to scope out her interest.[31]

Cunningham's response seemed promising at first: "I am in thorough sympathy with this movement," she wrote, "and firmly convinced that equal rights will ultimately prevail." There was a "but" coming. Cunningham could not help to organize an E.R.A. in her community, she explained. She was swamped with D.A.R. duties, but even if she had the time, she was not willing to give it to suffrage work. She heard that school suffrage in Lexington was repealed because twice as many black women as white had voted and the board of education was "practically controlled by negroes."

Concerned that she might be coming off a bit shrill, Cunningham noted that she never endorsed slavery, but she clearly supported efforts to make blacks second-class citizens and resented that they were getting uppity. "Disagreeable and impertinent" black picnickers monopolized Henderson parks, she complained. A plan to build a Carnegie library had to be scrapped when "gangs of negroes" threatened to go there "and read all day long." Cunningham concluded that it was useless to pursue rights for women. If it meant additional rights for African Americans, the cause was doomed.[32]

By the time the Klair Bill passed in 1902, Josephine Henry had retired from active suffrage work. She had always been a political junkie though, and she could not help but comment on events that spring. The repeal of school suffrage validated her claim that "piecemeal suffrage" was a flawed strategy. Four years earlier when making her break with KERA, she had warned Clay that fighting for anything less than the full ballot for women was a grave mistake. Now, she spoke up again, simply sharing "food for reflection" with readers of the *Woman's Journal*. Partial suffrage—be it presidential, municipal, taxation, or school suffrage—required "herculean" effort for little gain. Women claimed their rights only to see the "ring politicians" like Klair use them "as a club to retard and paralyze the cause" later. Men had never had to fight for "crumbs of justice," and women "weakened their title to their political heritage" by doing so, she argued.[33]

Henry's protest against partial suffrage reveals that it was more than just the *Woman's Bible* controversy that led to her ouster from KERA and NAWSA. Religious views mattered, but perhaps even more, so did competing tactical goals. Henry had no patience for suffragists who were content to fight for crumbs. She also resented suffragists who were unwilling to consider new ideas. Weeks after Henry wrote to the *Woman's Journal* to reflect on Kentucky's backward step, her ally Olympia Brown (who had also been pushed out of the National) offered a figurative "amen" to her indictment of partial suffrage. Brown's complaints further illuminate the philosophical differences at the center of the dispute. Suffragists spent too much of their time, she insisted, trying to win over timid clubwomen. Pursuing co-guardianship, age of consent, and anticigarette laws might appeal to the "fashionable women" but it was moving them no closer to their ultimate goal of winning full suffrage for all women. Henry, Brown, and others felt the movement should go in one direction, and Clay and her supporters felt it should go in another. The safe route, one that focused on making their cause as nonthreatening as possible to appeal to as many women as possible, won out.[34]

By 1900, NAWSA's priorities had narrowed and KERA's did likewise. Nineteenth-century suffragists had claimed the vote as a basic right of citizenship, but increasingly as the movement matured it would focus on equipping "deserving" voters and only in limited capacities. This narrowed focus, leaders suggested, would allow the movement to grow by making it seem less threatening and by appealing to a larger cross-section of women who might be scared off by bold claims of female equality. Kentucky suffragists would spend the rest of the decade trying to win back school suffrage, but only for women who could read and write the English language. Josephine Henry thought they were making a mistake, but no one asked her.[35]

7

All Women Cannot Be Heroes

With the 1904 KERA convention only a week away, Laura Clay was staring down a huge to-do list on Monday morning, November 7, but she set it aside when the mail arrived in her box. As usual, she had a thick stack of correspondence to thumb through. Between her state and national suffrage work, her WCTU responsibilities, church business, and running her farm, she kept the mailman busy. It was nothing for her to answer more than a dozen letters in a single morning. Today, her eyes settled on a small rectangular envelope with a Madisonville postmark. She had been waiting for Mrs. Franceway's response. She hoped what was inside would be encouraging.

For years, she had been trying to drum up suffrage support in western Kentucky, but the region had been impervious to her overtures. One of KERA's first auxiliaries had formed in Glasgow, a small farming community less than twenty miles from the already hopping tourist destination, Mammoth Cave. The town, named to pay tribute to settlers' Scottish heritage, was home to only two thousand residents, but thirteen Glaswegians had declared as suffragists. It seemed like a hotbed of activity in 1889 considering KERA had only ninety-three members in the entire state.[1]

But Clay's initial hope that Glasgow could serve as a base from which to plant additional suffrage locals across Kentucky's western reaches proved premature. The spark never managed to catch, and two years later the Glasgow group disappeared from KERA's short list of E.R.A.s (the state's first eastern Kentucky chapter located in Laurel County folded soon after). It could be that one of the guiding spirits of the group moved away, or took sick, or died. Or, the group likely just lost interest. It often happened. Too often, it seemed.

The further one traveled from Kentucky's major urban centers, the more difficult it became to generate and maintain suffrage enthusiasm. KERA's goal, of course, was to have active suffrage chapters working in every corner of the Commonwealth, all linked through a central state organization, which in turn worked under the direction of the National. Each year, they hoped to add new auxiliaries until all 120 counties were organized. Instead they found that losses constantly offset gains. Their recruitment efforts looked something like a Whac-A-Mole arcade game: each time they nailed down a community, another one popped out of reach. After fifteen years, suffrage work remained concentrated in just a few areas: 73 percent of Kentucky's 352 suffragists lived in Kenton County, Fayette County, or Madison County in 1903.[2]

As she opened her mail, Clay hoped for good news on the western Kentucky front, but she knew another polite rejection was likely. She had worked to make suffrage as palatable as possible, but it still left a bad taste in people's mouths. To declare for suffrage meant facing jeers, gibes, sneers, and scathing jokes. You had to have thick skin, letting the nasty words and queer looks roll off your back, and so did your husband and children—difficult to do in small towns where gossip was as thick as meringue on pies. Ella Porter, a young suffragist from Glasgow, feared she might not have the necessary gumption. She prayed for strength in 1889 as she took up the work begun by "worn-out pioneers." Sarah Millsop, MD, of Bowling Green refused to join KERA because she feared damaging her professional career. Being a "woman doctor" was outlandish enough, she insisted.[3]

Mary Barr Clay wished her fellow Kentuckians would show more bravery, but she understood their fears: "All women cannot be heroes," she concluded.[4]

Even women who believed firmly in suffrage hesitated to join the fight, fearing that suffrage work would distract from their never-ending housework. One correspondent told Clay that she could depend on her to help after her children went to college (a long time to wait—her son had just turned two). But even women with grown children struggled to balance motherhood and suffrage work, and often motherhood won out. With a daughter getting married soon and another "expecting a visit from the stork," Mrs. W. S. McLaughlin had to scrap her plans to attend KERA's annual convention in 1911. Then, there was Margaret Castleman who gave up her suffrage responsibilities when she found herself in an "interesting condition" (she was pregnant). Suffragists felt an extra responsibility to put their families first since anti-suffragists often warned that voting women threatened domestic tranquility.[5]

Mrs. Franceway, Clay's western Kentucky hope, was in her sixties with a grown son. Certainly, she didn't have to fear the stork! But she might be one of those women who lacked confidence. That was Laura White's problem. She was one of Ashland's most dependable and enthusiastic suffragists, but she was prone to self-doubt. She agreed to organize in Owensboro (where her sister lived), but quickly had second thoughts. First, she needed to gain more club experience and a knowledge of parliamentary law. Then, she would be ready, she assured Clay. Similarly, Emma Roebuck questioned her abilities when asked to oversee KERA's legislative work. "Perhaps someone else would be better," she suggested, warning that she would need to be advised at every step.[6]

Clay knew that Mrs. Franceway was highly experienced and perfectly capable of organizing her community. If anything, her excuse would be that she already had too much on her plate. Mrs. Franceway's priority was temperance work; this is how Clay—herself a "white ribboner"—had come to know her. Franceway led WCTU work, not only in Madisonville, but across the second congressional district. She was known for her gracious hospitality and charm, and she was on fire for temperance. Clay hoped that she could get her on fire for suffrage too.[7]

Clay tried to tap into her WCTU contacts whenever possible, but this proved a mixed blessing. The national WCTU almost from its inception endorsed suffrage and created a department of the franchise. President Frances Willard with her "do everything" philosophy believed the vote was one of the surest ways for women to achieve their reform goals. Many southern women, however, questioned the wisdom of mixing temperance and suffrage for fear doing so would discredit them in their communities. WCTU chapters, particularly the "ultra-pious kind," found themselves at odds concerning the vote and decided it was best not to muddy the waters. It was a legitimate concern. Linking the two issues also had repercussions for suffrage, too. By courting the WCTU, KERA antagonized the liquor industry, Kentucky's so-called Third House.[8]

Did Mrs. Franceway side with her conservative colleagues or with state WCTU president, Frances Beauchamp, who had reputedly stormed out of the Prohibition Party convention the previous year when delegates refused to include a woman suffrage plank? Clay hoped she was of the latter mind. She had big plans for the Madisonville woman.[9]

Laura Clay turned back to her convention to-do list. So many preparations still to make. Many details had to wait until the last minute, but she could work on drafting her address to the delegates. She had been scouting out typewriters, an innovation that would speed up her work considerably (and make the historian's job easier), but she still hadn't settled on a model. She would write out her speech in longhand as she always did. She carefully considered her tone. KERA delegates' moods might be a bit somber, still smarting as they were from the loss of school suffrage. Efforts to get it restored had failed so far. Clay needed to build enthusiasm. She needed to focus her colleagues' attention on key priorities. She knew there was one point she would make loudly and repeatedly during the convention: "Increase the Membership" would be her refrain.[10]

Clay looked over her words and added one more pen stroke, placing an exclamation point at the end of her last sentence: "Increase the Membership!" She was not one to use such boisterous punctuation, but this sentence demanded one. Usually, if she wanted to emphasize an idea, she would put it in all caps, but then only rarely. Exclamation points seemed inappropriate somehow. They suggested unbecoming exuberance or worse, unladylike insistence. But as a new century opened, she expanded her punctuation repertoire. Putting an exclamation point after those three words drove home the importance of suffragists' new marching order.[11]

Clay wanted to see their Kentucky work expand, for sure, but she had other, more selfish reasons for encouraging growth. By 1900, Clay was establishing herself as a national suffrage star. A changing of the guard was under way—Elizabeth Cady Stanton had already made her exit (not all by choice) and Susan B. Anthony announced her retirement as NAWSA's president that year. Anthony had prepared for this day. She had carefully cultivated the next generation of leaders, a crew, including Clay, that affectionately became known as Aunt Susan's Girls.[12]

These younger suffragists were not content with business as usual. They had new ideas and ambitious priorities, and one of their top goals was to expand their numbers. The suffrage movement had always struggled to grow. In 1893, NAWSA had only seven thousand dues-paying members, compared to the WCTU's half million members. It raised on average only $2,000 annually. It needed more money and more manpower if it ever hoped to achieve its goals.[13]

Carrie Chapman Catt, a relative newcomer to the movement, did not hesitate to point out NAWSA's shortcomings in a bold speech she gave at its 1895 convention. This speech led to a new organization committee, which Catt was asked to lead, and her work with the committee led her to the presidency a few years later.[14]

Catt had built her career by emphasizing enrollment growth, and Clay either consciously or subconsciously hoped to do likewise. Clay looked for every possible opportunity to advertise her expertise in this area. When a standing-room-only crowd showed up for Catt's 1898 organization committee meeting, Clay volunteered to lead a second overflow assembly. When NAWSA began naming a roll of honor in 1902, announcing the five states with the highest enrollment gains and dues totals (and also publicly reprimanding states that did not send dues), Laura Clay basked in the praise heaped on Kentucky. Her efforts paid off. When it came time to appoint a chair for a new Increase of Membership committee created that year, Clay got tapped. Her charge: to double national membership, just like she had done in her own state.[15]

She may have felt a little pang of concern or even guilt. It was true that the membership total Kentucky reported to the National in 1902 was more than double its 1901 number, but the growth was a little misleading. One reason its 1902 tally—287 members—looked so impressive was because the previous year had been so dismal. Clay's mother died after an extended illness, and that, combined with the impact of Josephine Henry's departure, had taken a toll on KERA's numbers. Membership had shrunk and the number of locals had dwindled to just five (leaving the mainstays—Madison County, Fayette County, Newport, Covington, and Kenton County). Still, the 1902 number was substantially higher than their best previous year, which had come in 1895 when they reported 176 members.[16]

Clay delighted in sharing her secrets of success. Soon, her ideas became known simply as the "method of Kentucky" or the "Kentucky plan." Suffragists across the country were encouraged, but not required to follow her recommendations (as a states' rights southerner, Clay emphasized that locals should determine their own policies). Clay's plan threw out existing membership requirements, making the process much simpler. Pledging membership had always involved three actions. One had to first sign a copy of a local chapter's constitution. Then, he or she had to pay a dollar for annual dues, of which thirty-five cents went to the state organization and ten cents were passed on to the National. Finally, the new member had to commit to work actively for the cause. Local auxiliaries were expected to hold regular meetings, usually monthly, and members were expected to attend.[17]

Maybe, this was asking too much, Clay argued.

With the repeal of school suffrage fresh on her mind, Clay understood keenly that their enemies were keeping score. Opponents sanctimoniously contended that women did not really want the vote. It was just a few "cranks" who were making a lot of noise and drowning out the many thousands of women who were perfectly content to let men do the politicking, critics alleged. Expanding the franchise would violate the rights of uninterested women, allowing a minority to trump the rights of the majority. Suffragists were quick to stress that no woman, if enfranchised, would be forced to vote, but their reassurances did little to soothe lawmakers, who were just looking for excuses anyway.[18]

If they wanted to engage in an "argument of numbers," Clay decided, so be it. NAWSA must offer numerical proof that millions rather than a few thousand Americans advocated woman suffrage if they ever hoped to advance. One way to do that was to crystallize existing support through better record keeping. Clay encouraged local treasurers to maintain updated lists of names and addresses of suffrage supporters. But she also went a step further. She argued that they must make membership less demanding.[19]

Clay found it hard to believe that any intelligent American, absent an ulterior motive, could deny the righteousness of her cause. She felt certain that hordes of unregistered suffragists existed, just waiting to be discovered. They simply must be asked to "stand up and be counted," Clay insisted. It was not lack of support, but rather lack of *proof* of support that was holding them back. She hypothesized that so far, they had only enrolled 1 percent of suffrage supporters, and that was a conservative estimate, she figured.[20]

But they would never get the 99 percent to commit if expectations were too high. Were meetings really necessary? Clay challenged. She knew how local auxiliaries struggled to maintain their momentum once the novelty of declaring for suffrage had worn off. They started strong—just look at the Glasgow local—but they soon fizzled out. Club presidents were left wracking their brains to plan monthly meetings. Busy men and women had to take time away from other pursuits to keep reiterating the simple point that women should vote. One meeting a year to collect the dues was enough, Clay reasoned. Names and dues, that's all that mattered, according to the Kentucky Method.[21]

There was a lot riding on Clay's call to "Increase the Membership!" As Kentucky's numbers grew, she understood, so would her stature within NAWSA. She planned to make her home state a model for suffragists across the country, demonstrating how easy it was to recruit if one simply approached the problem logically.

Clay looked back over the morning mail. It was the time of year when local presidents sent their chapters' annual reports along with the dues they had (hopefully) collected. Clay ran some numbers. Not bad. Their work seemed to be paying off. Besides introducing the idea that regular meetings were not necessary, KERA had adopted other new recruitment strategies the National had encouraged. Before Clay's appointment as head of membership, Carrie Catt had introduced what today would be called "best practices." States should, if possible, hire a paid organizer—a field-worker—to oversee recruitment. At the very least, they should spread the word by enlisting good speakers who were active club women as well as suffragists. They should also sponsor booths at county fairs and local chautauquas and make the most of press coverage. Directives from the National suggested not only new tactics but also potential new constituencies, such as female factory workers, church members, teachers, and students.[22]

Clay planned to incorporate every suggestion. Press work was already one of KERA's strengths. She could not be more pleased with the work Lida Calvert Obenchain—a struggling author about to make her big break—was doing. Obenchain took control of this department in 1900, and somehow, in between raising four children and writing a best-selling novel, she managed to pepper nearly one hundred Kentucky newspapers each month with pro-suffrage articles. She achieved some synergy by having her children fold circulars and address envelopes. Some columns she wrote herself, others the National provided. Many had to be reproduced by hand. Luckily, she was an early adopter of the typewriter.[23]

Despite her satisfaction with Obenchain's work, Clay had to grit her teeth when a letter from her press superintendent arrived. They were long missives, sometimes spanning twelve pages, and stuffed with complaints. Obenchain thoroughly detailed her dental woes in one letter: "I don't want to lose my teeth, for of course a woman who wants to vote mustn't be ugly." At least she always added a note of humor. Clay was willing to tolerate her grumbling because she was so useful to the cause. Not one to complain herself, Clay even used her correspondence with Mrs. Obenchain to wallow in her own self-pity every now and then. Her greatest woe was Kentucky's insufferable heat. "You thin people" have no idea how "we *fat* ones suffer" in this weather, she wailed as the summer inferno dragged into October one year.[24]

KERA followed other NAWSA directives. It introduced the issue of suffrage at the Lexington chautauqua during the summer of 1903 and invited the famous Anna Howard Shaw, minister, white ribboner, and future NAWSA president, to speak. A tent on the grounds (now the site of Woodland Park) served as a hospitality station, offering a resting spot to visitors, all of whom would go home with suffrage literature, of course.[25]

Writing under the pen name "Eliza Calvert Hall," Lida Obenchain (shown left) became famous for her "Aunt Jane of Kentucky" books. She also was active in suffrage in Bowling Green and on the state level. She appears here with fellow suffragist Lillian South, a physician who helped to eliminate hookworm in Kentucky. (Western Kentucky Library Special Collections)

Chautauquas were a useful platform because they attracted large crowds, but Clay understood that spreading the gospel of suffrage worked best when done face-to-face and close to home. In many small Kentucky communities, no one heard anything about suffrage except as something dreadful until a speaker came through to change their minds. NAWSA's number one suggestion for growing the membership was to hire professional field-workers to act as missionaries. Iowa (Mrs. Catt's home state) served as a model. Fourteen professional organizers, bankrolled by NAWSA, had established 250 new suffrage clubs, opened a state headquarters, and established a presence in almost every county. Clay longed to do something similar, but professional organizers were expensive. Free-will offerings, KERA's primary funding mechanism, were unlikely to cover the cost of putting someone on the payroll, but Clay was determined to try.[26]

KERA had experimented quite successfully with trained organizers when the National had sent them on loan in the past. Emma Smith DeVoe's short tour in 1897 resulted in the creation of seven new locals. But it was unrealistic to think that an organizer could give a speech and spend a day or two and leave a healthy, permanent organization. DeVoe left the state, and a year later only two of the new auxiliaries showed signs of life. Still, Clay was optimistic. The Kentucky Method made it easier to be a suffragist now that meetings were unnecessary. Clay expected this change would result in more growth (especially among men) and growth that would last.[27]

Clay stretched KERA's limited resources to hire Frances Woods for one month in 1904. The forty-year-old medical school graduate was a talented speaker and had previous organizing experience, having traipsed across Iowa, Kansas, and Arizona. She had even spent a few weeks in Kentucky in 1901. Clay decided that putting Woods to work in western Kentucky would yield the greatest return on investment. Woods began work in Paducah in mid-October. From there, she hopped over to Princeton, Hopkinsville, Madisonville, Henderson, and Hawesville. A week-long illness forced Woods to scrap her plan to go to Owensboro, but once her intestinal tract was back in working order, she visited Elizabethtown, Glasgow, and Cave City to round out her tour.[28]

When considering where to send Woods, Clay purposely picked communities with strong WCTU chapters, hoping to piggyback on that work. But her plan backfired. In nearly every report, Woods grumbled about the region's conservative values. Ministers were against them, but she found "W. C. T. U. narrowness" even more challenging. As soon as she arrived, Woods seemed ready to give up. Hopkinsville was a dead end, she reported. The right person might "accomplish something very gradually in a number of years," but she was not that person. In Paducah she ran up against fears that woman suffrage was "one of the forerunners of race-equality." Over and over, she met resistance. Whether discouraged by her illness, or because she was a sour person generally or perhaps a pragmatic realist, Woods expressed little confidence that western Kentucky could be organized without years of work.[29]

But some good had come from her effort. Paducah's E.R.A., established in 1895 but dormant since 1897, had sputtered back to life. In four communities—Princeton, Henderson, Hawesville, and Cave City—there was not enough interest to form an auxiliary, but someone did step up in each town to serve as a future contact. And then, there was Madisonville.[30]

The one bright note in Woods's gloomy reports was her announcement that Madisonville had organized a new and remarkably vigorous E.R.A. Fifteen members assembled, and even better, they paid their dues on the spot. Brimming with energy, each member pledged to recruit not just one other person, but *five* additional members by the next year. For as much as Woods had complained about WCTU women's "narrowness," Mrs. Franceway, the Madisonville local's new president, seemed different. Not only did she step up to organize her community, she also promised to leverage her temperance connections to recruit in other towns.[31]

The Madisonville E.R.A. did not have seventy-five members the next year as promised, but it managed to hold its own. The chapter, now calling itself the Hopkins County E.R.A., paid dues for fourteen members in 1905. But the report Franceway sent suggested its energy was waning. Following KERA's suggestion that regular meetings were not necessary, it held just one. Franceway was active even if her fellow suffragists were not. "*I* distributed three hundred pages of literature at the county fair," she was careful to note, before adding that she had also passed out leaflets at the local teachers' institute. The organization's one big activity that year was a talk they sponsored at the courthouse.[32]

Clay knew that fledgling chapters were prone to slip away unless carefully "mothered." How could she keep Hopkins County engaged? She had an idea. She would ask Madisonville to host the annual KERA convention. Conventions were thrilling events; they were filled with pageantry and camaraderie, and often featured displays of the latest technology (in 1894, it was Lexington's electric trolley; in 1915, it was the automobile). Locals could expect a substantial membership boost after hosting. Lexington recruited fifty new members when it hosted in 1904.[33]

Mrs. Franceway seemed a little uncomfortable with the idea, but with Clay's encouragement, she invited KERA to meet in Madisonville in 1907. Clay knew that it would likely mean lower than normal attendance as they had discovered the previous year when the convention met in Ashland. Hopkins County was even further afield, twice as far from Lexington as it was from Nashville and 250 miles from northern Kentucky. But the chance to build interest in western Kentucky, where KERA had always struggled, seemed a worthwhile trade-off.[34]

In the end, fate thwarted Clay's plan to use the annual convention to recruit. The 1907 KERA convention met in Richmond, not Madisonville. Mrs. Franceway's suffrage work largely ended that year. She found herself suddenly caring for a newborn when, in February, her daughter-in-law died in childbirth. With its driving force sidelined, Madisonville disappeared from KERA's auxiliary list. It would languish until KERA sent another field-worker to Hopkins County in 1913.[35]

Despite Clay's optimistic claim that suffrage supporters already existed, who were just waiting to be discovered and would pledge their undying support to the movement if they only knew how easy it was to do so, KERA struggled to win converts in rural Kentucky. Heavy workloads, sparse populations, and competing priorities prevented country women from organizing. A visit from Laura Clay or a famous national suffrage leader could sometimes stir up curiosity and weak pledges of support, but maintaining that interest was a different matter. Newly established clubs tended to be highly unstable and often quietly folded as soon as the charismatic NAWSA organizer left the area.[36]

But sometimes the seed took root. Case in point: the Ashland E.R.A., established in 1901 after Laura Clay spoke at the local Christian Church. Boyd County women managed to maintain a local auxiliary, with a membership hovering around thirty, without fail until suffrage was won. Some of that time, a second organization even existed in nearby Catlettsburg.[37]

The extremely well-educated and impressively tall (six foot two) Laura White was one big reason for the Ashland group's success. The sister of US congressman John Daugherty White, Laura was the first woman to earn a BS degree from Michigan State in 1874. Then, it was on to MIT and then the Sorbonne to study architecture. After graduation, she returned to eastern Kentucky to help run her family's business empire. Only later did she adopt her brother's interest in suffrage (he helped create a House Select Committee on Woman Suffrage in 1882). When Clay came to Ashland in 1901, it so happened that she spoke at a church that White had designed. White became a charter member of the Ashland local. On several occasions she served as the organization's secretary or treasurer, but she did most of her work behind the scenes.[38]

Besides suffrage, Laura White had another passion. She didn't just want the vote for the vote's sake. She wanted it so she could promote world peace. Her colleagues in the Ashland E.R.A. shared her interest. In 1906, the group reported that one of their most significant accomplishments was getting Peace Day recognized in local schools. White later led KERA's peace and arbitration committee.[39]

The Ashland E.R.A. remained a consistently vibrant group. They met often. In 1906, Fayette County suffragists met only three times, compared to the Ashland women who convened seven times. Their meetings were meaningful and intellectually stimulating, filled with discussion of current issues. Strong newspaper support (a suffragist's husband, a local feed store owner, bought a lot of ads and could pull some strings) helped educate new members, but the sense of purpose Ashland suffragists shared kept them engaged.[40]

Unfortunately, however, most suffrage auxiliaries were more like Madisonville than Ashland. One person was left to do all the work, and if for some reason that person had to withdraw, then all was lost.

Clay and her KERA colleagues grew weary, and who could blame them: converting suffragists one day, only to see them fall away the next. It was so difficult to maintain interest, particularly in rural areas. Every year they added new suffragists, but a healthy number always had to be subtracted from their tally when dues failed to materialize. In 1906, Clay took a second look at her Kentucky plan. Maybe they could relax membership require-ments even further. She had long argued that collecting dues was a sacred responsibility for state and local treasurers, the only way to prove they were gaining on the argument of numbers. But now she reconsidered. Perhaps there was a way to show advances but hide the losses.[41]

She proposed a radical solution. Let's make dues optional, she urged. She hoped that women would still want to do their part—maybe they would even voluntarily contribute more than the bare necessity—and if they didn't, wealthy women could help cover the deficit. Names were more valuable than dimes, Clay figured. New members should only be asked to sign their name to a card pledging their belief in the right of suffrage for women, nothing more. Cards would be easy to keep on file and pledges would remain in effect for life. An individual could officially withdraw his or her card, but that seemed unlikely.[42]

"We have been an overgrown woman's club long enough," Clay chided her fellow suffragists, urging the need to look more like political parties. To join a political party required nothing more than to state one's allegiance—no dues, no duties. It was organization in its simplest form. Extending this line of thought, Clay recommended that suffrage canvassing follow estab-lished political boundaries to ensure efficiency and full coverage: precinct, ward, city, county, and state lines.[43]

With this new and improved Kentucky plan, Clay hoped KERA would finally start to show the kind of growth she had promised when she became head of NAWSA's Increase of Membership committee. KERA's official membership (measured by dues paid to the National) had risen from 287 in 1902 to 442 in 1905, but it fell back to 351 in 1907. Never again, Clay vowed, would KERA show a loss. From here on out, it would be once a suffragist, always a suffragist.[44]

It had been several years since Miss Clay had last heard from Mrs. Franceway, but in January 1909, she took a deep breath, loaded a sheet of KERA letterhead into her typewriter, and tapped out a request. A huge task lay in front of Clay. She needed to draw on every contact she had, no matter how unlikely it was that person would come through. President Taft's recent offhand remark that he would give women the vote when they demonstrated that they wanted it, led NAWSA to hold him to that promise. They would show him how many women wanted the vote. Carrie Catt called for a "monster petition," containing the signatures of at least one million American adults. They would ceremonially present the names to Congress along with a demand for a federal constitutional amendment to enfranchise women.[45]

Apportioning the total among the states, Catt determined that Kentucky should provide one hundred thousand signatures. The goal stunned Clay a little, but the request also likely flattered her, a sign that Catt believed in her leadership. Ten years from now, Clay would go gangbusters to defeat a federal amendment, but in 1909, she was willing to commit her whole winter to see it advance. Clay's living room served as ground zero for the massive effort, which in the days before computers and photocopiers required tedious "pasting and classifying." They must demonstrate the utmost care, Clay warned her fellow volunteers. Antis would be looking for signs of fraud.[46]

Catt encouraged suffragists to work through existing organizations—the WCTU, the Grange, labor unions, any collection of people who might endorse their cause—letting them do most of the heavy lifting. Clay, preferring always to support local choice and local autonomy, decided instead to appoint a representative for each county and let them collect names however each saw fit. And so, she was writing to Mrs. Franceway to ask her to be Hopkins County's chair.[47]

Clay was used to hearing "no," but the petition drive tested even her fortitude. More respondents than not delivered an excuse for why they could not participate. Many begged off, noting that their friends and neighbors would not sign. Bowling Green's Mary M. Mitchell, for instance, declared that the time was not "ripe in the South-land for suffrage."[48]

Those who were on board unanimously agreed that their target goals were too high. If they were going to get anywhere close to one hundred thousand signatures (Clay herself believed this an impossible goal, though she hoped they could make a "creditable showing"), they would need to get as many names out of Louisville as possible. Emma Hast, Louisville's assigned petition director, tepidly agreed to take one thousand petition blanks. Clay sent the blanks and cheered her on but admitted to another correspondent that Louisville's actual quota was three thousand.[49]

Northern Kentucky had long been one of KERA's most fertile fields, but representatives appointed to head up the effort in those counties also swallowed hard when Clay announced their target numbers. Emma Roebuck had served not only as the president of the Campbell County E.R.A. but also as the recording secretary of KERA since 1901. No one could question her loyalty to the cause or her willingness to work, but she flat out told Clay that five hundred signatures from Campbell County was too much to ask. We only have "six or seven working members," she reminded Clay.[50]

Often, the success of the petition in a community hinged on the efforts of a single woman. Laura White, Ashland's peace-loving suffragist, tried to mobilize her fellow E.R.A. members, but hit a dead end. Not one to disappoint, White told Clay that she would try to visit every house in her county herself, "if the weather continues fairly good." She finally found another woman willing to help and they covered a lot of ground. The Ashland petitions were the first to come in and they were plentiful, Clay celebrated.[51]

Mrs. Franceway, meanwhile, apologizing for her lack of service over the past two years, agreed to direct the petition effort in her county: "My health is better now, and I want to do something for the cause I love." Her letter, penned in a neat, leaning cursive, brought excellent news. Clay needed more of these encouraging responses.[52]

Still, Clay's attempts to get women to stand up and be counted were largely unsuccessful. Only in Lexington did things go as she had planned. Lexington suffragists functioned like a well-oiled machine, dividing the city into districts to which teams of volunteers were assigned.

Perhaps if Clay had been on the ground to direct efforts, they would have been more successful. Clay was in Arizona during much of the collection period (as a National leader she was often called to assist in other state campaigns). Her sister, Mary Barr Clay, picked up the slack, but Clay's absence probably took a toll.[53]

The survey, so carefully collected, cut and pasted, checked and rechecked to avoid duplication, does not survive, nor does any record remain of the number of Kentuckians who ultimately signed. Clay would have surely leveraged the petition for its full promotional value had they reached their goal of one hundred thousand signatures or even come close to it. Many states reported their signature totals at the 1910 NAWSA convention, but not Kentucky. The correspondence preserved in Clay's papers suggests that the results were highly disappointing.[54]

Nationally, the outcome was only slightly more encouraging. After postponing delivery, NAWSA finally presented its scroll of signatures to Congress on a beautiful blooming spring day in April 1910. Fifty-two automobiles rolled up to the front of the Capitol and suffragists carrying the fruits of their labor—404,825 signatures—hopped out. They had hoped to deliver the names of 10 percent of adult Americans. Instead, their bounty represented less than one-half of 1 percent of the nation's population.[55]

In November 1909, the KERA executive board met just as it did every year to determine its plan of work for the upcoming year. No surprise, increasing the membership stayed at the top of its list of goals. But an approaching legislative session offered hope of bigger, more tangible victories like a co-guardianship bill to protect mothers' rights and a requirement that women be placed on boards of state educational, charitable, and penal institutions. KERA would continue to support the Kentucky Federation of Women's Clubs (KFWC) as it pushed for school suffrage for all women who could read and write. But one more objective rounded out the list. A new goal, demonstrating a new level of confidence: a state constitutional amendment.[56]

Clay believed her low-stakes approach to membership would be the breakthrough the Kentucky movement needed to grow. She assumed that white, affluent, educated Kentuckians would embrace her cause if doing so didn't require too much time or money. But what she failed to grasp was that many, especially rural Kentuckians, continued to see woman suffrage as a radical cause. Membership requirements were not the problem. Until suffrage lost its reputation for being a bit "cranky," KERA would flounder.

Clay expected that her Kentucky plan would boost Kentucky's suffrage numbers and, as an added bonus, would boost her national prominence. She aspired to lead the NAWSA as it entered its next phase—hopefully as it finally claimed victory. It turns out, she miscalculated on both scores, which events in Louisville soon revealed.

8

Louisville Awakens

Laura Clay always looked forward to October. It was a beautiful time to be in Kentucky. She rejoiced as the "debilitating" heat of summer finally broke and celebrated the fall harvest. In 1911, October promised another thrill: the NAWSA annual convention was coming to Louisville. For over a year, Kentucky suffragists had been planning, making sure every detail was just so, and now they looked forward to hosting their colleagues and friends.

Clay had tried her best not to micromanage the preparations. Louisville women should control the meeting details, she agreed. But she really wanted her home state to look good, so she weighed in frequently on decisions big and small. Many people are afraid of elevators, she reminded planners. Best to select a downstairs meeting space. She felt sure they would have a large attendance so conference rooms should accommodate between forty and eighty people. Knowing from personal experience that NAWSA officers would bring many trunks filled with books and files, she instructed the local women to reserve spacious suites for them with ample natural light. KERA had already promised to foot the bill, she reminded.[1]

The swanky, downtown Seelbach, the city's first "European" hotel, completed six years earlier at a cost of nearly one million dollars, would serve as the conference site. Its Beaux-Arts Baroque design lent just the right touch of old-world opulence while offering the best in modern amenities, including a telephone in every room. No detail had been overlooked in its design. Even the water fountain in the lobby, the largest piece of Rookwood pottery ever made, served to impress. When the hotel opened, observers billed it "the most elaborately equipped hostelry in all the South."[2]

Clay was not about to squander this opportunity to show off her native state to visitors. She knew Americans perceived Kentucky as an exotic far-off place, the stuff of legend and lore, and not all of it flattering. Part west, part south, a little polished, a little rough—visitors would see the state's multiple sides during the six-day convention. Arriving at the Seelbach, they would get a quick lesson in Kentucky's pioneer history as they studied towering hand-painted murals adorning the hotel lobby. Kentucky's southern credentials—its

Official seal of the 1911 NAWSA convention held in Louisville. (*Woman's Journal*)

hospitality, its lovely women and handsome colonels—would also be on full display. Planners arranged for the elderly Emily Todd Helm, Mary Todd Lincoln's Confederate-leaning half sister, to address the convention and for a quartet to perform suffrage songs set to the tune of "Dixie." A special "Votes for Women" excursion train would take attendees to Lincoln's birthplace and Mammoth Cave at the close of the convention.[3]

While Clay's frequent suggestions helped ensure the convention's success, it was Louisville suffragists who did the heavy lifting. Considering the perennial struggle to capture and maintain suffrage interest in the state's largest city, the convention was a remarkable triumph. Such a feat would have been unthinkable even five years earlier. How far they had come!

KERA did not offer a prize for the most improved chapter each year, but if it did, the award would have gone to the Woman Suffrage Association of Louisville (LWSA) in 1909, and then again in 1910 and 1911. "Splendid" suffrage "material" existed in the Derby City, Clay knew, but it had never managed to live up to its potential. Now finally, the suffrage spirit was building there, and its local was growing like gangbusters. Twenty-nine members in 1908 became sixty-seven members in 1909. And the news kept getting better: 170 members the following year and 225 in 1911. Louisville representatives proudly reported 425 members in 1912, making it the largest of KERA's eleven auxiliaries.[4]

It was a bit surprising that suffrage had been so slow to take off in Louisville. When suffrage speakers like Lucy Stone went on tour, even before the Civil War, they often chose to visit the fast-growing city. With its population approaching two hundred thousand residents by 1900, Louisville was significantly larger and more cosmopolitan than the rest of Kentucky. Many of its residents had moved there from other regions, and they tended to bring progressive ideas with them.[5]

Susan Look Avery was one of these open-minded transplants. Mrs. Avery came to Kentucky by way of upstate New York. She was shaped by the revivalism of the so-called Burned-Over District in the early nineteenth century. An abolitionist before the war, she remained a deep-in-her-soul reformer, even as she settled down with her husband, B. F. Avery, owner of a prosperous plow factory, to raise six children. For many years her activism remained at a low boil as she prioritized domestic duties. When her husband died in 1885, she took that event not as a sign that she should retire into quiet widowhood, but as the beginning of a new chapter of activism and intellectual exploration. Rather than snuffing the fire in her belly, age made her increasingly willing to question the status quo.[6]

Avery threw herself into advocating for a long list of causes, some appropriately feminine (missionary work, temperance) and others not (free silver, ending capital punishment). Her interest in woman suffrage developed naturally. Women could only be change agents if they had the vote, and Avery, now in her seventies, had every intention of leaving this world a better place than she had found it.[7]

In March 1889, the energized widow invited like-minded women to convene at her stately home at Fourth and Broadway to establish the Louisville E.R.A. (precursor to the LWSA). The small circle of women, soon numbering fourteen, knew each other well since there was significant

Susan Look Avery became active in civic work when she was nearly seventy years old. She was heavily influenced by the Chicago settlement house scene and its woman's club movement. Besides fighting for suffrage, she also spoke out against racism, which made her unusual for her time. (Property of Woman's Club of Louisville, used with its permission)

cross-pollination between civic organizations. The Presbyterian church, the WCTU, the Louisville Free Kindergarten, and the new Ramabai Circle, established to fund educational opportunities for children in India, were a few points of overlap.[8]

Caroline Leech, wife of a local banker, was one of the notable attendees. Described as beautiful, influential, impervious to ridicule, and accustomed to results, Leech was thirty years younger than Avery. In fact, she was almost the same age as Laura Clay, and they were likely classmates at Sayre Female Institute in Lexington. Clay and Leech continued to cross paths through their shared involvement in the WCTU, though it is not clear if one influenced the other and if so, in what direction.[9]

Not all of the newly pledged suffragists were as well-to-do as Mrs. Avery and Mrs. Leech, but most were quite comfortable. They also shared her tendency to be forward-thinking and to embrace the avant-garde. Shortly after joining the group, Dr. Helena M. Cady, one of the first female doctors in Louisville, divorced her husband and became a single mother of six. Another early member, Stanley B. Huber, husband of the organization's secretary, Marion Huber, embraced some of the era's newest novelties. He became a typewriter dealer and an avid bicyclist.[10]

The LERA seemed poised for success. Avery and her friends elected officers, created three standing committees, and pledged to meet monthly. It was a bad sign that its second "regular" monthly meeting had to be postponed for lack of attendance. When the group finally gathered a week late, the president, vice-president, and two of three committee chairs were missing. The committed few that did convene were not deterred. Instead of dialing back they voted unanimously to start meeting twice a month.[11]

The will was there but the way was not. To its credit, the group had a few moments of brilliance. It got a police matron added to the local force. Members passed the hat at one meeting and raised $10.75 ($300 in 2018 terms) to help fund Josephine Henry's legislative work. But the group lacked consistency. They went on hiatus from June to October each year since so many members summered elsewhere. The rest of the year, even after they reduced the quorum from five to three members, they struggled to keep active.[12]

Apathy was not the problem. The members of the LERA suffered from overcommitment. Susan Look Avery had a broad mind that wandered in every direction at once, it seemed. Explaining her proclivity for multitasking she stressed that women could not afford to consider one political question at a time: "We must take them all along as we go." The year after she set

LERA in motion, she established its much larger sister society, the Woman's Club of Louisville.[13]

Avery's oldest daughter, Lydia, had moved to Chicago, and her engagement in its lively reform community inspired her mother, too. Ideas from Chicago steadily flowed toward Kentucky through this channel. Chicago had a Woman's Club, and soon Louisville did as well. The Chicago Woman's Club created a subcommittee called the Emergency Association in 1893, and Louisville women followed suit, but with a twist. Instead of settling for assisting destitute families by helping jobless women find employment as the Emergency Association was created to do, the Avery women expanded its scope to address any national, state, or local emergency that might arise.[14]

In 1900, Louisville women knew they had a public emergency on their hands. They seized on the assassination of Governor Goebel to mobilize more than three thousand outraged women who were tired of seeing Kentucky "droop her head in shame." It was up to them, the women decided, to save the state's good name. Their demands: an end to gun violence, limits on concealed carry, and an end to partisan bickering. The Emergency Association raised a good ruckus, but soon it was on to the next crisis. By the next year, they were focused on combatting polygamy.[15]

The women of Louisville had too much to do to focus exclusively on suffrage. LERA persisted but in a severely emaciated state. A visit from Susan B. Anthony and Carrie Chapman Catt in 1895 popped its membership up to thirty-two, but it immediately shriveled again. By 1898, membership was down to six. Despite LERA's 1902 prediction that "a great suffrage revival" was expected soon, it did not materialize. Clay struggled to find even one person doing suffrage work in Louisville in 1906.[16]

It had been several years since LERA had sent a report to the state convention, and then only to say it had held no meetings, but suddenly in 1908 its radio silence ended. The auxiliary with such promise had proved a dud up until now, but with new leadership and a new name it sprung to life. Calling itself the Woman Suffrage Association of Louisville, in accordance with the National's revised naming guidelines, the new and improved LWSA highlighted its key goal: obtaining the vote. The group still did not have a permanent president, but Mrs. Charles A. Nield served as acting president. The signs were good all around.[17]

Winning Lucy A. "Lula" Nield to the suffrage fight was a bit of a coup. Back in the 1880s and 1890s, she had drawn widespread attention as the "girl orator." "Fearless," "fetching," "magnetic," her admirers gushed. She was a young mother then, in her early twenties and the wife of a coal operator, and she could expound on the evils of alcohol like few others. No suffrage work for her, she stuck to enterprises she deemed "sweet and womanly." "I want no higher sphere than wife and mother," she swore. Women did not belong on the stage, she argued, blind to the walking contradiction she represented. When her family moved to Louisville in 1888, she gave up speaking, but she remained active in the WCTU and in the Woman's Club. Her name first appeared in LWSA records in 1908, the year she agreed to lead the group.[18]

Nield pledged to support woman suffrage at the very moment that the Progressive spirit, offering an optimistic collection of solutions to an assortment of pressing problems, was sweeping America. As chair of the civics department of the Louisville Woman's Club, Nield saw some of the worst effects of industrialization. There is no telling whether her status as a coal operator's wife lent a sense of urgency to her efforts, but something clearly had opened her eyes to inequality. To those who blamed the poor's struggles on irresponsibility, Nield incredulously asked how a woman or a girl could possibly be expected to live and dress herself on $3 or $3.50 a week. She lobbied for tougher child labor laws, she helped secure pure food and drug legislation, and somewhere along the way, she decided that being sweet and womanly was not enough. She needed the vote.[19]

Nield kept her promise to only serve temporarily as LWSA president (she continued, however, to hold leadership roles in KERA), but she put it in good hands. Emma Hast agreed to take over, working closely with Virginia P. Robinson, president of the city's new chapter of the Collegiate Equal Suffrage League. Hast, a well-connected member of a prominent German immigrant family, had years of social reform experience. She also had a decidedly creative mind. She was not an inventor yet, but her life was heading in that direction—she secured patents for a toilet seat cover in 1919 and a new, improved roller skate in 1931. Robinson, a recent Bryn Mawr graduate, was significantly younger than Hast, but she too would do great things. She earned a PhD in social work at the University of Pennsylvania and wrote a book that revolutionized her field. But first, she helped to revolutionize the LWSA. Together, Hast and Robinson gave the Louisville work the vitality it had long lacked.[20]

College-educated women, like Robinson, helped drive the LWSA's growth. Many of these new members got their start at Female High School, one of the two original public high schools in the city, which opened in 1856. By the early twentieth century, it had a large and active alumnae association. Many female graduates did not stop with a high school degree. They went on to college, and some, like Robinson, returned to teach at their alma mater, where they had a platform to influence scores of future suffragists.[21]

With Louisville suddenly showing so much promise, Clay decided to hit it with a full-court press. One reason they had always struggled there, she concluded, was because of its hostile local newspapers. The rascally Henry Watterson had long dismissed suffragists as "crazyjanes" and "sillysallies." Lida Obenchain had tried unsuccessfully for nearly a decade to crack the Louisville market. Not a single paper would take the articles she peddled. How could the movement hope for success when it had no chance to tell its own story?[22]

Clay hoped a new press superintendent with connections in Louisville could work some magic. Mrs. Obenchain announced in March 1909 that she was stepping down. The strain was getting to her and she was sure that she was on the verge of a nervous breakdown: "It isn't the 'change of life' with me. I passed that . . . years ago," she confided. Her exit gave Clay a golden opportunity to turn things around in Louisville. She chose Margaret Weissinger, a local debutante, as Obenchain's successor, hoping her social connections would lead to more column space for their cause.[23]

Weissinger, like Nield, was a new convert to the movement. In the past, women of her station—what she called the "Home class women"—typically limited themselves to joining the Woman's Club, where they gathered for teas and bazaars and appropriately feminine activities. But now, speaking as a true Progressive, she noted that woman's "direct influence [was] needed in industrial matters, in affairs of sanitation, in bettering conditions in the slums, and in enforcing the pure food law." It was impossible for women to assist what she called the "helpless class" if they themselves were helpless too.[24]

Momentum was finally building, but it could stall at any time. A convention would be just the thing to lock in interest. Louisville had only hosted the KERA annual meeting once before, in 1891. Returning to the Derby City would reward the LWSA for its hard work. Clay, Robinson, and others predicted the spectacular growth that would follow. If these were betting women, they would have put money on the LWSA doubling its membership within the next year.[25]

KERA conferences rotated from town to town, but they always had a familiar rhythm and tone. The 1909 meeting, however, sang a new song. The business looked familiar—co-guardianship, school suffrage, with a state constitutional amendment thrown in to signal eternal optimism. The meeting opened, as usual, with prayer and devotions. Rev. Anna Howard Shaw, NAWSA president, was again their honored guest (she had spoken at every convention held since 1903). But beyond that, it was clear that this meeting would not be business as usual.[26]

One sign that change was in the air was the absence of many of KERA's longest-serving leaders. Vice president, Mary B. Clay, apologized for her absence, but she sent greetings and five dollars. Nancy S. McLaughlin, another vice president from Covington, was also missing. No one could fault Mary C. Roark, KERA's corresponding secretary, for skipping out. She had been selected to succeed her husband as president of Eastern Kentucky State Normal School after his death several months earlier. Learning the ropes and grieving were her priorities now. There had been very little turnover in the KERA slate of officers over the last two decades, so the absence of these stalwarts was immediately noticeable.[27]

Other signs suggested that the Louisville women had not planned a same-old, same-old kind of convention. The meeting's urban setting gave it a more cosmopolitan air and allowed new voices to be heard, like that of Rebecca Rosenthal Judah, who was scheduled to offer fraternal greetings to the delegates on behalf of the Council of Jewish Women. Unlike many KERA chapters whose members exclusively represented mainline Protestant sects—Baptists, Methodists, and Episcopalians—the LWSA drew Unitarians as well as Catholics and Jews. Later in the convention, Anna Howard Shaw gave her keynote address in the Temple Adath Israel.[28]

Working women, especially factory workers, though not well represented among the meeting goers, featured heavily in the conference programming. Lula Nield greeted attendees on behalf of "the professional women, who are not at present members of the Equal Rights Association," hinting at new priorities. Later, Nield proved why she had won the nickname "girl orator" (though few would have confused her for a "girl" anymore) by delivering an enlightening lesson on the dangers of a modern economy in her role as chair of KERA's new Committee on Industrial Problems Affecting Women and Children.[29]

From beginning to end, the convention paid homage to working women, reflecting not only Mrs. Nield's influence but also that of other

Louisville suffragists, many of whom were also members of Louisville's branch of the Kentucky Consumers League. Founded in 1901 to end sweatshop labor, the KCL encouraged women to scrutinize their shopping habits and to only buy goods that carried the National Consumers League stamp of approval. From there, they moved into advocacy work. The league helped to pass child labor legislation, arranged for inspectors to oversee the city's factories, and worked to clean up the city's slums.[30]

Extending these connections, many Louisville suffragists also had ties to Neighborhood House, a social settlement that attempted to do for Louisville what Hull House had done for Chicago. Neighborhood House served a diverse community, which included not only "Syrians and Italians and Negroes, [and] Russian Jews," according to one resident, but also "American whites who have seen better days." Living with the city's unfortunate and viewing their struggles up close allowed these Louisville suffragists to deeply understand the power of the vote and the benefits it could bring to all women.[31]

The Progressive spirit was so strong by 1909 that even leading capitalists like S. Thruston Ballard, co-owner of Louisville's Ballard & Ballard Flour Mills, were championing labor reform. Ballard argued there was more to business than just the bottom line; he won national acclaim for completely rethinking capital–labor relations. Together with his brother, he established one of the first profit-sharing plans in the nation for employees and adopted the eight-hour day before mandated to do so.[32]

Ballard and his wife, Sunshine, were initially drawn to the suffrage cause when they heard Madeline McDowell Breckinridge speak about school suffrage in 1909. They joined the LWSA and began injecting their concern for working women into the organization. The Ballards saw the 1909 convention as an important opportunity to reach out to this overlooked group. They invited Rev. Shaw and KERA delegates to tour Ballard Mills on the last day of the convention. Shaw, a fellow champion of working women, jumped at the chance to inspect the facility—a model operation, she proclaimed—and to instruct its female employees on the uses of the ballot.[33]

As predicted, hosting the 1909 convention boosted the LWSA's membership numbers. The group more than doubled in size in the following months. The convention helped, but other factors worked in the Louisville local's favor. Its demonstrations of how women's vote could advance Progressive causes resonated with a wide cross section of the city's white women and men. The Kentucky suffrage movement, distinctly homogenous up to this point, gained new constituencies, at least in one part of the state. Louisville suffragists were willing to think outside the box, even considering the merits of socialism (not the dirty word it would become later, but still controversial). Newcomers could feel the group's intellectual energy and appreciated its commitment to solving social problems.[34]

The LWSA gave Ethel Snowden much of the credit for its new birth. Snowden, the wife of a British parliament member and personal friend of Louisville suffragist Caroline Leech, first spoke in Louisville in November 1908. She received such rave reviews that LWSA invited her to return just days after the 1909 KERA meeting. Snowden proudly claimed the title of "suffragette"—not "the most militant type," she noted, not the type that broke windows or chained herself to park railings—but the outspoken kind nonetheless. Snowden was just radical enough to light a fire in Louisville women's bellies, but not so radical that she turned hearers off. Louisville women, it seemed, were primed for a bolder approach than Clay had traditionally advocated.[35]

Unlike many of her fellow suffragists who were swept up in the great questions of the day, Laura Clay's mind did not point that direction. Organized labor had always been a personal blind spot for her, a point she openly acknowledged. It was difficult, she claimed, for someone like her, "born and reared on a farm" and now making her living by farming, to understand the perspective of those who "labor in masses." She thought it best to let people who knew something about "manufacturing people" deal with their worries.[36]

Laura Clay had been leading the Kentucky suffrage movement for nearly thirty years by 1909. She was not a young woman anymore, with the mental agility that youth affords, but rather a sixty-two-year-old woman who had a clear and unbending view of the world. That view had served to create and inspire many suffragists over the years, but increasingly, Laura Clay's vision and that of her colleagues were at odds.[37]

Laura Clay wanted the Louisville chapter to grow, but it seemed to be growing into something that she hardly recognized. With its interest in urban problems, its diverse membership, and its willingness to consider more militant action, the new and improved Louisville branch did not look like its sister chapters in other parts of the state. Increasingly it would not be Clay's vision that dictated the movement's course, it would be Louisville women's vision. She had always predicted that Louisville would be the key to suffrage's success in Kentucky. Over the next decade, she would find out just how right she was.

October 1911, as expected, brought its promised cooler temperatures and a dazzling display of color as trees put on their end-of-year show. Clay had been looking forward to hosting the NAWSA convention for over a year, but now, she began to dread its arrival. Tensions had been building within the National. Laura Clay, the hero of the southern work, protégée of Aunt Susan, and NAWSA auditor for the past fifteen years, knew that a shake-up was coming, and chances were high that she would be shook out. The realization that her ejection could happen in her own backyard made the possibility extra painful.

In a show of hometown loyalty, the *Lexington Leader* speculated that Clay might be elected NAWSA's next president at the convention, but she knew that this was wishful thinking. She was much more likely to be *de*moted than *pro*moted. For months she had been mentally preparing herself to be ousted from the board. NAWSA had been in turmoil for several years, a result of Anna Howard Shaw's divisive presidency. Shaw felt that NAWSA had failed to keep up with the times, and she especially blamed conservative southern board members for its inertia. Shaw preferred universal suffrage won through federal means, while board members such as Clay wanted qualified suffrage secured on a state-by-state basis.[38]

NAWSA had been faking unity for several years, but its days of putting on a good face were over. Planned changes to the organization's constitution would determine its future course, and a battle—possibly spirited, but likely unfriendly—was sure to follow. Two main questions loomed: where would NAWSA's headquarters be located, and how much control would the National have over state and local suffrage work? Clay feared that NAWSA would be made a "mere N. Y. affair," but there were deeper, simmering points of disagreement. Factions disagreed on how democratic their movement should be. Some, like Clay, insisted that they must avoid antagonizing the South at all costs, while others demanded a more inclusive perspective, one that courted working-class women and that confronted the injustice of racism.[39]

The fight was getting ugly. Several veteran board members who lacked the stomach for dissension announced that they would not run again, and Clay thought about joining them but soon reconsidered. The organization needed representation from all regions, she reasoned, especially amid crisis. She knew she would probably be "cut out," but she pledged to stand for reelection anyway. The ship might be on the breakers, but she would not desert, she heroically promised.[40]

The swirl of conference activities probably took Clay's mind off the upcoming elections, or maybe she passed the time by doing some politicking. When the convention opened on October 19, attendees were in a particularly celebratory mood, intoxicated by news that California voters had voted "yes" to enfranchise women just days before. The glamorous Seelbach was decked out in sunny yellow, the official color of the suffrage movement. Delegates milled around sporting the fashions of the day—high-necked, lace-trimmed shirtwaists and slim skirts paired with elaborately plumed, feathered, and flowered hats. Each wore a white and gold button displaying six stars for the suffrage states won so far.[41]

Clay, however, could not help but feel a sense of gloom. On the fourth day of the convention, 133 delegates gathered to elect the next slate of officers. Much would stay the same: NAWSA would continue to be directed by Anna Howard Shaw, and the headquarters would stay in New York. But many other leadership changes were announced. Clay received an impressive 432 votes in her bid for office, but they were spread over seven different contests, not enough to carry any single election. Races for second vice president and first and second auditor offered her the best chances for victory, but, each time, an absentee candidate edged her out. It was a discouraging, though not surprising outcome.[42]

Clay had been replaced in what Carrie Chapman Catt later called "a much-needed surgical operation." The new officers represented America's Progressive superstars: Hull House's Jane Addams, University of Chicago professor of social economy and native Kentuckian, Sophonisba Breckinridge, and Belle La Follette, wife of Wisconsin's famous governor, "Fighting Bob."[43]

But there was still a speck of hope. The absent women might not choose to serve, Clay's southern ally Kate Gordon pointed out. Officials telegrammed the winners to see whether they would accept their respective posts. Breckinridge, upon learning of her appointment, quickly cabled Miss Clay to get her blessing before accepting her role as second vice president. Clay encouraged her to take it, relieved that a southerner would still be on the board.[44]

Clay's allies still hoped to see her elected should any of the other absentee winners refuse their positions, but Shaw shut down that possibility. In case of refusal, the new board would appoint replacements. Some Kentucky women publicly attacked the National, namely the eastern delegates who had orchestrated this "incivility"; other KERA members remained quiet, suggesting either a higher standard of decorum or a breach in loyalty. Clay took her loss, now confirmed, in stride. She still had work to do as the NAWSA convention wound down and as the ensuing KERA convention began.[45]

The biggest event of the 1911 national convention wasn't the election controversy; instead, it came on the meeting's final night, October 25, when Emmeline Pankhurst, a famous militant British suffragette, addressed the crowded hall. Delegates had been anticipating this event for days, their appetites whetted when on the first night Pankhurst breezed in, shaking hands and offering a few brief words. Pankhurst's reputation preceded her. Everyone wanted to catch a glimpse of the notorious woman.

Throughout the convention, little sparks of defiance, inspired by Pankhurst and her associates, crackled in the air. On the second day, a young vivacious suffragist from Philadelphia urged her colleagues to "rope people in," with vulgarity if necessary: "Anything to attract attention." She had disappointed her family, she admitted, by riding on a suffrage float in a parade—a stunt that seemed shocking in 1911, and even more scandalous when she cavalierly threw in, "They got over it." Louisville suffragist Jennie Mengel announced that she for one was ready for a "baptism in the militant spirit." When a collection was taken to cover a deficit in the treasury, one mother in the crowd, knowing precisely what she was doing, triumphantly pledged $5 on behalf of each of her "three little suffragettes."[46]

Pankhurst's admirers and critics alike looked forward to hearing her explain her controversial methods, especially after *Courier-Journal* editor Henry Watterson delivered a stinging denunciation of her and her ilk. Pankhurst met Watterson's assault head-on, defending militancy in a dignified, yet unapologetic way. Attacking property—breaking windows and trespassing on the homes of officials   had been good for their movement, boosting visibility and donations. "We threw only a few stones," she admitted, "just enough to let the men know we were in earnest." She never came out and said that American women should copy their British sisters' methods, but few could resist contemplating the possibility.[47]

Militants would not have the last word at the 1911 convention. Clay made sure that went to a southerner. Following Pankhurst's address, Kentuckian

Madeline McDowell Breckinridge, champion of school suffrage, took the stage to offer some final words before Shaw officially closed the meeting. Exhausted KERA delegates assembled the next day to hold an abbreviated state convention before heading home.

Laura Clay had spent much of October in Louisville. She was exhausted and she looked forward to a rest. She would go home to central Kentucky, check on her farm, and process the events of the last few weeks. She might no longer have a national executive position, but she had no intention of stepping back from the cause she loved. The work would continue, and she must be ready.

Before she departed, however, she decided to make a quick stop in Peewee Valley, just east of Louisville. Pulling up to the home for Confederate veterans, a stately Victorian mansion with sweeping porches and manicured lawn, she took a deep breath. She paused only briefly before heading inside to try to convince the aging residents to sign suffrage cards. It seemed a fitting place for Clay, herself a remnant of an earlier era, to nurse her wounds.[48]

9

Meeting New Work with New Methods

It was not a curtain that fell or a page that turned—time-honored symbols of an era ending—but rather for Laura Clay, it was a lid slamming shut that signaled the beginning of a new phase of life. In the summer of 1912, the lid of her desk, on which she had composed voluminous suffrage correspondence over the past quarter century, accidentally fell, slicing her face. Stitches followed, and the doctor ordered a week of rest. The mishap would not leave much of a scar, Clay assured worried friends, but it provided a useful moment to pause and contemplate the future.[1]

Clay's long tenure on the NAWSA board had ended the previous fall, a move that had not been her doing, but one that she resolutely accepted. When KERA met next, her run as its first and only state president would also conclude. This time though, she proclaimed to all who would listen, she was stepping aside by choice.[2]

A transfer of power had been in the works for nearly a year. In her presidential address at the 1911 convention, Clay proposed term limits, and delegates agreed that rotating offices, like women's clubs did, made sense. An officer reaching the end of a two-year term could run for a different post, but she could not continue in the same role. At least one delegate wanted to go even further toward redistributing power and proposed that the executive board include only one officer from each town, a move designed to limit central and northern Kentucky dominance. The motion failed.[3]

Still, the new policies were bound to shake things up. Clay was not the only officer with a long record of service. Seven board members together amassed 120 years of leadership. Four out of the seven (Clay, Mary Barr Clay, Mary C. Cramer, and Isabella Shepard) had served continuously since 1888. What began as valuable continuity somewhere along the line had become dangerous inertia. Certain officers tended to "throw cold water" on almost any ideas proposed, another officer protested.[4]

The changes that younger women in the National and that Progressives in the Louisville local were pushing had rubbed Clay the wrong way, but

133

Laura Clay campaigns in Topeka with members of the Kansas Equal Suffrage Association in 1912. Kansas women won the vote that October, stoking Clay's desire to make Kentucky a campaign state as soon as possible. (Kansas State Historical Society)

now she was the one suggesting a shift. She recognized that KERA's goals and tactics were necessarily evolving: "We ought to meet the new work with new methods," Clay ventured in a moment of inspiration. The suffrage fight was transitioning from educational to political work, and she feared that she was stuck in an "educational rut."[5]

From now on, rather than diluting their efforts by seeking a litany of statutory laws in each legislative session, Clay argued, they should focus on just one singular objective. Let other organizations work for school suffrage or to have women appointed to educational and charitable boards; KERA would zero in on the goal that no one else was bold enough to pursue—her holy grail of suffrage—a state constitutional amendment. It was time, she grandly announced, for Kentucky to become a campaign state.[6]

Clay was a veteran of state campaigns (Oregon, Oklahoma, Arizona, and most recently Kansas), and she knew what all-consuming effort they demanded. Even when they had ended in defeat, they had been exhilarating —the "most interesting years of her life," she declared. Round-the-clock action, friendships forged in the heat of battle, merry evenings spent planning strategy. She couldn't wait to do it again. Ohio was currently considering a state amendment. If it passed, Clay assumed her state would be next.[7]

She must be free when the time came to direct Kentucky's campaign. KERA, therefore, needed a new, capable administrator to oversee day-to-day operations. She should be a younger woman with fresh ideas, but one who understood the Commonwealth and honored its sacred traditions. She should have name recognition and access to powerful men, not to mention bountiful energy. Clay decided that her successor, if she could convince her to take the position, should be Madeline McDowell Breckinridge.

Laura Clay had won state and national fame for her suffrage work, and now she offered Madge Breckinridge an opportunity to be her heir apparent. Breckinridge, however, did not jump at the chance. Unlike Clay, who accepted that suffrage would be long in coming and who patiently swallowed defeats, working year after year without an end in sight, Breckinridge did not show the same endurance. She badly wanted to vote, but she could not imagine giving decades to the cause. She might not have decades to offer. Madge knew she had to make each day count because death was lurking at her door.

Just as being diagnosed with AIDS in the 1980s was considered a death sentence, the word tuberculosis had the same power to terrify at the turn of the twentieth century. Tuberculosis is one of earth's oldest diseases. It is not a fall ill in the morning, be dead by night kind of illness. It delivers its vengeance over years or decades, as its nicknames, "consumption" or "wasting disease," indicate. Before World War II, the best victims could do to thwart its effects was to rest, eat well, and imbibe the fresh air at one of the nation's many sanitariums. The introduction of streptomycin in 1944 finally ended the disease's reign as one of the world's greatest mass killers, but Madge would not live to see this miracle.[8]

Madeline McDowell, the great-granddaughter of Henry Clay who was once described as "all eyes and legs," received her dreaded diagnosis in 1896 when she was twenty-four years old. TB most often affects the lungs. Inhaled through spit droplets, the rod-shaped bacteria invade the air sacs of their human host. In 90 to 95 percent of cases, the body's immune system snaps to attention, sealing off the bacteria, and it is business as usual. But sometimes the bacilli multiply and sometimes they travel to other parts of the body like the brain, blood, guts, bones, or joints. Madge suffered from tuberculosis of the bone. Specifically, she carried the disease in her right foot. Doctors would eventually amputate it.[9]

Amputation, though life changing, was not a cure. The disease remained a "sword hanging over her head" or more like a strong wind blowing at her

Madeline McDowell Breckinridge served as president of KERA from 1912 until 1915 and again from 1919 until the movement culminated in 1920. (Library of Congress)

back. Madge, a descendant of both the famous Clay and McDowell families, learned two important life lessons: one, as a member of a leading family, she had a duty to contribute to society, and two, she must plan to do so quickly since death might very well cut short her plans. Outfitted with a new wooden artificial limb and equipped with a deepened empathy for suffering people, Madge became what her sister-in-law Sophonisba Breckinridge—herself an extremely accomplished woman—proclaimed Kentucky's "most useful citizen."[10]

Madge's transformation from carefree debutante to dedicated social reformer was complete when she married Desha Breckinridge, a Lexington newspaperman (and son of the disgraced congressman W. C. P. Breckinridge) in 1898. Using her husband's *Herald* as a platform, she became the driving force behind Lexington's good government and scientific charity efforts. She never became a mother herself, but she viewed the community's children as her own. She created playgrounds, kindergartens, and a juvenile court system and fought for stricter child labor laws. She also led Kentucky's efforts to treat and prevent tuberculosis. Her periodic need to seek the "rest cure" in warm, dry climates slowed down her work, but she made lemonade out of lemons, gleaning reform ideas from other communities to apply at home.[11]

Fighting for the vote for the vote's sake did not appeal to Breckinridge. But she recognized the vote could help her achieve her other goals and so she pursued it, though in limited ways at first. Between 1906 and 1912, Madge became Kentucky's most visible champion of school suffrage. She thought it utterly ridiculous that the men of the state said to its women on one hand, "your glorious mission is to bear and rear children," but then excluded them from decision making when those children entered the public schools. KERA had led the effort at first to restore school suffrage to Kentucky women, but Clay decided to turn it completely over to the Kentucky Federation of Women's Clubs in 1906 because it had Mrs. Breckinridge to oversee its education committee. KERA could do no better than that, Clay recognized.[12]

Reclaiming what had once been theirs, even with an added literacy requirement, proved astonishingly difficult. Each legislative session, women —black and white—rallied to the cause. Breckinridge accepted white women's assistance while discouraging black women from joining in. "One war was enough at a time," she later explained. Expedience drove her exclusionary approach, not racism. When they won the school franchise, Breckinridge sincerely hoped black women would share in the spoils.[13]

With each approaching session, white women, under Breckinridge's steady direction, redoubled their efforts to win the school vote. Of course, not all women were of like mind. Lawrenceburg, for example, sent two delegations to Frankfort to weigh in on the measure in 1908, one in favor and one intent on seeing it defeated. That same year, Covington women did their part by peppering their state representative with telegrams even as he sat at the bedside of his dying mother. Mass rallies, repeated every two years in Lexington and Louisville, demonstrated the appeal that school suffrage had, even among women who still opposed full suffrage.[14]

The reasons for defeat varied, but the outcome was always the same: 1906, 1908, 1910. The men of Kentucky, as the *Louisville Herald* noted, had decided "to continue their mismanagement of its schools unassisted." Even when interest in education was at an all-time high (the 1908 General Assembly was nicknamed the education legislature), when all parties seemed convinced that voting women would improve the schools, and when the cause was "far from revolutionary," victory still did not follow. Madge blamed the liquor industry, scared of what women would do with the vote, for orchestrating their repeated defeats.[15]

Going into the 1912 session, chances for victory looked good, but they had looked good before. The Republican and Democratic parties both pledged their support, but their promises that the bill would "certainly become a law" failed to soothe Breckinridge. She organized a campaign that, according to her biographer, "likely surpassed in intensity the campaigns of those running for state office, including the governorship itself." KFWC members sent out nearly one hundred thousand pieces of literature in preparation for the 1912 session. School suffrage proponents swayed reluctant lawmakers to their side and finally scored a big win. Even their archenemy Billy Klair, architect of the 1902 school suffrage rescission, backed the measure, although a desire to win positive press coverage from Desha Breckinridge, rather than any sincere interest in women's rights, explains his conversion.[16]

With school suffrage won, Kentucky women looked forward to reaping the benefits of their hard work. A spirited get-out-the-vote effort began statewide, to prepare women to use their new rights "with intelligence and with dignity." Suffragists spread their message through expected channels—the press, the pulpit, and women's organizations—but also through unexpected methods, such as in Louisville where they broadcast their message in bright lights. Several organizations cooperated to rent three large electric signs and positioned them in the business district reminding women they must register to vote on October 1 and 2.[17]

In most areas, suffragists directed their message exclusively to new white female voters, but in Louisville the message crossed race lines. Boldly ignoring the ill-fated history of the school vote when opponents claimed too many black women in Lexington had voted, Louisville suffragists, many with Neighborhood House connections, held meetings at the colored branch of the public library and at the black Beargrass Baptist church. Black women embraced their new rights alongside white women. When Louisville registration numbers came in, the results showed that 19 percent of the total registrants were black, which matched the city's African American population almost precisely.[18]

School board elections were not the only contests on suffragists' minds in the fall of 1912. The constitutional changes that KERA adopted the year before meant that at its next convention, members of the organization would install a new slate of officers. The president, vice president, corresponding secretary, and treasurer positions would all need to be filled.[19]

Breckinridge seemed like an obvious choice as Clay considered whom to tap as her successor, and not just because she was coming off her big school suffrage win. She had all the right qualities and connections. For years, observers had mistakenly identified Laura Clay as Henry Clay's granddaughter. Madge's ties to the Great Compromiser were real; she grew up in his home, Ashland. Having a newspaperman for a husband could also come in handy. At forty years old, Breckinridge was young, but not too young. She was forward-thinking, but not radical. And importantly, she had the administrative acumen necessary to lead KERA into its next phase.

Clay believed Breckinridge would be the perfect person for the job, but Breckinridge was not so sure. She kept Clay guessing throughout the summer of 1912 as to whether she would accept the position. Clay knew Madge was reluctant to take time away from her other causes. She was already terribly busy. Plus, she had to be mindful of her health. Finally, after Clay promised that she would have a full-time assistant (KERA allocated $300 to hire a stenographer), Madge agreed to lead the organization. She assumed office in November 1912.[20]

Clay's suffrage career did not end when she stepped down. Far from it. She stressed that she might not be president any longer, but she was "not going to stop working one bit." She assumed the role of KERA's corresponding secretary. When that term ended in 1915, she became a member of a newly created advisory board and, after that, vice president. Clay's name no longer appeared at the top of KERA's letterhead, but it always appeared somewhere. Clay also continued to be active in NAWSA. She served as chair of its membership committee and continued to advocate for suffrage work in the South during the remainder of its history. Clay did not intend to ride off into the sunset, and Madge was glad to keep her around. She frequently sought "Miss Laura's" advice.[21]

Breckinridge was appropriately deferential, but she fully intended to put her own stamp on KERA. The Kentucky movement began to look more urban and progressive under her direction and started to reflect the reform spirit that was sweeping the country. Exponential growth followed. KERA had always been a tight-knit, small-scale operation—a gathering place for a handful of brave and beleaguered women—but now it entered a new era.[22]

As a thoroughgoing Progressive enchanted by the power of numbers, Breckinridge brought her passion for data to KERA. When she had wanted to convince skeptics that school suffrage was a good idea, she compiled tedious research to establish a correlation between women's voting record and state literacy rates. Likewise, she offered proof that enfranchised women and stronger child labor laws went hand in hand. KERA began to turn over a new quantitative leaf under Breckinridge's direction.[23]

Madge argued that KERA must not hide its candle under a bushel anymore. Suffrage must be "a force to be reckoned with." As the wife of an editor and herself a frequent contributor to the *Herald* (she had begun writing a Woman's Page in 1905), she understood the power of the press. For years, poor Mrs. Obenchain had painstakingly typed articles and distributed them, knowing that they would likely end up in the dustbin. Even if editors believed in suffrage, they often did not find it worth their trouble to set the pieces in type. To fix that problem, Madge ordered eye-catching and informative premade press plates, and sent them to one hundred newspapers. It would be so easy for editors to pop in their pieces that they were sure to get more ink.[24]

Breckinridge decided that KERA needed an official state headquarters if it hoped to be taken seriously. In February 1913, the organization hung its shingle outside a suite in the McClelland Building, a new structure that had recently taken Lexington's skyline up a notch. Its location directly across from the courthouse at the corner of Short and Upper signified that

KERA operated not on the periphery, not from some woman's parlor, but in the center of action. Desha Breckinridge rented offices in that building, likely helping to keep costs down.[25]

Laura Clay had operated KERA on a shoestring budget, but Madge was prepared to take more financial risks. In 1906, delegates had voted to cap annual operating expenses at $125. The sum barely covered officers' travel to Frankfort, postage, and printing costs. Freewill offerings funded special projects like bringing in national speakers, but the women prided themselves on being exceedingly thrifty.[26]

Madge immediately signaled that she would not follow in her frugal predecessor's footsteps. KERA expenditures increased from $121.90 in 1912 to a whopping $1,450 the following year. Charges for the telephone, a new but necessary luxury, alone added five dollars a month to the budget.[27]

Breckinridge planned to spend money, and that meant they had to raise money. Laura Clay had made dues optional in order to boost membership, and Breckinridge initially endorsed her Kentucky plan. Madge encouraged women, particularly rural women, to simply "stand up and be counted," promising that just like political parties, KERA would ask for nothing more than a signed card. She quickly realized the limitations of this plan, however. A low-stakes approach might bring in new members, but it produced little revenue.[28]

Madge could have chosen to court women of modest means, adding up the nickels and dimes they could provide, but instead she set her sights on more affluent patrons. More and more, the National was relying on ridiculously wealthy women to bankroll its efforts, women like Mrs. Alva Belmont, flamboyant former wife of railroad magnate William Vanderbilt. Breckinridge hoped that her state could find its own Mrs. Belmont. It needed a fairy godmother.[29]

KERA had received one large gift during its history when Laura Sutton Bruce, a promising young Paris-trained artist and daughter of a successful Lexington hemp dealer, died suddenly in 1904, leaving the organization $5,000 (roughly $140,000 in 2018 dollars). Bruce's mother contested the will, but Laura Clay successfully defended the bequest, which provided her a nice little pot of money with which to fund her pet projects. Beyond this large gift and the regular contributions of the Clay sisters, however, few women had contributed more than five dollars at a time.[30]

Breckinridge hoped to make it fashionable to give large gifts, and she intended to bring giving out into the open instead of it being something one did quietly. Rather than taking up the traditional freewill offering at the 1913 convention, she challenged one hundred members to give twenty-five dollars each to create a "President's Fund." When Kentucky became a campaign state, she wanted to be ready. A $1,000 gift from Mrs. S. M. Hubbard, long-serving suffragist and wife of a very successful Murray businessman, jump-started their efforts.[31]

The 1913 convention offered KERA's rank-and-file members their first hint that a substantial remodel of the organization was under way. The meeting opened without an invocation, undoubtedly shocking many veteran suffragists. There were no devotional exercises, prayers, or scripture readings. Breckinridge shared Clay's Christian faith, but she did not feel compelled to put it on display. She adopted a more "ecumenical and bureaucratic approach," Claudia Knott explains, understandable since she had embraced women's rights to further her social reform goals and not out of religious conviction, like Clay. KERA had a large Jewish constituency in its Louisville local, host of the 1913 convention, and it is possible Breckinridge kept it in mind.[32]

The roughly two hundred convention attendees could not help but notice the Progressive winds blowing through the 1913 meeting. Invited speakers included some of the nation's most famous reformers. Greenwich Village bohemian poet and political activist, Max Eastman, headlined. Settlement school leaders offered words of encouragement. Robert McDowell Allen, noted champion of pure food and drug laws, addressed the delegates. The message was clear: women needed the vote so they could change the world—at least their corner of it. It was a message that Madge felt in her soul and that drove her to expend her limited energy to win the vote.[33]

Influenced by her sister-in-law, Sophonisba Breckinridge, Madge had become all too aware of the privileges she enjoyed: "I believe there are many comfortable women today who cannot remain long so comfortable," she stressed, "because they are beginning to realize that the leisure they have, the freedom from the household drudgery of their grandmothers is bought at the price of the work of little children and of other women working long and exhausting hours in unsanitary conditions, and for a mere pittance of wage." Unlike Clay, who fully admitted that she wore blinders concerning the challenges female factory workers faced, Breckinridge strived to put herself in their shoes.[34]

She also tried to picture herself in the position of black women. Depending on her audience, she sometimes reiterated popular stereotypes concerning black men, but women, she argued, were "the better element in the negro race." Their deep interest in their children's well-being would make them responsible voters. Having worked with plenty of black women in school elections, she confidently predicted that with instruction they would be a boon to American democracy. Breckinridge harkened back to the democratic foundations of the suffrage cause. As she declared in her address to the 1911 NAWSA convention: "I want the ballot and I want all other women to have it."[35]

Though Breckinridge brought many changes to KERA, one thing that remained consistent throughout its history was its commitment to racial segregation. Breckinridge was a racial liberal. She, along with Desha, joined the NAACP, and the *Herald* often took progressive stands on race matters. But even while Breckinridge believed that black women deserved to vote, she understood the political realities of the nineteen-teens. White southerners, she knew, used race as a "scarecrow" tactic to dismiss suffrage out of hand. She had no choice but to play their game. In the contest between principles and expedience, expedience won. KERA remained an all-white organization during Breckinridge's tenure.[36]

A theme resounded during the 1913 convention: women had been timid long enough. It was time to demand results. Breckinridge called her fellow Kentucky suffragists' attention to the British movement and the cloak of militancy it wore. While she did not suggest that Kentucky women should blow things up like their British sisters famously had done, she encouraged women to make their wishes known. For too long, they had been "trying to get suffrage in the most lady-like manner," without anyone finding out they wanted it. It was time to seek attention. Perhaps it was her age—she was two decades younger than Miss Clay. Perhaps it was her constant reminders that time was fleeting. Whatever the reason, Breckinridge pushed KERA members to embrace new ideas and to have a little fun. Wear official buttons and stamp your letters and checks with "Votes for Women," she encouraged.[37]

Laura Clay shrank from doing anything that might make KERA look radical even after the national movement began to rethink its tactics in the early nineteen-teens. She found British suffragettes' actions disgraceful. Clay carefully distinguished between the terms "suffragist" and "suffragette" to distance herself from militants. Correcting a well-meaning schoolgirl in 1911 who simply asked for leaflets so she could prepare for a debate at school, Clay explained that suffragists "depend upon peaceful arguments and petitions" to persuade. "There are very few 'suffragettes' in America," she added, "and none at all in Kentucky!"[38]

If it had been up to Clay, NAWSA would not have invited Emmeline Pankhurst to its 1911 convention. Pankhurst was a troublemaker—accused of breaking shop and business windows, blowing up mailboxes, and torching government property. But some of Clay's colleagues in the National believed that a troublemaker was just what they needed to rouse the suffrage question from its "somewhat dormant" condition in the United States, and they were right.[39]

Considering more militant tactics energized the movement but it also caused a split. Some suffragists broke away with Alice Paul to form the Congressional Union (later the National Woman's Party) in 1913. Even women who remained loyal to NAWSA and who shunned militancy, however, began to embrace new, splashy tactics. By the nineteen-teens, the pageantry we associate with the suffrage movement—the parades, the buttons, the sashes and banners—was on full display.

A few Kentucky suffragists began experimenting with new tactics as early as 1908, but they did so without KERA's sanction. When northern Kentucky women began holding open-air meetings, Clay gritted her teeth and remembered her commitment to local control. The concept had spread from England to New York, then to Cincinnati, and now it had crossed the river. Open-air meetings allowed suffrage to be agitated in the summer, "the dull season" when no one wanted to be cooped up in a stuffy parlor. They were also more democratic, offering anyone the chance to participate, not just those on a pre-selected guest list. Defending their decision to Miss Clay, the Covington suffragists stressed the dignity and legality of their event. They had secured the appropriate permits and attracted a courteous and well-behaved crowd, but Clay continued to question the wisdom of this line of agitation.[40]

Breckinridge, on the other hand, relished the opportunity to shake things up. She enjoyed a good publicity stunt and believed observers would as well. Women should deck out their automobiles with yellow flags, she advised, and motor across the state. When suffrage hikes (hiking from city to city, passing out pamphlets along the way) became the rage, Breckinridge proposed that KERA members hike from Covington to Lexington, following the Cincinnati Southern Railroad.[41]

These methods were all productive, but none could beat the attention-grabbing power of a good parade. Parades had long been associated with labor unions and armies, reserved for promoting thoroughly masculine causes. When Alice Paul concocted a scheme to recruit thousands of suffragists to march down Pennsylvania Avenue in Washington, DC, on the day before Woodrow Wilson's inaugural in March 1913, she raised more than a few eyebrows. She hoped their *procession* (a semantic choice that seemed more dignified than *parade*) would overshadow the following day's festivities and offer a powerful display of solidarity.[42]

Madeline McDowell Breckinridge thought it was a grand idea, and she encouraged every Kentucky woman who could make the trip to Washington to participate. Imagine it, Breckinridge mused: "women clad as heralds, mounted on white charges and blowing golden trumpets," outfitted in "picturesque and varying costumes." No male parade could possibly compete with the aesthetic scene the women could deliver.[43]

Suffrage leaders wanted publicity, and they got it, beginning months in advance and continuing well beyond the parade day. The women's plan to play on emotion rather than argument and reason worked, bringing out the worst in male observers. A plot by (presumably male) college students to release thousands of mice and rats into the lines of marchers was foiled in advance, but unruly men stepped in to intimidate the women in place of rodents, heckling the estimated five thousand female marchers along the route. One participant recalled that she had never heard "such vulgar . . . scurrilous language" as they endured. Arms were broken, bodies scarred. According to the anti-suffrage *Courier-Journal*, the "bedraggled" suffragists had to fight their way "foot by foot up Pennsylvania Avenue" until the US Cavalry swooped in to offer protection.[44]

A few Kentucky women heeded the planners' call and provided "a militant representation of the fair sex to march behind a Bluegrass banner." Kentucky's delegation included at least two northern Kentucky women: Jessie Firth, president of the Covington E.R.A., and Mary Light Ogle, a well-known artist and suffragist also from Covington. Ogle later threatened to sue the US government over the brutal treatment she received at the hands of the police during the march.[45]

No Louisville suffragists apparently joined Kentucky's parade delegation, but they were still inspired by the idea. Alice Castleman, former president of the LWSA, decided that the city's Oliver Hazard Perry Centennial Celebration, scheduled for October, should include a "Suffrage Brigade," akin to the inaugural. Castleman drew on her many social and reform connections and soon had a team of Louisville women prepared to make it

No images of the 1913 Louisville parade survive, but this picture of a 1915 parade, likely in New York City, gives a sense of the pageantry involved. (Library of Congress)

happen. A float committee went to work building a replica of the DC parade's centerpiece. A finance committee began collecting donations. To ensure a respectable showing, they instructed prospective marchers to reserve a spot by postcard.[46]

On the day following the celebration, the *Louisville Herald* reported that the women had done well. The turnout offered "gratifying proof" that the suffrage movement in Kentucky was alive and well. Two hundred women participated, cheered on with every step, especially in the business district, where managers and employees leaned out of windows to offer encouragement. "I'm for you, girls" and "Let 'em have it," supporters shouted. Only once did some out-of-touch man yell out, "Say, can you cook?" "You vote, and you can't," a quick-witted marcher returned. Representatives of the female sex, including the elderly down to small "suffrage babies," enjoyed the attention.[47]

Breckinridge reported that it was the first suffrage parade south of the Mason–Dixon Line, but it wouldn't be the last. KERA established a parades committee at its annual meeting the following month.[48]

It took Clay time to adjust to these new methods, but even she begrudgingly came to see their merit. When a group invited her to speak at an openair meeting in Lancaster in 1915, she agreed, admitting that she in fact preferred open-air over indoor events. For Clay, always tortured by summer heat, it was less about image and more about comfort. If they must move out of the home and into the streets to find a refreshing breeze, then so be it.[49]

New leadership provided a much-needed shot in the arm for KERA as it passed the quarter-century mark. Madeline McDowell Breckinridge embraced modern methods and, more importantly, she could explain in tangible ways *why* the vote mattered. She did not dwell on issues of fairness or God's intention for woman to be man's equal. She focused on what women—the "mother sex"—could do with the ballot to make the world better.[50]

When Breckinridge began writing her "Woman's Sphere" column in the *Herald* in 1905, she adopted a sweeping tagline: "Whatever a woman can do, that, by divine ordination she ought to do, by human allowance she should be privileged to do, by force of destiny in the long run she will do." She was ready to see destiny fulfilled. Breckinridge did not completely forsake her other causes. She continued to fight tuberculosis, to improve southern schools, and to assist Lexington's unfortunate; but increasingly, suffrage became her main priority.[51]

With a state constitutional amendment on the line, 1914 would be a big year for Madge and the Kentucky movement.

10

The Pink Tea Stage

Laura Clay was accustomed to media requests, but one she received in February 1911 made her pause. Mary Holland Kinkaid, a writer for *Good Housekeeping*, requested that she please send a photo of herself—that part was expected—and could she include a note about her "favorite line of home activity?" Did she prefer meal planning or mending or perhaps tending the garden? What domestic art most satisfied her? Kinkaid hoped to include Clay's response in an article documenting the "Feminine Charms of the Woman Militant."[1]

"I recognize that home-making will always occupy the great majority of women," Clay began her response. "Therefore, I think our schools and colleges should provide educational facilities to prepare girls and young women for home-making as a life work." Female house managers, she argued, should be taught scientific methods, turning "mere drudgery" into a "skill intelligently directed." Even better, she hoped that soon modern mechanical appliances would free women from domestic burdens altogether. Clay wished Kinkaid all the best with her article but insisted that she could not help. She lived alone and occupied herself "not at all in housekeeping."[2]

Kinkaid's request demonstrates how much had changed by the nineteen-teens. Suffrage had begun as a movement marked by "bitter protest, ridicule, ostracism, and martyrdom," but now it was entering what Madeline McDowell Breckinridge called the "pink tea stage." Sure, there were still people who turned up their noses and dismissed voting as unladylike, but all in all, suffrage had become stylish. Across Kentucky, even in small towns and rural areas, women and men were growing accustomed to women having a say in civic matters. But as Kinkaid's request indicated, as suffrage became a fashionable cause, it was also stripped of its potency. It became less about the demands of woman militants or even about revising expectations that limited women's options and more about celebrating traditional female roles.[3]

In June 1913, the Kentucky Federation of Women's Clubs officially endorsed suffrage, a sure sign that the cause had achieved mainstream appeal. Going into its annual convention, some questioned whether the organization, a bellwether of "home loving" Kentucky women, would take up the issue, with some warning that it might be forced by a few individuals. The decision was not unanimous, but thirty-four women, spurred on by Louisville's Caroline Leech, voted in favor of the suffrage resolution, with only ten opposed. Applauding the KFWC's big decision, Miss Hebe Hamilton, a snappy short-haired reporter for the *Paducah News-Democrat*, triumphantly proclaimed that the days of locking the door and speaking in a whisper when discussing votes for women were over. "A bully fight" (borrowing Teddy Roosevelt's expression) still loomed, but women would be voting in no time, she predicted.[4]

Women's club members stood in good company. The following year, the Kentucky WCTU also finally declared its support. The National WCTU had come out in favor decades earlier, but Kentucky's teetotalers took much longer to get on board. Its other resolutions that year—compulsory teaching of the Bible in schools and a ban on tobacco—suggest that its moral standards had not changed but its view of women's roles had. By 1914, organizations representing farmers, bakers, and printers all declared their support for voting women.[5]

All over the country, people were shifting from raising an eyebrow when "Votes for Women" was mentioned to raising a toast (lemonade, for Kentucky's dries). All those years NAWSA had struggled to grow the membership and to win the argument of numbers, and now it seemed to be happening: its membership almost tripled between 1911 and 1912, topping 171,000. More importantly, three new suffrage states were added in 1912, raising the number of electoral votes tied to states where women voted to fifty-five. Suffrage, at last, was in vogue.[6]

Progress was palpable in Kentucky, too. KERA membership stood at 1,779 when Breckinridge took office in 1912, with only eight counties organized. By the end of 1914 it had more than 10,500 members dispersed among sixty-four local clubs.[7]

Madeline McDowell Breckinridge made membership growth a key priority of her presidency. She ambitiously announced her plan to organize every one of Kentucky's 120 counties in preparation for a state campaign. "No great effort" had been given to organizing work previously, she claimed, an allegation that surely rankled Clay. "The woods in Kentucky are full of convinced and instinctive suffragists," Breckinridge noted. She just needed to "burrow" into the forests and "pluck" them out.[8]

VOTES FOR WOMEN

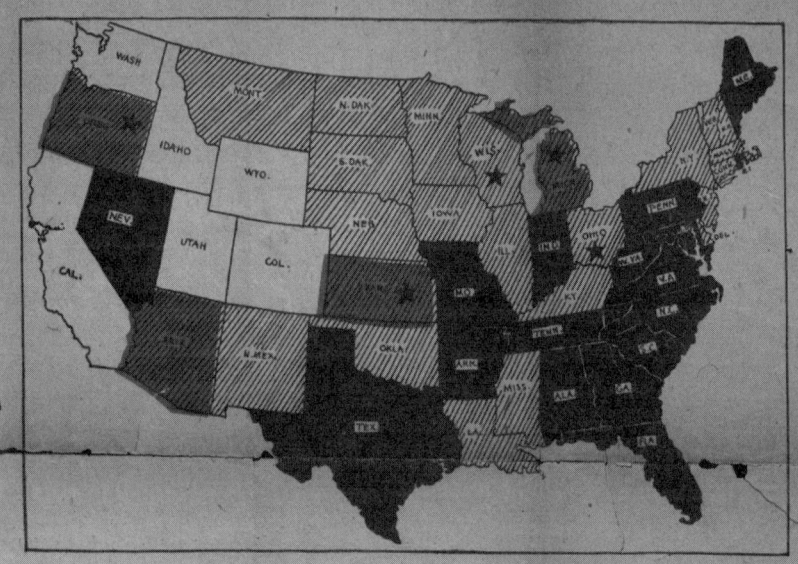

White states, full suffrage; shaded, partial suffrage; black, no suffrage. ★ States where the question will be voted upon this year.

Red States—Victories This Year!

WOMEN HAVE FULL SUFFRAGE IN

ARIZONA, KANSAS, MICHIGAN, OREGON, Won November, 1912

WHITE STATES	Date granted	Number of women eligible to vote	Percentage of women who do vote
Wyoming	1869	34,000	80 to 90
Colorado	1893	160,000	75 to 85
Utah	1896	55,500	85 to 90
Idaho	1896	68,000	75 to 85
Washington	1910	175,000	85 to 95
California	1911	670,987	90 to 99

Why Not Make Yours A White State, Too?

NATIONAL AMERICAN WOMAN SUFFRAGE ASSOCIATION
505 FIFTH AVENUE   **NEW YORK CITY**

A 1912 NAWSA broadside reports on progress toward adding new suffrage states. It notes that four states enfranchised women that year, but Michigan's referendum actually failed. (University of Virginia Library)

Burrowing in required sending representatives—actual human messengers—to the far corners of the state. Who better to do that than Kentucky's most famous suffragist, Laura Clay? Now that she was no longer president, Clay offered to serve as a missionary for the cause and embarked on an extensive speaking tour in April 1913. Setting her sights once again on western Kentucky, she visited fifteen towns in two weeks. She recruited new members in Russellville and Hopkinsville and wrangled tired groups in Owensboro, Henderson, and Hawesville back into operation.[9]

Interest was increasing, but skeptics still abounded in rural Kentucky. Trustees at Owensboro's Carnegie Library refused to allow Clay to speak there—a fortuitous roadblock, she decided, because the space would not have been large enough to hold the crowd that ultimately gathered. Even though she reiterated constantly that KERA and the American suffrage movement were much different than its British counterparts, Clay still frequently met women who were quite afraid of the question and its radical implications.[10]

Clay's trip to western Kentucky may have felt a bit like déjà vu, a repeat of a sweep she made in 1904. Her audiences, mostly club women, looked familiar, as did the arguments she employed: "equal rights to all and special privileges to none," "no taxation without representation." For Clay, voting was a simple matter of justice. She employed methods from a previous era, even as times were changing. Knowing that she would have a stopover in Bowling Green on a Sunday, Clay asked Lida Obenchain to find a local church where she could give a Bible reading.[11]

Breckinridge, meanwhile, targeted new constituencies. She did her fair share of traveling the state in 1913, carrying Clay's trusty membership cards with her from stop to stop. Building on her interest in education reform, she spent much of her summer addressing teachers' institutes. She did not manage to send a speaker to every county as planned, but she and other KERA members covered nearly fifty, some in remote mountain areas. When they couldn't get on the Kentucky Education Association's annual meeting program, Breckinridge hoisted a tent in a nearby yard and distributed materials from there. She knew their message would play well with teachers, particularly their arguments concerning equal pay. Plus, teachers could inspire the next generation of suffragists simply by being role models for young men and women.[12]

Clay and Breckinridge were the heavy hitters, but getting the word out required more manpower. To extend its reach, KERA created a lecture bureau, staffed with talented public speakers, including among others, Clay's sister Sallie, former Lexington school board member Ida Withers Harrison, and the Louisville labor advocate Lucy Nield. Still, demand outstripped supply. Breckinridge knew they needed to bring in paid organizers if they hoped to achieve full coverage across the state.[13]

Working with limited funds, Breckinridge sought professional organizers who could deliver the greatest return on investment. She understood all too clearly that a state suffrage amendment could not pass without male approval, since men constituted both the legislature and the entirety of the voters. Madge didn't care whether men were invited to join existing locals or formed separate leagues, but she wanted them "herded" in. She urged the Louisville group particularly to "enthuse the men and swell the membership."[14]

Men were the best weapon to recruit men, Breckinridge figured, and with that in mind she hired Urey L. Estes of Chicago as a field secretary in 1913. She admitted that she rather liked the idea of bossing a man around, but her motive was pure. Not only would putting a man in the field win over necessary male supporters, but it would also get them noticed: "Why, in a small town," she remarked with a bit of a drawl, "he ought to attract almost as much attention as a fire engine." In February and March 1913, Estes stumped central and western Kentucky, forming new clubs as he went.[15]

Breckinridge knew how powerful male advocates could be because she lived with one. Her husband, Desha, had not started out an ally, but she had managed to win him over. He had once looked askance when his sister Sophonisba announced she was buying a bicycle. He would not call himself a suffragist for a long time, but he always supported his wife's work, allowing her space in the *Herald* to promote women's rights. Her well-reasoned arguments swayed him. He finally went on record in 1909, declaring suffrage was bound to come "sure as the day follows the night." From then on, KERA could count on his full support.[16]

If duels had still been in style by the nineteen-teens and if Henry Watterson, editor of the *Courier-Journal* had not been so "old and infirm," Desha's defense of suffrage might have inspired one. Instead, the two editors chose to spar in writing. Following a particularly galling editorial in 1913, in which Marse Henry attacked "the woman who does not find her highest happiness and usefulness at home," Desha snapped to attention "like a knight charging off in defense of fair ladies." He confronted Kentucky men and demanded they pick a side: "In Which Army Will You Enlist?" he queried.[17]

Madge Breckinridge hoped to win men over with persuasive arguments delivered by respected figures like her husband, but she was not averse to using the "public pocket-book" to advance their work. With woman suffrage rapidly gaining in popularity, groups of commercially minded men hoped to capitalize. "Every suffragette means another customer for the baker," the National Association of Bakers astutely noted in 1912. Suffragists were only too happy to play the "you scratch our back, we'll scratch yours" game. Women might not have political power, but as the nation's primary consumers, they had purchasing power, and they schemed how to best use it.[18]

When cotton farmers hit hard times in 1914, KERA encouraged each of its members to "get the bales moving again" by buying a bolt of cotton cloth. Decorations at the 1914 KERA convention included a bale of cotton and signs reminding women to support planters. The Fayette County local got clever and held a "Cotton Ball" the following spring. Attendees wore cotton gowns and donated the proceeds to struggling farmers. In return, Breckinridge expected the cotton industry not only to endorse suffrage but also to "abolish the blot of child labor," one of its cardinal sins.[19]

Breckinridge hoped one day soon she could use her vote to eradicate evils like child labor. Their greatest shot to win the ballot would come during the 1914 legislative session, and she began gearing up early. Her efforts to recruit men were an important first step and continued through the summer of 1913 at booths KERA sponsored at county fairs in Louisville, Lexington, Mason County, and McCracken County. Madge credited their state fair presence for bringing nearly one thousand new members into the organization, many of them male.[20]

It would not matter how many Kentuckians were on their side, however, if the ones that mattered most—the lawmakers who controlled the fate of a suffrage amendment—were not. Using part of Mrs. Hubbard's large contribution, KERA reached out to every candidate for office during the summer, sending them copies of the *Woman's Journal*. Following the general election, when they knew who would represent them at the next session, suffragists continued to woo them with letters and literature.[21]

They privately lobbied the men and put the squeeze on them publicly, too. "An Appeal to Legislators," written anonymously but clearly Breckinridge's work, appeared in newspapers across Kentucky. "Are you a member of the coming Legislature?" she asked. "Are you going to prove that you represent the women of Kentucky as well as the men by allowing them to submit their case to the voters?" One must not believe in woman suffrage, she insisted, to believe in fair chances.[22]

KERA's "invasion of the Capital City" was complete by the time the session began in January. Suffragists vowed to "come early and stay late." Setting up temporary headquarters at the Capitol Hotel was an "extravagant" move, Breckinridge admitted, but it gave them easy access to their prey. Either the president herself or one of her "corps of assistants" was on hand every day. Once a week, they invited the legislators to drop in for tea and cookies, following the recommendation of one wise woman who urged them to "feed the brutes."[23]

The session began as sessions do with a furious fight by lawmakers to get their pet legislation considered. KERA was relying on John G. Miller in the House and J. H. Durham in the Senate to act on their behalf by introducing the suffrage amendment that Robinson A. McDowell, husband of one of their officers and Madge's cousin, wrote. Before their allies had time to act, however, the suffragists were blindsided when an opponent, a representative from Allen County, introduced a bill to have school suffrage repealed. Fortunately, the measure did not gain traction. At least there would be no repeat of 1902.[24]

Breckinridge knew they could not hope to pass their amendment in either house without winning new supporters. Lawmakers at least showed some interest in listening. They passed a resolution (on the second try) to invite Mrs. Breckinridge and Miss Clay to address them in joint session. It was the first time a woman was ever accorded this courtesy and was a "grand social occasion," according to the *Cincinnati Enquirer*. Suffragists came from all over the state to witness history being made.[25]

It turned out it did not matter how charming or convincing Breckinridge and Clay were. It did not matter whether suffragists served legislators' favorite snacks. Nothing mattered because their amendment fell victim to poor timing. The two amendments that had passed during the previous session—one that allowed convicts to work on state roads and another pertaining to property tax classification—had been ratified but then later invalidated due to sloppy paperwork. Since only two amendments could be considered in any election cycle, lawmakers claimed they were obligated to make the measures that voters had already endorsed the chosen two. It was just the excuse reluctant legislators needed to brush women off once again.[26]

The defeat was not completely unexpected, but it still stung. Kentucky women would have to wait at least three more years before they could win a state constitutional amendment (two years for the next session, plus another year for voters to ratify). They would likely have no say in electing at least one more president, one governor, one US representative, and numerous state officials.

It was hard not to feel gloomy. KERA's legislative defeat was followed in July by news of a Great War in Europe. Breckinridge remained optimistic, at least concerning matters that were partly within her control. She was too busy to wallow anyway. In addition to her frequent speaking engagements in Kentucky, she gave thirty-two talks outside the state during 1914 as her role within the National grew. She was serving as a vice president, and many saw her as a leading presidential contender.[27]

Madge could point to the growth KERA was experiencing as proof it was moving in the right direction. New clubs were forming in areas of the state where previously they had never found success.

Even Owensboro, target of years of work, was finally coming around. Ever since Susan B. Anthony had visited in 1879, suffragists had eyed its potential as a starting point for organizing western Kentucky. Anthony returned in 1895, this time accompanied by Carrie Chapman Catt, her eventual successor as NAWSA president, and this time Owensboro residents, a few at least, decided that they were ready to endorse suffrage and formed the Political Equality Club of Owensboro. The response the club generated in the newspaper, however, indicated that the cause was still too radical for most members of the community. What will happen to the babies, one writer in the *Owensboro Messenger* asked, "with both parents hustling for a favorite candidate or for the spoils of office?" Two years later, the Owensboro local disbanded.[28]

An attempted reset in 1906 also fizzled, but by 1913 when Breckinridge sent Urey Estes to Owensboro, the time was finally right. No memory of previous suffrage speakers or an earlier club survived. The *Messenger* incorrectly noted that the first suffrage address in Owensboro would be given in March.[29]

Soon after, the Daviess County Equal Rights Association formed with 107 members, including many prominent citizens. Instead of men and women organizing separately, as they did in most communities, the Owensboro local started as a joint association. Local schools held speaking contests, which helped to build interest and attract new members. The Owensboro Woman's Club's decision to endorse suffrage also helped it to grow.[30]

Interest from Owensboro spilled over, leading to the formation of satellite chapters in the tiny nearby towns of Utica and Hawesville (population one thousand) that summer. Suffrage still had its opponents—a teachers' institute in adjacent Ohio County adopted resolutions "condemning immodest dress, woman suffrage and such dances as the turkey trot"—but the number of Kentuckians who saw suffrage as ridiculous was shrinking steadily.[31]

The schedule of the 1914 KERA convention, hosted by the new Owensboro local, however, offered a quiet reminder that racism still threatened suffrage's chances of becoming a mass movement in certain parts of the state. The program highlighted its now-standard litany of Progressive Era topics, but it also gave space to Kate Gordon, "states' rights suffragist," vehement racist, and president of the Southern States Woman Suffrage Conference. Including Gordon on the program reminded participants that one could support suffrage and still protect the southern racial order.[32]

Suffrage was not just a simple matter of justice and convincing women that it made good sense. As historian Sara Egge reminds us, the fight for the vote was also tangled up in "complicated local and regional issues." People living in the same vicinity, Egge shows, often had "vastly different experiences with woman suffrage." KERA could only win rural women's support by understanding and acknowledging these regional variations and meeting women where they were.[33]

Laura Clay's well-worn arguments, that women should vote because America promised liberty to all, did not play well in conservative rural communities. Emphasizing equality inflamed racial fears and collided with strongly rooted beliefs that women were in fact different from men, created for a unique purpose. Many women across Kentucky did not want to throw off the "Lords of Creation" as Mary Barr Clay had urged them to do. They could, however, agree with Rev. G. L. Morrill that every woman should have "a wedding ring on her finger and a ballot in her hand."[34]

Only by acknowledging deeply rooted values centered on God, family, and community would the suffrage movement gain headway in rural Kentucky. The Hopkinsville local's 1915 report said as much. The Sunday School Convention of the Christian Church in Madisonville had recently taken up the issue of suffrage, and, "strange to say," the motion passed without a dissenting vote. "This movement is taking on a new phase," the anonymous correspondent explained. "It is no longer its highest aim to acquire powers in politics, to be on an equality with men, but a desire in the heart of every good woman . . . to fight the great moral evils which have been a blot to civilization and a disgrace to American liberty." The writer applauded the awakening under way—"an awakening in the way God has prescribed."[35]

For many women, the vote had always seemed irrelevant, but when the Kentucky legislature passed school suffrage in 1912, it suddenly mattered much more. It had moved from the realm of the hypothetical to the real, and it promised to advance women's work as mothers. Rural women who had not given a thought to voting before now snapped to attention.

Maysville women were a perfect example. They invited Laura Clay to speak on school suffrage in July 1912 as they prepared to vote for the first time that fall. A suffrage organization did not emerge right away—Maysville women had only organized a woman's club a few months earlier—but interest in women's rights grew quickly, especially with voters across the river in Ohio considering a state constitutional amendment that November.[36]

The Mason County Woman Suffrage League formed the following summer and immediately went to work. Their first activity involved running a booth at the Germantown fair, where Laura Clay again spoke. Hoping to generate more interest, they invited Ida Withers Harrison, chair of KERA's Committee on Church Work, to conduct a "Whirlwind Campaign" through the county in October, speaking at five churches along the way. Newspapers gave the new club generous coverage, and the organization's president, Alice Lloyd, took full advantage of the publicity. By the fall of 1913, the Mason County local had 241 members.[37]

Having a whiz-bang president with more spark than Henry Ford's newest Model T helped the organization to grow. Alice Lloyd was something of a celebrity—one of Kentucky's two famous Alice Lloyds. This was not the one who created a school to train mountain kids in Pippa Passes. Mason County's Alice Lloyd, known as the "Joan of Arc of the Burley tobacco growers," became famous during the tobacco wars for standing up to the governor and the tobacco trust and for eloquently defending Night Riders. She transformed from teacher to crusader and never looked back. Now suffrage, the "right that protects every other right," became her main priority.[38]

The Mason County E.R.A. grew quickly under Lloyd's exacting leadership (in newspaper notices of upcoming meetings she warned members to come promptly: "Don't waste the time of others by being late"). By 1914, it had a full slate of ten officers, far more than mature clubs like Madison County, which only had seven. Its membership grew rapidly, reaching 456 members in less than two years' time. Following the lead of bigger cities like Louisville, Mason County suffragists took steps to organize down to the precinct level.[39]

School suffrage provided the catalyst other locals needed to form as well. The Bell County E.R.A. organized in 1913 to support a female school superintendent candidate, and the chapter proudly noted that four hundred women turned out to vote in school board elections that fall. The Anderson County local also owed its rapid growth to school suffrage. It formed after Mrs. Breckinridge spoke at a teachers' institute in the summer of 1913. Its real energy, however, came from supporting one of its members, Mrs. Lee Maddox Campbell, first in her bid to become school superintendent and then, once she won election, by defending her right to hold the position.[40]

New suffragists were popping up in every corner of the state. With their fight for a state constitutional amendment coming to a premature end in 1914, Madge Breckinridge turned instead to advancing the awakening under way. They would ask for a state amendment again in 1916, and the more documented suffragists they had on their side, the better. The key to shaping public opinion, Madge argued, was to hire as many paid organizers as possible. She and Laura Clay could not do it all alone. Reaching some counties required a thirty-five-mile trek on muleback. Miss Clay, though spry, was no spring chicken, and Breckinridge had her health to consider.[41]

That summer, KERA contracted with six field-workers for varying lengths of time. The combined cost—$800 (salary and expenses)—represented a significant investment, but these organizers extended KERA's reach significantly. Together they visited ninety-four teachers' institutes, gave addresses at fifty citizens' forums, and converted 4,720 new suffragists.[42]

Traversing Kentucky required flexibility, creativity, and stamina. During her eight-month assignment, Lily Ray Glenn traveled by autos, mail hacks, and boats and even forded the Cumberland River when necessary to reach forty-five counties. To get to Hyden, she carried her clothes (one suspects she meant her extra clothes!) in her mule's saddlebags. The rough ride into Leslie County was worth the effort. A very supportive minister greeted her, and 110 residents signed cards. Agents sought not only to recruit new suffragists but also to strengthen the "weak-kneed apostles of the faith."[43]

The weak-kneed remained a problem. KERA was gaining in numbers, but few members stepped up to become active workers. Every year they added new locals, but most, Breckinridge reported with frustration, were "not worth the powder that would blow them up." Miss Clay had promised suffragists that they need not do anything more than "stand up and be counted." The majority were content to take her at her word, it seemed.[44]

There was so much to do and so few to do it. Suffrage work was becoming increasingly strategic, demanding the skill and dedication of savvy professional lobbyists. Following the lead of the National, Breckinridge hoped to compile biographical information—"a life history"—of each lawmaker. For Kentucky, this meant doing detailed research on eleven representatives and two senators and then consistently deluging them with letters, telegrams, and suffrage material. There were petitions to circulate, party platforms to influence, and *Woman's Journal* subscriptions to sell. The work of dividing the state not only into county units but even further into precincts was just beginning. They needed hundreds of women, particularly women with political skills, to step forward and lead. Signing a card was just not enough.[45]

Breckinridge opened the new year in 1915, the final year of her first term, by writing to the president of every local across the state. She urged them to "turn over a new leaf" and to begin "active work" for suffrage. As suffrage entered its "pink tea stage," becoming trendier and less radical, complacency grew, maybe not in the larger cities, but in many rural areas. "Suffrage is not going to be handed to us on a silver waiter in Kentucky," she stressed, but requires "effort and sacrifice," both in terms of time and money. Breckinridge advised local clubs to hold regular meetings and to pursue a study course in civics. She also encouraged members to pay their fair share toward the work. Support must be "expressed in dollars." Clubs should make it their New Year's resolution, she urged, to contribute financially.[46]

It was about to become even more difficult, however, to focus women's attention on the work that lay ahead. The war in Europe that many assumed would be over in a matter of months had defied predictions. With the conflict about to enter its second year, American women felt torn between fighting for their rights and caring for the world's hurting people. Their time and money were about to become even more precious.

11

Working for Peace

Saturday morning, May 7, 1916, dawned in Lexington a lovely spring morning awash in the soft colors of blooming flowers and trees. The state was gearing up for the Kentucky Derby, but it would not run until the next week. This Saturday, it was all about suffrage. NAWSA had designated May 7 as "National Suffrage Day," and central Kentuckians planned to do it up big.

Any bashfulness suffragists had felt about making a public spectacle of themselves had disappeared by 1916. Relying on Alice Paul's playbook from the great 1913 parade, Lexington women hoped to match its pageantry and to surpass Louisville's parade three years earlier. Planners, however, had learned from some of Paul's mistakes. Suffrage was becoming a mainstream cause, but there were still those who might want to harass or embarrass marchers. Police would be on hand to prevent disruptions.

Organizers spent weeks fine-tuning the parade lineup to ensure spectators saw suffrage as a dignified cause with widespread appeal. They carefully organized the estimated one thousand marchers who assembled in Gratz Park into divisions of men and women, with children at the front. Miss Dorothy Fitzgerald, a pretty blond teenager with what might someday be called Shirley Temple dimples, served as lead bugler and rode with her younger sister in a gilded chariot at the head of the line. The Camp Fire Girls, the Fresh Air Children (organized to combat tuberculosis), and the Lincoln School baseball team came next. No one could accuse suffragists of being antifamily. Men followed, sorted by profession. Then, the women came. Planners similarly tried to organize women according to occupation—teachers, businesswomen, nurses—but also added a category for "miscellaneous female marchers" to cover those who did not work outside the home. Plenty of participants carried American flags to emphasize suffragists' patriotism, magnified now by the possibility of war.

To make sure no one missed the purpose of the event, organizers splashed yellow, the color of the movement, everywhere they could. Women, nearly to a person, dressed in white and sported yellow sashes. Men pinned yellow badges to their coats. Colorful "Votes for Women" banners floated by. Music provided by two brass bands gave the parade additional oomph.

The highlights of the event were two elaborate floats, each reportedly filled with "pretty young women." One depicted all the US states where suffrage had been won and compared them to Kentucky, represented by a blindfolded woman. The second float drove home the point that voting women made society better. Mothers who could vote, one sign emphasized, would support baby registration, finally making Kentucky's record keeping as effective for its children as it was for its livestock.[1]

At 10:30 a.m. it was time to proceed. The parade left the park, turned down Third Street, and soon reached North Broadway. Navigating one of the city's main north to south arteries, marchers passed noted landmarks— the Centenary Methodist Church with its soaring white spires on the left and the elegant Opera House to the right.

Next the procession swung left onto Main Street and began traveling east. It moved slowly enough that participants could admire the businesses lavishly decorated in solidarity with the cause. As the sun came out and the morning heated up, some participants may have made a mental note to stop back later at Calagis and Co., which promised the "best soda fountain in the city." They advanced past the new sixteen-story Fayette National Bank building, past the US army recruiting station, which beckoned more insistently to young men now that America's involvement in the Great War was looking likely, and past the Ben Ali and Strand theaters, sure to be packed with moviegoers later that evening. Once it arrived at its southern terminus, the handsome and bustling Union Station, the parade pivoted and returned the way it had come back up Main Street.[2]

Arriving at Cheapside shortly before noon, Walter J. Millard, a former Socialist lecturer turned suffrage organizer, addressed the crowd of nearly five thousand onlookers. The site, which had once held penned slaves awaiting sale, now became a place to claim women's liberty, though Millard did not note this irony. Comparing the reverberations felt that day to those that brought down the walls of Jericho, Millard predicted that suffragists were destined to decimate prejudice soon—well, sexism, at least. "The hour has struck," Millard dramatically declared just as the courthouse clock delivered twelve well-timed strokes.[3]

The suffragists "had the town for the morning," the *Lexington Leader* reported the next day. The songs, signs, and speeches marking the occasion all carried a message of urgency. Suffrage had been a long time in coming, but finally victory was close at hand. At least that was what Kentucky suffragists were telling themselves.[4]

Just months earlier, KERA had experienced another crushing defeat when a state suffrage amendment failed again in the legislature. Suffragists knew the governor, A. O. Stanley, a staunch "Wet," would likely put his weight behind the amendment's defeat, but they did not expect last-minute trouble from Washington, DC. When US Senator Ollie James and US Congressman James Cantrill, Antis who admitted they had no justification for sticking their noses into the state legislature's business, did just that, sending a well-timed telegram to the governor, which he leaked to the press, it spelled the bill's doom. The Wets, Breckinridge reported, had foiled them again.[5]

Suffragists took this defeat particularly hard, not only because it signaled their work was far from over but also because they could not rely on their ablest representative to direct it moving forward. Breckinridge's term as president ended in the fall of 1915, and Sallie Clay Bennett's daughter, Elise Bennett Smith, took over, allowing Breckinridge to become chair of the campaign. But soon after, Madge's fragile health sidelined her. She had failed to rest as instructed. Now, she was paying the price. For the next two years, well-being must come before work, doctors' orders.[6]

That meant women with the last name of Hubbard would be the driving force behind the 1916 fight for a state amendment. Fulton County's Sallie Hubbard underwrote its costs with her $1,000 contribution, and May Hord Hubbard (unrelated, it appears) became chair in Breckinridge's stead. Admirers described May Hubbard, the wife of a "railroad man," as a "political woman." Beyond directing the 1916 state amendment campaign, she also served as congressional chairman for Kentucky. Beginning in 1914, at the request of the National, she organized the state according to congressional districts to prepare for federal action on suffrage. Hubbard also managed—single-handedly to hear some tell it—to get a suffrage plank added to the state Republican platform in 1915. Democrats, despite her best efforts, refused to budge.[7]

They were making progress, but it was infuriatingly slow, and signs did not point to it speeding up anytime soon. By mid-1916, Kentucky suffragists could see that it was not lawmakers beholden to special interests that represented their greatest challenge. Nor was it the loss of Mrs. Breckinridge's leadership. The biggest factor that threatened to derail their efforts was unfolding thousands of miles away. The Great War was about to make their fight much more complicated.

Barbed wire, mustard gas, submarines. Kentucky women shuddered at the macabre horrors the first modern war spawned, but at least they were insulated from its direct impact. Only in retrospect did the event that ignited a world crisis, the assassination of Archduke Franz Ferdinand of Austria in June 1914, seem destined to change the course of history. Kentucky suffragists followed news of the unfolding crisis, but their interest in it largely centered on how it was harming women and vulnerable children across the globe. At its fall 1914 convention, KERA members took up a collection for Belgian relief.[8]

Suffragists had long embraced pacifism. It seemed to be in their blood. KERA members, heeding the call of Peace and Arbitration Committee chair Laura White, recommitted themselves to bringing women's priorities of negotiation and compromise to world affairs. "The conservers of life and the peace-loving half of humanity" needed to vote, they reiterated. Women would be the ones to end this war, achieve disarmament, and prevent future violent disputes, if only given the chance.[9]

Throughout 1915, most Kentucky suffragists demonstrated a firm anti-war commitment, joining the Woman's Peace Party when urged by KERA leaders to do so and embracing its principle of "aggressive passivism." That fall, the KERA convention invited Rosika Schwimmer, a Hungarian activist working to end the war, to be its special guest of honor.[10]

While deeply held principles informed suffragists' response to world events, their larger goal of gaining the vote never left their minds. Madge Breckinridge, for one, kept her focus pointed like a laser on her main objective. When governor James B. McCreary appointed eighty-five women to serve on a war preparation committee in the fall of 1915, Madge took a principled stand but one that also gave a nod to the bottom line. "Kentucky women are not idiots—even though they are closely related to Kentucky men," she snapped in an open letter rejecting McCreary's call. "You can't ignore them and treat them as if they were kindergarten children, and then when work is needed expect them to do a man's share." Still smarting from seeing the state suffrage amendment go down in defeat, she reminded the governor of the lack of charity shown to her and her colleagues by the legislature the previous year. Asking women to assist when they were getting nothing in return was unfair, she reasoned.[11]

Suffragists keenly understood that the war, if America were to become involved (and they still hoped it would not), could do one of two things for their cause: it could either derail their progress or it could suddenly propel them over the finish line. If they were lucky, American leaders would recognize the hypocrisy of asking women to help defend a nation that did not grant them full rights and would correct the injustice. But savvy suffragists understood that continuing to pursue their suffrage activities during the war could backfire, making them appear selfish and unpatriotic. The decisions they made carried grave implications. War could be their golden ticket, or it could once again set them back decades. It was anyone's guess which way it would go.

At first, the United States' position of strict neutrality made questions about the war's impact on "Votes for Women" hypothetical. But by the summer of 1916, despite Woodrow Wilson's reelection promise to keep the nation out of war, Americans began preparing for the worst. Preparedness became the watchword, even among pacifists, who argued that the most effective way to prevent war was to be ready for it.

Coming right on the heels of the mammoth suffrage parade held in Lexington in May 1916, Kentuckians organized elaborate community preparedness parades. Marchers, including suffragists who sported their yellow banners alongside their American flags, called for expanding the US armed forces and encouraged young men to enlist. The popularity of preparedness parades dissipated quickly after someone planted a suitcase containing a bomb at a similar gathering in San Francisco in July, killing ten people, but the martial spirit continued to grow.[12]

When Germany announced that it would resume unrestricted submarine attacks in February 1917, American involvement seemed imminent. Carrie Chapman Catt, serving a second term as NAWSA president, understood that the winds of public opinion had shifted. Americans who had not long ago insisted on neutrality had become rigidly pro-war. Toleration for dissent evaporated. Catt was a master strategist, and she hoped to capitalize. She usually insisted that suffragists must not jeopardize their work by allowing other causes to sidetrack them. But the war was a different story.[13]

Catt called an emergency meeting in late February to hammer out a plan should war come. It was an agonizing choice, but NAWSA delegates decided that prioritizing war work over suffrage work offered the best path to the vote. Women wanted to be trusted as full citizens. How would it look if they refused to support their government? By committing themselves fully to the war, by doing everything they were asked to do and more, women could prove they deserved a full measure of citizenship's rights and rewards.

America, if thrust into war, could depend on two million suffragists, Catt grandly offered Woodrow Wilson. They might not have a political voice, but they had patriotic spirit and intended to do their part to whip the kaiser. Catt had been a founding member of the Woman's Peace Party. She despised the thought of war and of soiling her hands to promote it, but if supporting the war was the way to achieve her goal of winning the vote, that's what she would have to do.[14]

Not all suffragists, however, were as willing as Catt to sell their souls to the Devil. Members of the National Woman's Party, led by the young, intelligent, and awfully impatient Alice Paul, also saw the war as an opportunity to achieve their goals but chose to approach the conflict very differently. NAWSA subscribed to the adage "you can win more flies with honey than with vinegar." Paul preferred to stick to vinegar.

The daughter of a Quaker suffragist, Paul moved to Britain after college to study social work. She also received an education in militancy by apprenticing with Emmeline Pankhurst's notorious suffragettes. When she returned to the States in 1910, she joined NAWSA. The National's painstaking approach to winning suffrage state by state, however, left her uninspired. And its decision to leave a federal woman suffrage amendment to gather dust for over thirty-five years left her bewildered.

Paul volunteered to breathe life back into NAWSA's moribund congressional committee and to work for the Anthony Amendment. NAWSA invited Paul to direct this effort but failed to commit the resources she thought it deserved. Before long, Paul was leading her own breakaway suffrage faction, which she called the Congressional Union (later renamed the National Woman's Party).[15]

Ever since the two organizations split in 1914, National leaders had wished Paul would go away. She offered some useful ideas, including her flair for adding drama to suffrage work and her emphasis on federal action, but these benefits came at a high cost. Paul's willingness to call a spade a spade and to embarrass public officials if necessary did not sit well with Catt and her colleagues. Too much vinegar for their taste.

In January 1917, as America teetered on the verge of war, Alice Paul's forces, calling themselves "silent sentinels," took up positions outside the

National Woman's Party pickets call on American leaders to live up to their promises to protect liberty across the globe in 1917. (Library of Congress)

White House. Their goals: to spotlight American hypocrisy and to shame Wilson into supporting a suffrage amendment. The pickets continued, issuing their quiet accusation, "Mr. President, how long must women wait for liberty?" even after Wilson signed the declaration of war against Germany on April 6, 1917. His promise that the "world must be made safe for democracy" encouraged suffragists—those picketing and those not—but the question was, would he make good on it?[16]

Most Kentucky suffragists considered the NWP's actions unladylike and ill-advised, and once America declared war the pickets seemed downright treasonous. KERA's new president, Christine Bradley South, daughter of former Republican governor, William O. Bradley, certainly felt that way. She agreed with Carrie Catt that suffragists' full energies must now go to the American war effort. NAWSA had identified three main priorities: working with the Red Cross to conserve food, protecting working women, and Americanization. South promised to support these efforts along with any other win-the-war project that arose.[17]

By the nineteen-teens, women were well educated, and they were highly organized, making them an obvious choice when the nation needed a "second line of defense." Suffragists wanted an expanded role in society, so they seemed especially good volunteer prospects. We're known as "people who accomplish things," the Franklin County E.R.A. proudly reported. A few

Christine Bradley South became president of KERA in 1916 when Elise Bennett Smith resigned to become recording secretary of NAWSA. (*Woman's Journal*)

Kentucky women signed on for active service in Europe; many, many more worked stateside to stretch America's human and industrial resources.[18]

The first Kentucky Red Cross chapter formed in Lexington in March 1917, and women made up a significant portion of its membership. Within six months a chapter existed in nearly every county. Volunteerism was popular and especially appropriate, it seemed, in a war to defeat autocracy. Kentuckians eagerly rallied to do their part. In Boyd County, for example, ten thousand of thirty-five thousand residents joined the Red Cross.[19]

Not everything, though, could be handled through volunteerism; some coercion would be necessary. When enlistments did not meet need in early 1917, Congress passed a Selective Service Act. June 5, 1917, was selected as Registration Day, the date by which all men between the ages of twenty-one and thirty-one must fill out a draft card. Women became a key part of the process, both by encouraging the men in their families to sign up and also by serving as unpaid clerks to record names and process paperwork.[20]

Suffragists proudly emphasized that their work to win the vote had taught them valuable skills their country now needed. Helping with Registration Day was just the first of many contributions they would make. When the Committee of Public Information began recruiting "Four Minute Men" to provide short pro-war spiels (four minutes is how long it took theaters to change reels), Louisville suffragists insisted they could do better. They would be "Three Minute Women." After all, an effective suffrage speaker had a lot of practice in being concise.[21]

They were also accustomed to selling unpopular causes. Even before the United States declared war, policymakers worried that America's food reserves would prove inadequate to feed its citizens and soldiers as well as its Allies, especially following a poor wheat harvest in 1916. Food could win the war, experts argued, but only if Americans treated it like a precious resource. Americans must voluntarily conserve, and suffragists argued that they were the ones to convince them.[22]

Suffragists became an essential part of Herbert Hoover's food conservation efforts by changing the way they fed their own families and also by collecting pledges from other women. KERA members were particularly adept at the work of going door to door to solicit promises. In many ways it felt like a repeat of previous efforts to get suffrage cards signed.

In most cases, women worked within their social and racial circles to seek pledges, but not always. Patty Semple, a white Louisville suffragist known for reaching across race lines to promote school suffrage, now did so

Madison County E.R.A. members show off their "suffrage potato patch." (Eastern Kentucky University Special Collections and Archives)

again. As second in command to Kentucky's federal food administrator, she specifically and personally encouraged black women's participation, vital since so much food consumed in the South was prepared by black domestics. Semple organized at least fifteen events, including a massive rally attended by four thousand black Louisville residents. War work, like suffrage work, however, remained deeply segregated just like nearly every facet of life in Kentucky, even as America fought to defend liberty.[23]

Efforts to conserve food—participating in "meatless Mondays" and "wheatless Wednesdays"—were important, but many suffragists went a step further, taking up farming to expand the nation's supply. As residents of an agricultural state, Kentucky women felt especially called to serve this way. Laura Clay had years of farming experience, and she capitalized on it, encouraging her fellow suffragists to bring more acres under cultivation. She loaned Madison County suffragists land on which to plant potatoes. They cut, dropped, and gathered the potatoes "with [their] own hands," about eighty bushels, they proudly announced. Beds of weeds across the state turned into baskets of produce under suffragists' careful direction.[24]

Many women, however, wanted to serve their "boys" overseas more directly. The Red Cross asked women to knit warm clothing for soldiers, and Kentucky suffragists stepped right up. Even Laura Clay, knitter though she was not, agreed to make one set of woolens (including a sleeveless jacket, wristlets, and scarf). Christine Bradley South committed KERA to providing five hundred sets of garments, enough to outfit every man on board the USS *Kentucky*.[25]

Even though some critics questioned whether hand producing garments that could be quickly made on machines was the best use of limited resources, women protected their turf. They did not knit for just any American soldiers; they insisted that their products go directly to the men of their community, the boys they knew and loved.[26]

Suffragists wrote letters to soldiers on the front, they sent books to cheer the injured, and they sold war bonds, lots of war bonds. "Don't be a miser," they urged, "throw in your change and lick the Kaiser." Kentucky suffragists held some of the most visible leadership positions in all four Liberty Loan campaigns, and their efforts were essential in helping Kentucky raise over $200 million to help fund the war.[27]

Madison County suffragists did not just sell bonds, they chipped in to purchase one, which they signed over to the Richmond Infirmary. Yes, they could have kept the $100 bond as an investment for their own cause, they acknowledged, but they felt that unnecessary. Surely, Kentucky women would be enfranchised before it would have time to mature.[28]

As its most substantial war-related project, KERA contributed to NAWSA's "war baby," a plan to build and equip two Allied European hospitals. KERA went even further, pledging to fund the purchase of an ambulance for the Barrow Unit, a facility in Great Britain run by Lexington medical professionals. The ambulance would be named the "Laura Clay" to honor their leader "who had done so much for the cause of human liberty and human betterment." Louisville women began fundraising to cover Kentucky's pledge to NAWSA's overseas hospital, and Lexington women began raising the $2,000 needed to purchase the ambulance. They hoped that each of the injured soldiers who had their broken bodies put back together at one of these hospitals or who were carried in their ambulance would come home ready to repay the debt of gratitude they felt to suffragists.[29]

Kentucky suffragists cheerfully shifted their attention from vote work to war work in 1917 and for the duration. They did so not as individuals, but collectively under the KERA mantle. Combining war work with suffrage work allowed E.R.A.s, now refashioned as "patriotic units," to continue meeting without guilt or fear of embarrassment. The Fayette County local pledged to multitask during its meetings. Members' fingers might be knitting, but their minds would be on suffrage.[30]

Louisville native Edith Callahan had no intention of knitting her way through the war. She had too much on her plate as a student and a busy socialite. As the daughter of P. H. Callahan, president of the Louisville Varnish Company, she was used to living a life full of travel and excitement. She and her mother were caught in Europe when war broke out in the summer of 1914, leaving friends and family back home to fear for their safety, but luckily, they made it back without incident.[31]

Under normal circumstances, Edie Callahan would have been getting ready to head back to New York in August 1917 to continue her training at the Comstock School of Music, but an accident earlier that summer interfered. She was driving her father's roadster through the streets of downtown Louisville, too fast according to reports, when she struck and killed a crossing pedestrian. The unfortunate victim died within minutes. Callahan turned herself in to authorities who charged her with involuntary manslaughter. With cases pending in both the criminal and civil court (the victim's family later sued Callahan for $25,000), Edie found herself stuck in Louisville longer than she would have liked.[32]

Luckily, she had friends who could help keep her entertained— Henrietta Bingham, the flamboyant daughter of Robert Worth Bingham, was one of her close associates, and there were the constant rounds of teas and bridge games to attend. But Callahan craved excitement. When the National Woman's Party announced that it was sending a field-worker to Kentucky, one of the only states where it had no local branch, Callahan's interest was piqued. She knew all about the NWP and its antics.[33]

The NWP had likely saved Kentucky for last because it seemed a hopeless case. Southerners generally rejected the NWP's argument that the best route to the vote was by federal amendment won through civil disobedience. Kentucky, however, seemed even harder to win because it had such a long history of suffrage work and such strong existing leadership. Indeed, KERA representatives were ready to pounce when the NWP announced in March 1917 that it would begin recruiting on their home turf.

KERA members' disdain for Alice Paul and her organization had been festering for several years. Miss Clay, increasingly firm in her support for "states' rights suffrage," could not accept Paul's claim that only a federal amendment would do and that state campaigns were "wasteful." Mrs.

Breckinridge was intrigued by the NWP's attention-grabbing tactics, but she shared Clay's belief that southerners would never go for a federal amendment, if it ever managed to get through Congress. She was not personally opposed to the Anthony Amendment; she just did not see it as likely to work.[34]

By 1917, many KERA members were coming around to the advantages of a federal amendment, but they were repulsed by the NWP's militancy and its potential to jeopardize their efforts. When the NWP placed announcements in Kentucky newspapers in March 1917 describing plans for its "Dixie Drive," KERA officers distanced themselves from Paul's group, worried that an undiscerning public would throw them all into the same suffragette stew pot. Their ties were to the NAWSA, which endorsed "patient, dignified and earnest" action, Julia Henning, KERA's chair of congressional work, explained. "There is no organization of militant suffragists in this State," KERA president Christine Bradley South added. "It is our wish that there may never be one."[35]

Despite South's best efforts to keep it at bay, militant suffrage work did come to Kentucky a few months later. With only eight women attending the NWP's first conference, however, it would not make a noticeable splash. Its membership never grew beyond twenty members, but it did establish a presence.

Edie Callahan, refusing to cool her heels after her motor accident, attended the NWP organizational meeting at the Seelbach on August 19 and offered to serve as chairperson for Kentucky. A few weeks later, she showed up on the picket line outside the White House alongside another Kentuckian, Cornelia Beach, a teacher from Louisville's Neighborhood House.[36]

Since the United States had entered the war, NWP protests had become a profound embarrassment to the Wilson administration. What once could be brushed off as free speech now appeared an act of treason. The White House began arresting the silent sentinels in June 1917, charging them with disorderly conduct, unlawful assembly, and disrupting traffic. Callahan and Beach knew the risks when they volunteered to go to DC; during the meeting to organize Kentucky, a telegram announced that a judge had just sentenced a group of pickets to thirty days in jail.[37]

It appears that Callahan may have lost her nerve when she arrived in Washington, or perhaps she was just one of the lucky ones (or unlucky ones, depending on your perspective) to avoid arrest. Cornelia Beach, however, found herself in the center of the action. On August 29, a front-page headline in the *Courier-Journal* announced that a local woman had been arrested the day before as a "'suff' picket."[38]

Authorities took Beach into custody along with nine other suffragists, including Alice Paul's close friend Lucy Burns. The women had not committed any serious disturbance, the paper admitted, but they had displayed their offensive banners. Beach was released on $100 bond later that day. The *Courier-Journal* noted that although Beach had lived in Louisville for several years, they could find no one "who knew when she came to this city, or where from." Beach's radical actions were the work of an outsider—not representative of well-behaved Kentucky women—the paper implied.[39]

Unlike European women who felt the ravages of war directly every day, American women had the luxury of experiencing World War I at arms' length. The extra distance allowed them to focus on the promise of the war rather than on its hardships. The war not only offered an unprecedented opportunity to expand liberty at home and across the globe, an opportunity that both NAWSA and the NWP hoped to seize, but it also gave women a chance to attack male vices that had perpetually irritated them, all in the name of patriotism, of course.[40]

Men's appetite for whiskey and prostitutes were two of women's greatest frustrations, and now it seemed they had a chance to knock them out for good. These vices, US officials agreed, posed a threat to America's fighting force. When soldiers started training at Lexington's Camp Stanley in 1915, city authorities passed an ordinance that shut down the city's red-light district, including Belle Brezing's famous brothel. The US War Department's Commission on Training Camp Activities encouraged similar crackdowns nationwide.[41]

KERA cheered these efforts. In 1917, it promised to cooperate fully in efforts to suppress the "social evil" (prostitution and venereal disease). Its members also grew louder in demanding prohibition. They argued that alcohol weakened soldiers, endangered women and children, and siphoned off grains that could be used to feed people instead. "Bar the barley from the bar, and bake it into bread instead," agile-tongued Fayette County suffragists demanded. Women were sacrificing by supporting wheatless Wednesdays. Shouldn't men have to sacrifice with "drinkless" and "smokeless" days, temperance leaders asked.[42]

The war drew attention to other problems that women hoped to solve. Illiteracy and disease left too many draftees rejected as unfit. Women argued that the next generation must be made stronger and smarter. They mobilized to better record American births and deaths and to have 1918 proclaimed "Children's Year." In Kentucky, known nationwide for its low levels of literacy, suffragists cooperated with one of their own, Cora Wilson Stewart, to support her Moonlight Schools movement.[43]

Suffragists also used the war to promote 100 percent Americanism and encouraged immigrants to shed their native culture. Although the Kentucky legislature took steps to prohibit schools from teaching German (vetoed by the governor), the state had a small immigrant population and so Americanization did not inspire the zeal it did in other places, Louisville and northern Kentucky excepted. Abby Meguire Roach, a member of the LWSA, wrote a series of articles for the *Courier-Journal* titled "We Americans." In Kenton County, a member of its E.R.A. did her part to promote Americanization by adopting a poor homeless French refugee boy. Showing his allegiance to his new country, the boy taught American soldiers how to "parlez-vous" before joining the army himself.[44]

Nineteen months after the United States committed to fight alongside the Allies, the war ended. American soldiers began returning home as Woodrow Wilson worked to ensure that the Great War would be the "war to end all wars." Suffragists, long proponents of an international court of arbitration, rallied behind the president's ill-fated League of Nations.[45]

Kentucky suffragists hoped that America would emerge from the war a kinder, gentler, healthier place, a place where women shaped decision making and raised moral standards. Most of all, they hoped the war would finally provide them the political rights they had so long chased. European countries, in quick succession, gave women the vote as a reward for their service. Many believed it was only a matter of time until American women became voters too. "The war," an editorial in the *Owensboro Messenger* declared, "has changed everything."[46]

But even as the Susan B. Anthony Amendment gained ground, some Kentucky suffragists wondered whether this was for the best. For the Kentucky suffrage movement, the war might be over, but its greatest battles were yet to come.

12

Ignis Fatuus

In August 1918, with the end of the war mercifully in sight, Kentuckians watched and waited to see whether Ollie James, their larger-than-life US senator, would live or die. Praise gushed forth from his supporters, both in Kentucky and across the country—"a magnificent specimen of manhood," "massive of body and brain," and "magnetic" were just some of the compliments they paid the sickened congressman. Admirers fervently prayed that James would make a full recovery, win reelection to his Senate seat, and serve his state and country for years to come, possibly as US president.[1]

But their prayers likely were not the only ones being said. Suffragists were not so coldhearted as to wish James dead, but they understood that his demise would mean a big boost for their cause. They had been working for months to see him defeated in November.

"Big Ollie" (he stood six foot four and weighed over three hundred pounds) had long seemed unbeatable, but now suffragists saw a glimmer of hope. Hospitalized since June, the senator had been diagnosed with everything from a nervous breakdown to tonsillitis to lumbago. The poor man had been poked and prodded, declared healed, and written off as a goner, often in reports issued on a single day. He had endured surgeries, tooth extractions, and blood transfusions, his suffering made worse by the oppressive summer heat. By late August, his condition was grave.[2]

James had many admirers, but Kentucky suffragists were not among them. In March 1914, when the US Senate began considering the Susan B. Anthony Amendment in earnest, James had helped to spell its defeat. Teaming up fellow racists J. Thomas Heflin of Alabama and Mississippi's James K. Vardaman, he outlined the danger voting women posed to white supremacy. A federal suffrage amendment would enfranchise seventy-five thousand black women in Kentucky, and he predicted that they, unlike white women, would all vote. James was not concerned about federal authority like some of his colleagues, at least he claimed he was not (and his support of the Sixteenth and Seventeenth Amendments, which established

175

Ollie Murray James represented Kentucky in the US House from 1903 to 1913 and in the Senate from 1913 to 1918. He was a staunch opponent of women's suffrage. (Library of Congress)

the income tax and direct election of senators, proved as much); James's reservations were rooted in racism, pure and simple.[3]

Suffragists blamed James not only for undermining the federal suffrage amendment but also for blowing their shot at a state suffrage amendment in 1916. The underhanded telegram he sent with Cantrill to the governor, claiming that the entire Kentucky congressional delegation in Washington opposed the measure, killed its chances for passage.[4]

And now, lying flat on his back, James continued to be a thorn in suffragists' sides. In June 1918, the federal suffrage amendment came up again in the US Senate for consideration. There was more riding on its vote now than four years earlier since the House had passed the measure in January. One vote would likely decide whether the amendment would die again or go to the states for ratification. James, though a very sick man, insisted on controlling his vote. It was a long-standing tradition in the Senate to allow an absent lawmaker to "pair" with someone on the other side of the aisle. The senator who agreed to pair would abstain from voting, thereby offsetting the vote of his (the Senate was all male until 1922) indisposed colleague. Pro-suffrage forces believed they had the votes necessary to win, assuming the right people showed up to vote that day, but when negotiations over a pair for Ollie James broke down, managers withdrew the bill. James had stymied suffragists again.[5]

But mercifully that was the last time he would block woman suffrage. On August 28, 1918, the Big Man died. Suffragists across the country could not help but see his tragedy as their gain. Assuming they could persuade Governor A. O. Stanley to appoint a pro-suffrage man in James's place—and boy, would they try—they would have one more vote in the aye column the next time their bill came up.[6]

Their scheming worked. Stanley, who had designs on becoming a US senator himself, appointed George B. Martin, a pro-suffrage lawyer from Catlettsburg, to fill the position. To suffragists' delight, Martin voted for the amendment the first chance he got.[7]

That was not the only good news suffragists received. The *Stanford Interior Journal* ran two encouraging announcements back to back on August 30. First came news that Ollie James had crossed the "Great Divide," immediately followed by the headline "COURIER-JOURNAL BECOMES SUFFRAGETTE."[8]

Robert Worth Bingham, left obscenely wealthy after the death of his wife, used his riches to purchase Louisville's most powerful opinion shaper. He immediately announced that the paper, which had long opposed suffrage and prohibition, would do a 180-degree turn on both issues. The *Courier-Journal* no longer would be the mouthpiece of the whiskey ring, suffragists' hated nemesis. With glee matching that shown by Oz's munchkins after the witch's destruction, the readers of the *Woman Citizen* ecstatically bid Marse Henry goodbye.[9]

Not everyone, however, was buoyed by these reversals of fortune that made a federal suffrage amendment suddenly more in reach. For Laura Clay, the grand dame of Kentucky suffrage, these announcements were like a canary in the coal mine. The Susan B. Anthony Amendment, a measure that gave her serious pause, was inching closer to changing the Constitution forever. Clay swallowed hard. She must take action to stop it before it was too late.

Laura Clay had not always lived in fear of a federal amendment. While many of her southern colleagues, the so-called states' rights suffragists, warned that it would destroy life as they knew it, Clay disagreed. She argued for a then-Sixteenth Amendment before a committee of the US Senate in 1908, an adjustment that would not only eliminate voting restrictions based on sex, but, Clay added with a dramatic flourish, would allow women to "imprint their convictions upon the Constitution." When NAWSA collected its monster petition in 1909 supporting a federal amendment, some southern women refused to participate, but not Clay. Years later, when her old friend Eugenia Farmer heard that she had denounced the Anthony Amendment, she was shocked by Clay's about-face: "Well! I thought you always favored [it]."[10]

To be fair, Clay had long-standing reservations about federal authority run amok and a strong preference for local control, but she made no bones about it: she would happily support a federal constitutional amendment if it proved the quickest way to win the vote.[11]

Clay's tolerance for a federal amendment, however, began to erode in the early nineteen-teens. Her shrinking role within NAWSA was one reason for her shift. After she was voted out of office in 1911, southern suffragists, including dyed-in-the-wool states' righter Kate Gordon, courted Clay and soothed her bruised ego.

Kate Gordon and Laura Clay had much in common. Both came from prominent families filled with sisters (Kate was one of three). Neither Clay nor Gordon had to worry about resources and neither married. Each committed her life to suffrage work. Gordon was to Louisiana what Clay was to the Kentucky movement. She founded the Era Club in New Orleans, which she admitted stood for "Equal Rights for All," though she really didn't mean *all*. White women, yes, but certainly not black women; Gordon did not hide her prejudices. Clay and Gordon served together on NAWSA's board after Gordon was elected corresponding secretary in 1901. As the collective voice of the South within the National, they became partners.[12]

When Gordon organized a separate Southern States Woman Suffrage Conference (SSWSC) in 1913, she chose Clay to lead it: "My dear Miss Clay, I really and truly need you," Gordon stressed. Clay declined the offer and did not go to the SSWSC's inaugural meeting, but she did accept its vice presidency.[13]

Southern suffragists wanted to claim Clay for their own, but she held their "flank movement" at arm's length. A separate organization, requiring extra meetings and publications, was a waste of resources, she felt. The daughter of abolitionists, she also struggled to feel at home under its racist banner. The cover of SSWSC's monthly magazine *New Southern Citizen*

Louisiana's Kate Gordon encouraged Laura Clay's states' rights view of suffrage. (Library of Congress)

boldly stated its goal: "MAKE THE SOUTHERN STATES WHITE." As a resident of a state where white supremacy was safely established, Clay hesitated to antagonize black voters, who were always skeptical of any effort that might jeopardize their rights, she explained. Clay felt that it was best not to stir the race pot publicly, but in private she did not hide her deepening racism.[14]

America in general was becoming a less tolerant place by the early twentieth century. Segregation seeped into all parts of life, North and South, and the practice of lynching viciously ensured that blacks stayed "in their place." Communities rallied together under cover of darkness and at gunpoint, as they did in Marshall County, Kentucky, in 1908, to achieve racial cleansing. Racism had the nation's collective stamp of approval: blockbuster hit *The Birth of a Nation* (originally titled *The Clansman*), became the first movie shown in the White House in 1915.[15]

Clay had once argued that black Americans should not be disfranchised wholesale but that the nation should adopt literacy clauses, giving all members of all races the opportunity to become educated and valuable citizens. Like her peers across the country, however, she began to doubt that African Americans would strengthen the country and began to see them as a growing threat as a new century began. Laura was not as blunt as her sister, Sallie, who asserted that white women needed the vote to protect themselves from black rapists, but she did not hide her simmering resentment. Members of "a childish and irresponsible race" had the vote and white women did not, one of the greatest indignities imaginable in Clay's estimation.[16]

On that point, she and southern suffragists completely agreed. And while it was not a concern in her own state where African Americans made up only 11 percent of the population, she fully sympathized with southern women's fear that suffrage won by federal means would undo white supremacy. For Kate Gordon and her Deep South neighbors, there could only be one route to the vote: it could only come as a state measure. Any other path spelled doom in their minds; the more Clay considered NAWSA's policy shift toward favoring a federal amendment, the more she saw it as a deal-breaker.[17]

NAWSA had always been equally committed to pursuing state and federal routes to the vote, as its constitution stipulated. Granted, its federal congressional efforts had always been a little puny. On the last day of their annual convention (when held in DC), leaders would trek down to the Capitol to deliver their plea. Alice Paul's efforts to revive NAWSA's congressional committee caused leaders to notice the possibilities of federal action, and even when they parted ways with Paul, their interest in a federal amendment continued to grow. State action was looking less and less promising, especially after five of seven state campaigns conducted in 1914 failed. State campaigns were grueling and costly. The thought of enduring thirty-seven more understandably left leaders seeking an easier option.[18]

As NAWSA tilted toward a federal amendment, Clay began to tilt sharply away. The more she allowed Kate Gordon and other southerners to gain her ear, the more she decided the National was barking up the wrong tree. Clay focused on a federal amendment's likelihood of failure. It must pass with a two-thirds vote in both houses of Congress and gain support of three-fourths of the states. Clay did some simple math. There were forty-eight states in the Union, so thirty-six must ratify. Even if the amendment squeezed its way through the House and Senate—and Clay believed that unlikely with Woodrow Wilson, a principled southern Democrat, in the White House—it could never clear the ratification hurdle. Twelve southern states would act as an impenetrable bulwark. NAWSA leaders claimed the federal amendment was a shortcut. Hardly, Clay maintained. It would be "a very long way round," if it ever came at all.[19]

Clay did not feel the same level of panic as her fellow southerners when contemplating the impact of a federal amendment, but she understood their concern. South Carolina senator Ellison "Cotton Ed" Smith summarized the danger: a vote for the Susan B. Anthony Amendment was a vote to ratify the Fifteenth Amendment, which no proud southerner would ever do unless coerced (Kentucky when given a choice did not voluntarily ratify the Reconstruction amendments until 1976). Savvy Antis capitalized on southerners' deepest worries and made apocalyptic predictions. Woman suffrage would "reopen the entire *Negro Suffrage* question." It would impose a new set of "reconstruction horrors." The amendment's enabling clause, giving Congress "the power, by appropriate legislation, to enforce the provisions of this article," was not harmless boilerplate language, they warned, but rather the keys to destruction.[20]

Southerners would never go for it, Clay decided. No way, no how. The outcome was too uncertain and the stakes too high. Without their support, the amendment was a dead letter. So, Clay looked for other ways to achieve suffrage through federal means without antagonizing the South. While some of her colleagues were promoting the Shafroth–Palmer Amendment in Congress, which would have made state amendments easier to secure, Clay put her energies behind what she called the United States Elections law.[21]

During the nineteen-teens, Laura Clay became less willing to consider a federal amendment giving women the vote. This photo (c. 1916) shows an older, more rigid Clay. (University of Kentucky Special Collections)

The "Clay Bill" became associated with Laura, but it was really the brainchild of her sister, Sallie. With five children to raise, Sallie Clay Bennett could not do much for suffrage, so she focused her energies on one goal: convincing Congress that it had discretion over who could vote for representatives and senators based on provisions of the Fourteenth Amendment. Every year, starting in 1895, Sallie Bennett presented a memorial to Congress asking it to take a simple vote to give women these rights. Laura had never paid Sallie's pet project much mind, although KERA had dutifully agreed each year to keep pursuing it. Now, however, with a slight adjustment to its constitutional justification (she focused on the Constitution's Preamble and Article I, Section 2), Laura began to see its merits. The United States Elections bill, which she first proposed in 1914, would not rattle southerners—they could still limit the electorate according to other criteria, just not gender—but it would give women a way to begin voting and to prove themselves worthy.[22]

Clay thought her United States Elections bill was suffragists' ticket forward—a measure that could satisfy everyone. But national leaders saw the matter differently and consigned it, much to her consternation, to the "limbo of lost causes." National leaders had always recognized there was more than one way to skin a cat and that pursuing multiple strategies made good sense, but now the organization committed to a singular approach. By 1916, NAWSA identified the federal amendment as the one and only path to the vote.[23]

When Carrie Chapman Catt was called back into service to lead NAWSA in December 1915, she decided the time for dillydallying was over. Suffrage's moment had come, and she did not intend to miss her chance to finally finish off what she had started three decades earlier. Strategy had never been the organization's strong suit; rather, its approach had been to throw everything it had at the problem, hoping something would eventually stick. Catt could see how well that had worked. She vowed instead to pick a specific goal and center their entire fight around it. Catt planned to build a lean, mean suffrage machine.[24]

One reason the National had always preferred to pursue a hodgepodge of goals, even at the risk of diluting its energies, was to avoid hard feelings and tough decisions. By picking one objective and refusing to deviate from it, Catt risked alienating many suffragists who would be asked to sacrifice their own priorities for the greater good.[25]

She would have to sell them on the merits of her plan. Like a good traveling salesman, Catt hit the road in the spring of 1916, moving from city to city to "sound her trumpet call for mobilization." One of her first stops was Louisville.[26]

Catt's decision to stop in Louisville involved cold calculation. When she considered the threats to securing a federal amendment, she knew the South was one of its biggest obstacles, and Clay stood for the South. Going to Louisville represented a flanking maneuver, a chance to undercut Clay on her own turf. Although Kentucky suffragists looked united to casual observers, tensions had been building within KERA, and Catt hoped to capitalize. The Louisville club, now more than four thousand members strong, had a mind of its own, a mind that Clay described as Republican and Progressive. Catt hoped that Louisville women would be of one mind with the National and would carry Kentucky in the right direction.[27]

Clay understood exactly what Catt intended when she invited suffragists to attend a "Congressional Congress" at the Seelbach hotel that March. She hoped they would promise to put their full energies behind the Anthony Amendment. Clay, however, wanted to protect her right to keep working for her United States Elections bill; she had to find a way to thwart Catt.

Clay jumped out in front as the congress convened, offering a vague resolution that promised only to "support the Federal bill." That was not good enough for Catt, who was only interested in the amendment. Catt finally squeezed out the firm promise she was seeking from the assembled women, but only after "a sharp argument." She won the showdown, but any hope she had of Miss Clay falling obediently into line disappeared.[28]

Catt believed so strongly in the merits of her plan and in Kentucky's vital importance to it that she chose to publicly spar with one of her oldest colleagues. Catt's arguments for an amendment often specifically referenced Kentucky, which she classified as one of several "very difficult states." States, namely Kentucky, were barking up the wrong tree, Catt argued, by chasing state suffrage measures, which were nothing but a ruse by Antis to delay progress. Why else would newspapers known for being openly hostile to votes for women endorse them? Catt saw Kentucky as a critical battleground—a "Northernized" southern state where the federal amendment had a fighting chance.[29]

Catt's hunch that it could all come down to Kentucky likely made Clay seethe, but it lit a fire under many of her KERA colleagues who quite liked the idea of their state being the deciding factor. KERA had sponsored a

Carrie Chapman Catt, president of NAWSA, introduced her "Winning Plan" in 1916, which made state interests secondary to national goals. (Library of Congress)

congressional work committee under the direction of Sallie Hubbard since 1914, but she had made little progress toward the goal of organizing Kentucky by congressional districts. State work preoccupied KERA members. By 1916, however, interest in federal suffrage was growing, and Josephine Fowler Post, president of the McCracken County E.R.A. and new congressional chair, began to see progress. "The real beginning of Congressional Work," she grandly declared, had begun in March when Mrs. Catt came to town. Kentucky suffragists, especially Louisville women, more and more, started to see a federal amendment as their best chance for the vote.[30]

It required an emergency convention in Atlantic City in September 1916 for Catt to get NAWSA "securely on the Federal Amendment trolley." Even Woodrow Wilson, so staunchly committed to Victorian ideas of woman's proper role, announced that he was along for the ride, winning a "tumultuous ovation" when he addressed the gathered women. His endorsement was cautious. He promised that he would not quarrel with the method by which suffrage came, leaving the state route open, but at least he didn't mention states' rights.[31]

Coming into the meeting, Catt suggested that NAWSA's future course was still to be determined. They would conduct a "three-cornered debate," considering all the possible plans—a state-only approach (argued by Miss Clay), a federally oriented approach, and one that contained elements of both. At the conclusion of the debate, suffragists would select the winning argument, which would determine NAWSA policy.[32]

It was an act of subterfuge. Catt knew from the start how she planned to proceed, and she played it masterfully. As Catt intended, the delegates decided that "all forces [should] be concentrated on the Federal Amendment" and urged the national board to do whatever necessary to achieve this end. State campaigns would still happen, but only if they reinforced the end goal. The NAWSA board would choose which states would get the green light and which would be told to cool their heels. This way, they could focus all their energy on lobbying lawmakers. It was a "Winning Plan," Catt promised.[33]

Laura Clay and Kate Gordon smelled a sham. "A well-oiled steam roller has ironed this convention *flat*," Gordon muttered under her breath when it became clear that the federal amendment would win out. Catt's promise that the national board would go easy on states that refused to fall into line did little to mollify the southern dissenters. Catt understood that the fact

Fifteen members of the Fayette, Franklin, and Madison County E.R.A.s represented Kentucky at the 1916 Democratic National Convention in St. Louis. (University of Kentucky Special Collections)

that she was asked how the National would respond to disloyalty suggested it was not a hypothetical question.[34]

Kentucky suffragists who favored a state constitutional amendment and who were looking forward to trying again for one in 1918 wondered what NAWSA's policy change meant for them. Would KERA bow to National demands? Would they take one for the team? Fortunately, immediate answers were not necessary since the next legislative session was more than a year away. The United States' entry into the Great War also made the question less pressing as Congress called a moratorium on all nonemergency legislation in April 1917.

Clay was not taking any chances. She began working immediately and at every turn to keep KERA steered toward state amendment work. At the very least, all methods of winning the vote, especially her United States Elections law, should receive consideration alongside the Anthony Amendment, she insisted.[35]

Keeping her colleagues on the straight and narrow would not be easy. She hated to admit it, but many of KERA's board members were as much carried away by the amendment—*ignis fatuus* (deceptive goal or hope) though it may be—as was Mrs. Catt. The hard work of first Josephine Post and now Julia Duke Henning to divide the state into eleven congressional districts and to recruit a chairman for each was coming along nicely. Kentucky women were helping Catt crank her suffrage machine. They sent out questionnaires to every sitting lawmaker and to every candidate for office. They would permit "no possible convert to escape," they pledged. Louisville suffragists by 1918 were ready to declare their state and local work finished. They had "quite outgrown" it, they explained. Their efforts would "be entirely concentrated upon . . . a Federal Amendment" from here on out.[36]

Clay could see troubling signs, not just in Kentucky, but across the South: weak women were ready to sacrifice their states' rights principles for a federal amendment. In Louisiana, Kate Gordon's home state, a rogue suffrage organization in favor of federal action had emerged. The SSWSC had withered by 1917 as even southern suffragists began to rally behind the Susan B. Anthony Amendment.[37]

Clay and her KERA colleagues agreed to disagree throughout 1917. To skirt disagreements, they settled on an unwritten policy: they refused to act as a body on controversial matters but allowed members to take individual action. With the next legislative session approaching, however, Clay and her colleagues found themselves on a collision course. Like it or not, they would have to make tough choices at their November convention.[38]

The war that had threatened to freeze suffrage work suddenly put it on the fast track that fall. Woodrow Wilson thrilled suffragists when he shed his lingering reservations about the Anthony Amendment and declared it "a very wise act of public policy." The House followed by creating a Woman Suffrage Committee, removing the amendment from oversight of the unfriendly Rules Committee. A complete reversal was under way; the cause's most committed foes suddenly became enthusiastic champions. J. Campbell Cantrill, US representative from Kentucky's seventh district, called on his congressional colleagues to "catch the spirit of the times," apparently forgetting all the years he had spent blocking suffragists at every turn.[39]

As victory began to seem inevitable, an endgame dynamic developed. Every woman who gained the vote became a force to enfranchise other women by voting out Antis, and thus as Alexander Keyssar explains, "The potential political cost of a vote against enfranchisement rose dramatically." Everyone wanted to claim credit for the amendment's ratification. Just as Clay once predicted, women went from "the seekers to the sought." Political leaders realized they must "jump on the bandwagon, or at the very least, to get out of the road." Cantrill served as exhibit A of this bandwagon effect. He claimed he wanted to reward women for their war contributions, but his real motivation was thoroughly partisan. He warned fellow Democrats that they risked losing plum committee chairmanships if they did not get on board.[40]

With so much momentum behind them, especially after New York voters approved a state suffrage amendment in November 1917, Catt decided she could afford no missteps. They must adhere strictly to her winning plan. Kentucky, however, was not falling into line. Catt firmly believed that a state campaign could not succeed there, but Miss Clay was hell-bent on trying. An opportunity came only every two years, she reminded. Rather than follow instructions from "some Board in New York," they must seize the day.[41]

The state route to the ballot had become an obsession for Clay, but it remained to be seen whether her Kentucky colleagues felt similarly. The decision to hold the 1917 KERA convention in Lexington gave Clay homefield advantage. Louisville women were Kentucky's most vocal proponents of the Nineteenth Amendment—"completely under the influence of the National," Clay charged—but the LWSA was sending only four delegates, compared to Fayette County's twenty-one. Louisville's impact would be greatly reduced, even considering that five out of ten executive board members were from the Derby City.[42]

The nine Louisville women who made the trip came ready to square off with Clay. When it came time to consider a state amendment, which the majority report advocated, Julia Duke Henning answered with a carefully prepared minority report. Her measure called for acquiescing to the National's demands by forgoing a state campaign. It was the first time since Mrs. Henry's ouster back in 1898 that the body considered competing reports. A telegram from Mrs. Catt, begging Kentucky suffragists not to go into campaign, did not change the outcome. After several "stormy" sessions and with twenty-one abstentions, the convention finally agreed to support the majority report. Clay had won. Kentucky suffragists would seek a state amendment. It was an empty gesture, but they also pledged to "cooperate generally" with the NAWSA.[43]

Christine Bradley South, KERA's president, recognized that she was in a pickle. She had an obligation to carry out the convention's wishes, but to do so, she might single-handedly sink the federal amendment, a significant worry after it passed the US House in January. Besides, she realized she was in an impossible situation. How could she follow the convention's decision to support a state campaign and to also cooperate with the National? The two objectives were completely at odds.[44]

An attorney helped South find a way out of the mess, though it would mean defying Miss Clay and her "cherished plan." KERA's executive board could override the convention's decision, and South decided it must. She called an emergency meeting in January. The meeting was poorly attended; board members preferred to steer clear of the controversy. Only by allowing two members to call in by telephone did they achieve a quorum. Mrs. Breckinridge acknowledged that it sickened her to vote against a state campaign, knowing it was probably the only chance she would have in her lifetime to win the vote. "The National Association," she stressed, "will never know what they asked us to give up." She just hoped that she wasn't also giving up her friendship with Miss Clay. The war—the Kentucky one, not the European—was not over.[45]

For a moment in January 1918 after the House passed the suffrage amendment at Woodrow Wilson's urging, it looked like Clay would call a truce. "It is futile," she confided to her sister Sallie. "A great statesman and head of the Democratic Party" had dismissed the concern that the amendment violated states' rights and had gone so far as to declare it "necessary to the prosecution of the war." Clay pledged to Catt that she would be a good soldier from here on out: "I am unwilling to jeopardize any chance for my enfranchisement by opposition to it," she promised.[46]

Once Gordon got to her, however, Clay's reversal did not last. Gordon—who had once been called the "petty dictator of a personal clique" for trying to divide Louisiana suffragists—urged Clay to hold her ground on a state amendment campaign. Split KERA, if necessary. Catt deserves it! Gordon spewed, calling her actions "dishonorable," "unscrupulous," a "form of Kaiserism," really. Gordon's attempts to reel her best ally back in worked. Clay promised she would never give up on finding an alternative to the Susan B. Anthony Amendment. Until it was a done deal, she would work to stop it. It was exactly what Gordon wanted to hear.[47]

Laura Clay drew a line in the sand that spring, a decision that had less to do with deep philosophical principles, or even with racism (although Clay was content to limit the vote to white women). Her resistance had more to do with her fading identity as a suffrage leader. Her role in KERA had shrunk since she turned the reins over to Madeline McDowell Breckinridge in 1912, and she could see that she was becoming less and less relevant with every passing year. When Kate Gordon offered her a chance to become the hero of southern resistance, she jumped at it.

Clay could see that the suffrage movement, her life's work, the root of her identity, was reaching its end and reaching it in a manner that she had vowed would never work. A fierce sense of commitment and a willingness to go against the grain seemed to be hardwired into members of the Clay family. Her father had been ready to fight to the death for abolition; she was prepared to do the same for suffrage, but only on her terms. There was "an element of melodrama" in Clay's resistance to the Nineteenth Amendment, historian Claudia Knott concludes. Perhaps for her, like her father, "the fight was everything and she could not bear to end it."[48]

When Carrie Chapman Catt announced that she would make a return visit to Kentucky in June 1918, Clay prepared again to face off. Catt would be giving war lectures in four cities, but Clay knew she had an ulterior motive for coming to the Commonwealth. She was really coming to generate "home pressure" on behalf of the amendment. Catt ended her Lexington speech by urging listeners to support a resolution endorsing federal suffrage action. The large crowd, swept along by the spirit of the moment, roared its approval. Only one negative vote was heard, but it rang out very clearly. "That was the one I cast," Laura Clay later reported to Kate Gordon.[49]

Clay no longer cared whether Kentucky suffragists presented a united front. After Catt left town, she penned an editorial explaining the dangers of the amendment and asked Desha Breckinridge to publish it in the *Lexington Herald*. Now, he was in a pickle. He was afraid that Clay's outburst would hurt the cause so dear to his wife's heart and that it would hurt Miss Clay's reputation. In a response laced with chivalry, he demurred. He would publish her piece if she insisted, but he felt he must be "frank." Her opposition would jeopardize the suffrage amendment, which he supported, and besides, with the war under way he had very little room left for other news. Paper and manpower were scarce. She would be doing him a favor, he humbly concluded, if she would withdraw her request, which she did.[50]

Clay's resistance to the amendment, once reasoned and measured, became shrill and downright paranoid by June 1918. Harmonizing her tune to that of Kate Gordon, she now argued that the Anthony Amendment, and the "inexperienced" women voters it would add to the electorate, were a threat to national security. Depending on her audience, it was "German Propaganda," the work of "collusion," or a plot by Republicans in the West to shore up their influence with Japanese voters driving the amendment. Voting women would introduce Bolshevism and socialism, she warned. Clay's arguments did not just highlight the weaknesses of the federal amendment, they raised serious questions about women's fitness to ever vote by any means.[51]

So long as the Senate did not pass the suffrage amendment, they were safe, Clay believed. After the Senate voted the measure down again in October 1918, the KERA board agreed to write an open letter to Kentucky senator J. C. W. Beckham, protesting his recent negative vote. Condemning this action as a partisan move and a violation of KERA's policies, Clay immediately resigned from the organization that she had founded. She didn't seem to really want to cut ties, however. She insisted that her resignation be put to a vote of the board. After they asked her to remain on the board, which she surely expected, she calmed down and withdrew her resignation.[52]

Clay would not abandon KERA, at least not yet, but she would not bend either. She remained firmly opposed to the Nineteenth Amendment, even as her KERA colleagues and others vigorously denied that it would undermine white supremacy. States' rights was a morally suspect position that only served the Antis anyway, they declared. Why else would lawmakers who had refused to consider a suffrage amendment on states' rights grounds support a prohibition amendment? (Clay later rationalized that a prohibition amendment, which she supported, was acceptable because it dealt with interstate commerce).[53]

Southerners' concern that a suffrage amendment would destroy their way of life was overblown, Catt and others argued. Giving women the vote would only lead to black rule "if the white race . . . is a puny, pusillanimous and degenerate one." A NAWSA publication asked, "If your race is superior, what do you fear?" But Clay did fear what it would do, both to the South and to her personally.[54]

KERA's next convention was sure to produce some fireworks. The influenza crisis, which began killing millions across the globe in fall 1918, provided an excellent excuse to postpone the inevitable confrontation. The quarantine was lifted in time to meet the following March, but few attended. In recent years, there had been over one hundred delegates at the annual convention; now, just thirty-six came. Once again, they had to consider the pesky question of whether to pursue a state constitutional amendment at the next session, and again, they kicked the decision down the road. It made sense, they agreed, to wait until the National met later that month and to send a representative to St. Louis to seek NAWSA's blessing. If they got the go-ahead, the executive board could authorize a campaign.[55]

KERA leaders did not shut the door on a state amendment, likely because they wanted to pacify Miss Clay, but all signs indicated that they would support a federal amendment over any other strategy, especially now that speedy and successful passage in the Sixty-Sixth Congress seemed assured. Alben W. Barkley, US representative from Kentucky's first district, promised women that he and his colleagues would pass the amendment at the "first opportunity." J. Campbell Cantrill, nemesis turned friend, followed by seeking forgiveness for "the sins of his past." Suffragists should begin to work "with the end in view," he encouraged.[56]

KERA delegates followed that advice. They voted to organize study classes to train new women voters. When it came time to elect a chair of a state campaign, they agreed to leave the position vacant. For president, the delegates elected Madeline McDowell Breckinridge, who was fully on record as backing federal enfranchisement.[57]

Now that Madge's doctors had declared her cured of tuberculosis, she was eager to cash in on her bill of good health to secure the vote. Women could only "fight the battles of civilization," she argued, if they had "every aid and advantage that men have had." They must have the ballot, and Breckinridge was sure that the federal amendment was the way to get it. The sooner, the better. She had other things she wanted to do.[58]

Breckinridge did not feel like going to St. Louis in March 1918 to present the "Kentucky matter" at the NAWSA convention, but a promise was a promise. It was not just the cost of the trip that bothered her; it was the inconvenience of it. Returning from the KERA convention in Louisville with her good friend Mary Lebus (who also happened to be her husband's mistress), she had been involved in a serious car accident. Now, just ten days later, Breckinridge admitted she was not strong enough to travel to St. Louis alone. Jessie Hutchinson, a fellow Lexington suffragist, agreed to accompany her so she would have someone to comb the tangles out of her hair and button her dress. Dutifully, Madge mustered her strength, presented the situation to the National, and then reported back its decision: the National wanted them to put a state campaign on hold, at least until after the Senate reconsidered the amendment in an upcoming special session. The KERA board acquiesced to its request.[59]

Then, in June 1919, the moment for which most suffragists waited arrived. The House had renewed its approval of the Nineteenth Amendment, and the Senate was preparing to vote again. Suffragists knew better than to hold their breath. They had the votes, but illness, death, or fraud could interfere again. While suffragists prepared for the disappointment of defeat, which always seemed to come, Clay braced for the disappointment of success. She had done everything she could to block the amendment. Now, the only thing to do was to wait. It was in God's hands, Clay reminded Miss Gordon.[60]

The US Senate met in special session on June 4, 1919, finally approving the measure introduced forty-one years earlier. In its understated way, the *History of Woman Suffrage* documents the milestone: "Thus ended the struggle for the submission to the Legislature of an amendment to the National Constitution . . . a struggle that has no parallels in history." Kentucky's A. O. Stanley voted in favor. J. C. W. Beckham stood opposed to the end. Women were "entirely too good" for the ballot, he continued to maintain.[61]

Clay had already considered what she would do if this moment came. Now that it was here, she did not hesitate to act. On June 5, the morning newspapers delivered the blow. "SENATE VOTES FOR SUFFRAGE; MAJORITY IS TWO," the *Courier-Journal*'s front-page headline announced. The Nineteenth Amendment would be added to the Constitution as long as thirty-six state legislatures agreed to ratify.[62]

Clay immediately loaded a piece of paper into her typewriter and addressed a note to Madeline McDowell Breckinridge, her friend and president of KERA. Dispensing with formalities, she composed a crisp letter of resignation. KERA's priorities were no longer her own. To continue her involvement would be "inconsistent" with her principles. Now that the amendment had passed, KERA would be focused solely on its ratification, which its constitution did not allow and which was a prospect Clay could not stomach. She followed this letter with a second one, echoing the same points, and resigning her position as president of the Fayette E.R.A. With those unpleasant tasks out of the way she prepared to start her workday.[63]

Barely a mile away on Linden Walk, Madeline McDowell Breckinridge was also beginning her day. Her scan of the newspapers brought a spasm of joy rather than a feeling of gloom, though she felt similarly daunted by the hard work that lay ahead. Miss Clay was ready to stop ratification at all costs. Madge was ready to sacrifice her last energy to see it succeed. Kentucky's two talented and committed suffrage leaders would go head-to-head, but only one of them would lead Kentucky to victory. It promised to be a historic showdown.

13

Twenty-Four

The doctor may have declared her cured, but those close to Madge Breckinridge could see that she remained far from healthy in 1919. She was entering what she hoped would be the final stages of the fight for voting rights, and she would need all the strength she could muster, especially since she was now fighting not only chauvinistic men and close-minded anti-suffragists. She was battling with her friend and mentor, Miss Clay.

Clay's colleagues in the National were astonished by the turn of events they witnessed. "It is too dreadful to believe," NAWSA president Carrie Chapman Catt confided to Breckinridge. She wondered if her old friend was quite in her right mind. How could a "splendid woman" like Clay work for a lifetime to win the vote only to turn around and fight it?[1]

Closer to home, Kentucky suffragists were also dismayed by the developing schism, but they were not surprised by it. Clay had been threatening to jump ship for many months. Still, it was hard to fathom a Kentucky suffrage movement without her. Miss Clay—the "original woman suffragist," the woman who had "mothered and nursed the equal rights movement through its infancy and its days of unpopularity in Kentucky"—would not be with them as they crossed the finish line.[2]

As president of KERA, Madge Breckinridge knew it was up to her to marshal her forces, to prevent additional defections, and to bring home victory. Leading Kentucky into the ratification column would require expert skill and massive energy, especially under these strained circumstances. Breckinridge had the skill. The energy was another matter.

No one could predict how many suffragists Clay would take with her when she resigned on June 5, but events during the spring of 1919 made Breckinridge think the damage could be great. Support for states' rights suffrage seemed to be growing, so much so that Madge compared Kentucky to Sodom and Gomorrah. God had destroyed those Biblical cities when he could find not one faithful soul. In Kentucky's case, not one "federal suffragist" appeared to remain. In March, loyalists had nominated Clay for several state offices at the annual KERA convention. She declined to stand for election there, but she agreed to serve as the Fayette E.R.A.'s president. If she wanted to lead suffragists astray, directing one of the state's largest locals positioned her to do so.[3]

In May, even as the Anthony Amendment remained hypothetical, Clay began to rally her forces. Kentucky suffragists had kept their feud quiet until now, but no longer. State Republicans were meeting to write their party platform, and KERA representatives hoped the party would put its full weight behind the Anthony Amendment. Clay instead wanted it to uphold its 1916 pledge to support suffrage by state means only. Accompanied by about fifteen Lexington suffragists, she went to the convention, not as a representative of KERA, but as head of a separate "committee of citizens." Party leaders ultimately pledged to support suffrage by any means, just as KERA wished, but the rogue force's appearance reminded Breckinridge that Clay and her supporters were a valid threat.[4]

Though she had hoped the day would never come, Clay was prepared when the Senate passed the amendment and she set her plan in motion on June 5. She had considered aligning her counterinsurgency with the Southern States Woman Suffrage Conference (which, according to historian Elna Green, existed "only in the person of Kate Gordon" after 1917), but just as quickly she dismissed the idea, afraid that its racist reputation would not play well in a border state like Kentucky. Bringing in the "negro question" was likely to confuse the issue and divide its friends, she admitted.[5]

Instead, she invited opponents of the "Anthony so-called suffrage amendment" to join a new Citizens Committee for a State Suffrage Amendment, an independent organization designed to be the "voice of the people." The great majority of suffragists, she claimed (offering no verifiable proof), had never asked for a federal amendment; it was the work of only a few national and state associations. Her group would pursue suffrage, but by a "safer and saner" route, Clay promised—"self-government as laid down by the framers of the United States Constitution."[6]

Three dissenters, all officers of the Fayette E.R.A., attended the Citizens Committee's inaugural meeting on June 11, exactly one week after the amendment's passage. They jotted their battle plan down on recycled KERA stationery. Each woman, like Clay, resigned from KERA and pledged to do everything in her power to defeat the amendment. It would be a small force, Clay reported to Kate Gordon, but she consoled herself that "numbers are not what we need." A "working committee" was enough.[7]

Clay's "faithful followers"—Alice Bronston Oldham, Dunster Gibson Foster, and Elizabeth Burgess McQuaid—had several things in common. They were all officers in the Fayette E.R.A., they all had husbands who agreed that women should vote but only by state means, and they all had strong Confederate or Democratic ties.[8]

Dunster Gibson Foster was, aside from Clay, the most visible and outspoken member of the committee. Her roots were in central Kentucky—she proudly claimed heritage in several pioneer families—but she spent most of her adult life in the Midwest and West. Her husband, Harrison Gardner Foster, was a successful coal and timber baron, enterprises that required the family to bounce between St. Paul and Tacoma. Foster's residency on the West Coast meant that she became a legal voter when Washington became the fifth state to enact woman suffrage in 1910. By 1919, she had years of voting experience under her belt, and she had even served as a delegate to the Democratic National Convention in 1916, distinctions that she wore like a badge of honor when she moved back to Kentucky. Better than other women, she argued, she knew the importance of voting, but she was willing to forgo the right if gaining it meant squandering American liberties.[9]

Breckinridge need not have worried that Clay's exit would substantially thin KERA's ranks. Her best efforts to recruit Kentuckians to join the Citizens Committee failed miserably. It had the trappings of a viable organization—a headquarters in Mrs. Oldham's son's building supply store and eventually its own letterhead—but it never formed additional locals across the state as Clay intended. In fact, it never grew beyond its original membership of four.[10]

Miss Clay's influence had evaporated, leaving her a relic instead of a revolutionary.

The "Laura Clay Movement," though small, still created serious headaches for Breckinridge. Steering Kentucky toward ratification was challenging enough without Miss Clay making it harder. Too often, Breckinridge found herself a step behind her rival in the race to pin down lawmakers. KERA members might not agree with a thing she said, but they had to admit that Miss Clay was "magnificent" when denouncing the Nineteenth Amendment. No one could deny that her powers of persuasion remained intact, even if her sanity seemed questionable.[11]

Clay believed the best way to thwart the federal amendment was to get states to pass their own amendments as quickly as possible. Then, federal action would be unnecessary. Clay was undaunted by her own admission

Suffragists pointed to Dunster Foster (center) and her husband, Harrison Gardner Foster, to argue that giving women the vote would not disrupt homes. The Fosters disagreed on politics while remaining "entirely congenial," the *Chicago Daily News* reported. (Library of Congress)

that, based on the number of states added in 1918, it would take eleven years to complete the task. Momentum, she cheerfully surmised, was in their favor. She called on legislators and governors both in her home state and in key western states (she assumed that southerners already knew the magnitude of the situation), imploring them to enfranchise their mothers, wives, and sisters rather than relying on the federal government to do so. "We know the Men of Kentucky will do this for us," Clay sweet-talked.[12]

Time was of the essence. With every state that ratified the Anthony Amendment—and within a month, eleven already had—their states' rights fight became less winnable. Clay pledged to do something she had never done before. She told her "fellow sufferer" Kate Gordon she would stay in Lexington instead of spending harvest season at her farm to focus her energies on their cause. Besides, staying in Lexington would allow her to deal with another pressing headache: she had recently learned that the US Treasury Department was auditing her taxes.[13]

Clay promised to fight the good fight, but she could not do it alone. She relied heavily on her three lieutenants to champion their cause. Together, they made sure that every Kentucky legislator and legislative candidate received a copy of their open letter. Foster and Oldham visited as many central Kentucky towns as possible to sway election results. Helping candidates who supported states' rights suffrage win in November was their best way to avoid ratification. Additionally, Foster wrote to governors and legislators out West, since she was well-connected there.[14]

Breckinridge insisted that most Kentucky legislators backed the federal amendment, and she had a promise from current Democratic governor James D. Black that he was ready to support ratification. Still, she knew she could not take any chances. For a time, she had toyed with trying to get a special legislative session called in fall 1919 to bring their fight to an early end, but Mrs. Catt advised against such a move. There was no need for a special session unless Kentucky could become the thirty-sixth state, and that was highly unlikely. With Kentucky's next regular session coming soon in January 1920, it made sense just to let nature take its course, but that would require more effort to keep lawmakers pointed in the right direction and out of Miss Clay's clutches. Clay was beating the bushes, and Breckinridge would have to do the same.[15]

Breckinridge set out with Mary Scrugham, a Lexington teacher and history PhD candidate, on July 4 to promote the amendment in eastern Kentucky. Shaping the incoming legislature was their priority, but along the way they organized new KERA chapters in coal towns like Jenkins and

Mary Scrugham became a history teacher after her graduation from the University of Kentucky in 1906. Here, she appears as a "co-ed," posing in the Chi Epsilon Chi sorority house. (University of Kentucky Special Collections)

McRoberts, for good measure. Breckinridge and Scrugham's interest in these areas was as much about educating new voters as it was about creating suffragists, since that role was hopefully soon to be obsolete. Citizenship training was Scrugham's passion. When KERA began creating "suffrage schools" across the state in the fall of 1919, she developed the curriculum.[16]

Scrugham and Breckinridge's tour was productive but exhausting. They rose at dawn and traveled continuously, speaking in a different town each afternoon and evening. Madge's sister-in-law, Sophonisba, compared the rigor of the tour to the travels she made back in 1915, before her TB got the better of her.[17]

Clay meanwhile was also doing everything in her power to fashion a legislature that would favor her position. She rejoiced when she heard that Governor Black had shut down the possibility of holding a special session. He was a "Governor Who Can't Be Driven at the Crack of the Suffrage Whip," she cooed, sounding a lot like anti-suffragists. The way she saw it, every week that passed without a vote on the amendment gave her more time to talk sense into Kentuckians who might be tempted to pursue suffrage "Any Old Way," instead of the right way.[18]

Clay held out hope that the Kentucky Democratic Party, her party, would honor its principles and its 1916 pledge to pursue suffrage by state means only. She could have gone to the Democratic state convention in September as a delegate—its first female delegate—but at the last minute she decided to go as a representative of the Citizens Committee instead.

Clay was disappointed by the outcome. Woodrow Wilson sent a telegram urging his fellow Democrats to "serve mankind and the party" by supporting the Anthony Amendment, and they complied with his request. They did, however, promise to pursue a state suffrage amendment if ratification looked unlikely, offering Clay at least a glimmer of hope.[19]

KERA members and Citizens Committee representatives were locked in a zero-sum game throughout the fall of 1919, and they found themselves forced to meet awkwardly in the same spaces as they sought lawmakers' support. KERA matched Clay tit for tat, sending its own large delegation to the Democratic Convention. Observers who had not followed news of the schism closely must have scratched their heads, wondering why suffragists seemed to be at war with each other.[20]

Suffragists themselves struggled to understand the finer points that divided them. Alice Lloyd, firmly in the federal camp but seeking to appreciate Miss Clay's concerns, wondered whether she really had her argument down fully or if she had "just enough of it not to understand." Another colleague who struggled to grasp the heart of the matter concluded that Clay saw things differently because she had a "lawyer's head," and others did not.[21]

A public debate could resolve the confusion, leaders decided. Clay and Breckinridge agreed to go head-to-head. They were originally slated to meet at the Democratic Convention, but Madge's worsening health interfered, requiring her to rest during most of August and September. Maysville's Alice Lloyd offered to stand in for her KERA colleague, but for reasons unclear, the plan was scrapped at the last minute. Instead, Clay and Breckinridge would match wits in October.[22]

Kentucky's two most famous suffragists met on October 18, 1919, at the Woman's Club of Central Kentucky to consider the merits of the Nineteenth Amendment. Miss Clay went first, arguing that it was unnecessary to change the fundamental law of the nation to give women the vote when it could be accomplished through the states. Worse, the US Constitution would be desecrated to secure an unsatisfactory form of suffrage. The federal amendment might invalidate state election clauses that denied women the vote, but it would leave the word "male" in place to serve as a "silent witness" that men and women still were not equal before the law.[23]

Clay spent most of her allotted time discussing the amendment's "Enforcement Act," which she claimed made women "a pawn in a sinister political game." The party in power would be able—and you could be sure it would happen, she thundered, since power always corrupts—to railroad elections, skirt the checks that framers so wisely included, and overthrow American democracy. It was a skillful piece of fearmongering, enough to win her victory over Breckinridge, though the judges, an assortment of lawyers, law school deans, and local businessmen, reported that their decision was not unanimous.[24]

Following the debate, the victorious Clay published her remarks in a pamphlet. She did not include Breckinridge's points, nor does a specific record of what the younger woman said that day survive. One assumes that she repeated claims she had made over and over when asked to defend the federal amendment. She undoubtedly challenged claims that this amendment, or any amendment for that matter, violated states' rights since three-fourths of the states were required to ratify. "In fact, the method of amendment . . . is a distinct acknowledgement of the principle of States' Rights," she explained. It was too late to start quibbling with the amendment process now anyway, Madge insisted. That ship had sailed.[25]

Breckinridge dismissed comparisons of the Nineteenth Amendment to the hated Fifteenth Amendment, though she agreed it had been a mistake. States had been coerced to ratify the Reconstruction amendments as a condition to reenter the Union, but now states were free to act independently. Attempts to draw parallels between the two amendments, a favorite point of Miss Clay, were misguided according to Breckinridge. She likewise dismissed concerns about the so-called enforcing clause. The first article to the Constitution already provided Congress all the powers it needed to uphold the Constitution, she crisply reminded.[26]

One suspects there was no mention of race during the debate, though anyone familiar with the matter understood its relevance. Clay rarely referenced the impact the amendment would have on the race question in her home state, reserving that point for other audiences. Breckinridge certainly let the matter lie. She had nothing to gain by playing the race card, and though she was on the side of justice and hoped that one day black women would prove themselves excellent citizens alongside white women, she was a pragmatist who believed it best to fight only one battle at a time.[27]

Breckinridge was a Progressive at her core with a deep desire to improve society. To do that, women must have the ballot. Was any other argument needed? There is no way to know if she ended her remarks with this point, but in her mind, it was the most important reason of all. The Nineteenth Amendment was the most efficient route to the vote, and women with the vote would be a force for good.[28]

On her good days, Breckinridge optimistically imagined her state sailing through the ratification process to victory. The odds appeared in their favor. Both contenders for governor, Black, the Democrat, and Edwin P. Morrow, the Republican—had pledged to fast-track ratification. But on her bad days, Breckinridge worried that she was wasting her time. In December she reported to Catt that she was working "all day and a good part of the night—much against my will" to secure ratification, but she could not help but be uneasy about what lay ahead in January. She was having a hard time forgiving and forgetting what Clay had done to the movement, she admitted.[29]

Breckinridge knew better than to become complacent. Kentucky was, after all, a southern state in its soul, and the South had made its position clear: it would stand united against the Nineteenth Amendment. So far, results showed they meant business. Suffragists across the country were following ratification news carefully—Georgia, no. Alabama, no. Doing the math, they knew they could sustain only so many losses before their work was sunk. The first states had come like a nice steady rainfall, but now it had switched to a slow drizzle. Who knew when the rain might stop?[30]

The election of Edwin P. Morrow, sworn into office on December 9, 1919, helped boost Breckinridge's spirits. He was a devoted champion of woman suffrage, a first cousin of former KERA president Christine Bradley South, and a good friend of Madge and Desha. Following a meeting with Morrow on December 18, Breckinridge reported that her confidence was higher than it had been even a week earlier. She was sure that Morrow would deliver the Republican vote, and polls indicated enough pledged Democrats to make ratification all but guaranteed. Madge had originally intended to wait until the second week of the session to introduce their bill, but she decided to go for it on the first day instead. It would be an unprecedented accomplishment, if they managed to pull it off.[31]

Breckinridge's forces were not the only ones ready to ring in the New Year with a suffrage victory. So were representatives of the National Woman's Party. Paul's organization had kept a low profile in Kentucky during the war. Only a handful of Louisville women claimed membership in its militant forces. The NWP continued to scandalize throughout 1919, staging "riotous scenes" in front of the White House and burning Woodrow Wilson in effigy. They were "unwomanly and reprehensible" creatures, according to most Kentucky suffragists.[32]

Not surprisingly, the NWP's announcement that it was sending two organizers to the Bluegrass in December to assist ratification rankled KERA members. They urged Breckinridge to respond on their behalf. The NWP would bring unwanted controversy at a moment when their cause could ill afford it. Plus, it seemed unfair that outsiders should steal their thunder. Breckinridge, however, refused to denounce the NWP. She did not plan to ask for their help, but she would not fight them either. "The less said, the better," she concluded.[33]

Three groups of white women would be ready in early January to watch lawmakers decide their fate. Three distinct groups of women who shared the same goal—to make women voters—would congregate separately in Frankfort in a few weeks, each endorsing very different strategies.

Was victory as certain as it seemed? Breckinridge was holding her breath. There was no way to tell what Miss Clay had up her sleeve.

Tuesday, January 6, 1920, dawned a cold but promising morning. The Kentucky legislature was set to convene, and it was sure to be a historic day, a day that many women had been anticipating for years or even decades. Suffrage pioneers like Susan Look Avery, Mary Cramer, and Sarah Sawyer, faithful until the end, had not lived long enough to see victory. Others, like Mrs. Farmer, had left Kentucky years before. The small but mighty Josephine Henry never mended fences with the movement, and though she may have celebrated privately, she would not share in the glory. Of KERA's original "big three," only Miss Clay would be a witness, and she would not be celebrating.

KERA hoped to flood the galleries of the legislature with its representatives. For efficiency's sake, Breckinridge timed the final KERA convention —a "victory convention"—to coincide with the session's start. Suffragists would gather in Lexington the night before to kick things off. The next morning, they would travel to Frankfort on a special interurban train. Members of the Franklin County E.R.A. would meet them and serve them lunch at the YWCA. Well fed, they would make their way to the capitol. They did not want to miss a minute of the action. The new governor was slated to do something novel: he would offer his opening address to the general assembly in person rather than in writing.[34]

Morrow hoped to shake Frankfort from its lethargy, and he carefully chose his words to inspire action. Kentucky stood at "the parting of the ways—it must go forward or it must go backward," Morrow insisted. He called for funding good roads, tax reform, curtailing mob violence, and finally, the point that made the women erupt: creating a government "of the people by the people" by ratifying the Nineteenth Amendment. Party loyalty and chivalry required the assembled gentlemen not just to act but to act fast. Morrow encouraged them to "break all previous speed records" to finally secure justice.[35]

Usually it took the legislature time to get its ducks in a row at the start of the session, at least a couple of days to get past the how do you dos and to get down to work. Electing presiding officers normally consumed the first day. But this year, the assembly hit the ground running. Kentucky might just set a speed record for ratification after all. It would not be easy, but Kentucky lawmakers seemed eager to try.[36]

The House, with its Republican majority, would be no problem. Joseph Lazarus of Louisville introduced the suffrage resolution there, and it passed 71 to 25 in just seventeen minutes. But the same bill hit a snag when it went to the Democratic-controlled Senate and got caught in states' rights forces' snares. Three senators took the floor to present the danger in the starkest terms possible, though due to cloture, they only had fifteen minutes each to present their tales of doom. "Caesar and the dead empire of Rome were called up from the seventh century to typify the inevitable result of indulging a federal government," the *Lexington Herald* reported. States' righters tried one final time to substitute a state amendment for a federal one, confusing freshman senators in the process. The "veritable state of bewilderment" that followed made the final vote count anticlimactic. "It was several minutes before many of those present, both among the spectators in the gallery and legislators on the floor, realized that the ratification was an accomplished fact." The final tally: thirty in favor, eight opposed.[37]

And with that, shortly after four o'clock, Kentucky "stepped into the suffrage line." Breckinridge had achieved a historic first-day passage. News came in that Rhode Island ratified just minutes before Kentucky. With states twenty-three and twenty-four added in a single magnificent day, there would be much for suffragists—with the exception, of course, of Clay and her supporters—to celebrate that night.[38]

14

An Instrument to Help Humanity

Ratification week passed in a blur. On Tuesday evening, following a quiet celebratory dinner at Ashland, elated suffragists and community members gathered at the Phoenix Hotel to hear Democratic and Republican Party leaders woo the victorious women. Wednesday brought an afternoon reception, a larger banquet, followed by a historic address by infamous British suffragette Emmeline Pankhurst at the Opera House. Madge had invited Pankhurst despite Carrie Catt's reservations. She was the "best Barnum circus drawing-card" they could find, and her war work had replaced "the bad odor of militancy" she once carried, Breckinridge reasoned.[1]

It was not all play that week, however; the victorious suffragists had work to finish. On Wednesday morning, they reconvened at the Phoenix to conduct the business of their thirtieth and hopefully final convention. Kentucky had ratified, but there was no certainty that the other necessary twelve states would follow. Ratification could happen quickly, or it might not succeed at all. KERA delegates strategized what to do either way. They agreed that they would ask the Kentucky legislature for one more thing that session: they would ask it to pass a bill giving women presidential suffrage. That way, no matter what, they could vote in November.[2]

Their most pressing decision involved what to do when ratification finally became a fait accompli. With ratification still incomplete, KERA had a continuing, though reduced purpose, but soon, if all went as planned, its reason to exist would be entirely gone. What then? Delegates voted unanimously that when this happened, it would become the Kentucky League of Woman Voters, an organization committed to making sure women used their new privilege effectively. A committee began writing a new constitution.[3]

On Thursday, with their hard work concluded, they returned to Frankfort to attend the bill signing. Suffragists packed the room carrying pennants and sporting sashes, and Morrow added his signature, with Madeline Breckinridge and his wife, Katherine, peering over his shoulder.

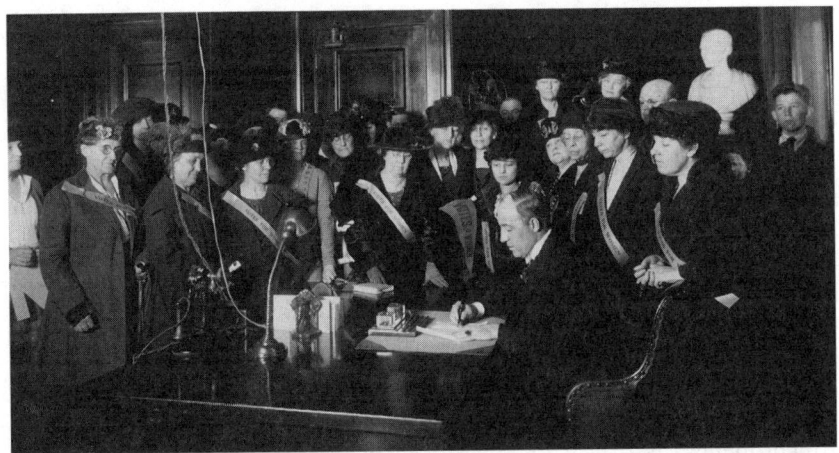

KERA paused its convention business to allow members to travel to Frankfort on January 6, 1920, to watch Gov. Edwin P. Morrow sign the Anthony Amendment, making Kentucky the twenty-fourth state to ratify. Suffragists, including Madeline McDowell Breckinridge, Caroline Leech, Josephine Fowler Post, Eleanor Offut, Rebecca Judah, Jessie Firth, Frances Riker, Fannie Rawson, Jessie O. Yancey, Virginia McDowell, and Katherine Morrow, among others, witnessed the historic event. (Library of Congress)

As suffragists across the country waited to see history made in the spring of 1920, they grappled with how to record that history. Work on volume six of the massive *History of Woman Suffrage* began, and Catt announced she would present certificates to every current and past state president at NAWSA's upcoming conference in Chicago. But writing an ending to the movement raised sticky issues. Catt solicited Breckinridge for guidance: "Whatever are we going to do about Laura Clay?" It did not seem quite right to honor a woman who "ceased to march forward" with them "when the last turn of the road was reached," but omitting her did not feel right, either.[4]

Even though Miss Laura had caused more headaches for Madge Breckinridge than for anyone else, the younger woman graciously urged that her place in history be determined by her lifetime of work rather than her final actions. Breckinridge remained on friendly terms with Clay. She even asked her to check over the Kentucky report before she submitted it for inclusion in the official NAWSA history. Clay added a few names and corrected several details. Her most substantial suggestion concerned her colleague's claim that the Kentucky movement had been brought to a "successful close" with ratification. Clay believed that the report should begin by noting that they had failed to accomplish their main purpose—a state amendment—a suggestion that Breckinridge quietly ignored.[5]

Kentucky had ratified the Anthony Amendment, which should have signaled the matter closed, but weeks later Clay was still gunning for a state amendment. The Nineteenth Amendment would make women voters, but it would not make them "the political peers of men," she emphasized. The word "male" was still emblazoned in the state constitution and would remain there symbolically taunting women even after it lost its force. The federal amendment, Clay noted, placed white women in a protected class with "negroes and other colored races." Only a state amendment could fix this indignity. Clay denied charges that her opposition to the Nineteenth Amendment was driven by racism, an accusation she heard often. She would oppose the Nineteenth Amendment even if there "were not a [single] negro voter in the country," she insisted. It was clear to many of her peers, however, that race absolutely mattered to Clay.[6]

Throughout the 1920 session, Laura Clay made good on her promise to Kate Gordon that she would fight to defeat the Nineteenth Amendment until no possible hope remained. A few Kentucky lawmakers were happy to play along and introduced Clay's legislation. Governor Morrow sought Breckinridge's counsel. Did she want the state amendment bill to go forward? Kill it in committee, Breckinridge urged. It was "too late by about 127 years."[7]

In the spring of 1920, while Laura Clay remained fixated on defeating the Nineteenth Amendment, everyone else moved on to considering the changes it would bring. Many predicted that it would be business as usual come fall. Women would stay home or just vote like their husbands did. Others predicted that women would band together to trigger comprehensive reform.

Male politicians were especially uneasy now that the rules of the political game had changed. Both parties hoped to secure the allegiance of women voters, who numbered some fourteen million across the country and more than half a million in Kentucky. "Hardly was the Amendment ratified," the *Woman Citizen* reported, "when the political leaders began showering marked attention upon the suffragists." Republican and Democratic leaders clamored to be the first to congratulate KERA delegates on their victory and to welcome them into their ranks.[8]

Republicans and Democrats alike offered women a place at the table, but they did so by providing constant reminders that women were newcomers and a novelty. Nearly every district sent at least one female delegate to the state party conventions in March 1920. Mrs. Annie Simms Banks, a schoolteacher, noted "race worker," and wife of a well-known publisher, made history by becoming the first black woman to serve at the Republican state convention. The "lady from Clark [County]" was treated just like any other delegate, *New York Age* reported, ignoring the fact that by highlighting her attendance, observers reinforced that she was *not* like any other delegate.[9]

Republicans and Democrats, acting as if women had been welcomed all along, competed to see who could lure the most to their national conventions. Only three women attended the 1916 Republican convention (in an official capacity); 160 would be included this time, party officials bragged. The women would be conspicuous in a sea of bald and gray heads, kind of "like a silk hat in the bleachers of the ballpark," one news outlet suggested. These were not "debutantes" or "frivolous" women. They were serious politicians, and leaders in their communities. But they were still women and the strain might be too much. "Rest rooms" would be available, just in case, news coverage assured.[10]

Democrats promised to do Republicans one better. They would give women *equal* representation at their national convention in San Francisco—one woman for every man—surpassing the small "handful" that the RNC attracted. Democrats fulfilled their pledge in some states, but in Kentucky they could not quite bring themselves to split things fifty-fifty. Leaders finally agreed to double the number of at-large delegates, giving each half a vote, and then named women to fill three of the eight slots. One of the slots went to Laura Clay.[11]

Clay had passed up an opportunity to become Kentucky's first female delegate at the 1919 state Democratic convention, citing her nonpartisan principles, but now she wanted very badly to go to San Francisco. A chance to convince so many influential men to support state suffrage, even if it meant crossing a continent to do so, did not come often.

Clay made the trip but found it a supreme disappointment. The National Association Opposed to Woman Suffrage—no longer her rival, but an ally—claimed Clay was "strangled," while "the Koreans, the Hindus, and whatnot" got to speak. Clay did not win support for state suffrage, but she could at least boast that she had been nominated for US president. She

Kentucky delegates to the 1920 Democratic National Convention take time out of official duties to have a little fun. Laura Clay is at the far left, Nora Layne of Fort Thomas is beside her, and Cora Wilson Stewart is in the center. (Photo courtesy of John Rhorer)

and fellow female delegate from Kentucky, Moonlight Schools' founder, Cora Wilson Stewart, each received one vote.[12]

Heading into the fall, both parties leaned heavily on female speakers to agitate for their candidates. Former KERA president Christine Bradley South became Republican candidate Warren G. Harding's main Kentucky spokesperson. A "soft voiced southern woman," with luminous auburn curls, milky white skin, and a bit of a "spicy temper," South had "literally grown up in politics." She stressed to female audiences that it was up to them to "turn the tide" and stop future calamities by choosing the right candidate. She urged them to oppose American participation in the League of Nations, which she warned would force mothers to sacrifice their sons to fight other nations' wars. Fellow KERA officer, Julia Duke Henning, argued just the opposite. To prevent war, women must vote Democratic. They must support James M. Cox.[13]

Parties understood that they had to speak women's language, and there was no better way to do that than to have women speak to other women. Campaigning had always been something of a sport for Kentucky men.

It was rough and rowdy—a thoroughly masculine pursuit. But with women's addition to the electorate, it would have to change. Taking the stump would never be the same again.

The addition of female voters to the electorate coincided with the end of World War I, a moment when America shook with turmoil. "100% Americanism" became the rallying cry, and hypernationalism was at its peak. New immigration restrictions were gaining favor. Bolshevism and anarchy appeared poised to destroy American democracy, and a Red Scare was under way. It was perhaps not the best time to be adding millions of new voters to the rolls.

Women might be inexperienced, but they promised that they would not arrive at the polls unprepared. Citizenship schools, designed to educate new voters, proliferated in the spring and summer of 1920. Hosted by black and white school groups, civic organizations, and women's clubs, these programs indicated that women would vote and that they would do so with an unprecedented seriousness of purpose. Most citizenship classes, like one held in Owensboro that spring, followed a fifteen-week curriculum developed by KERA's Mary Scrugham. Students read and digested the Constitution, they considered current social problems, and they reviewed the basics of American government and history.[14]

African American women, just like white women, wanted to be ready when it came time to cast their ballots, but their efforts to prepare themselves raised alarm in some communities, particularly in western Kentucky. Democrats feared anything that would encourage black women, known for being staunch Republicans, to register. It would not matter whether there were many more white voters than black voters across the country if the oft-repeated prediction—black women would vote, and white women would stay home—proved true. Kentucky was a two-party state, and it had never disfranchised blacks like its Deep South neighbors, making black women voters "a live issue."[15]

White women, suffragists or not, had a responsibility to "rally to the standard" and to register, Democrats urged. If Republicans won in the fall, taking the presidency and control of the Senate, apathetic white women in the border states would shoulder the blame. Voting was not a privilege; it was a matter of "self-preservation," the *Owensboro Messenger* warned.[16]

Black women had not been active in Kentucky's suffrage movement for several decades, choosing to prioritize other reforms instead, especially

Poll workers from the National Association of Colored Women prepare new voters in Louisville, 1920. (University of Louisville Archives)

when it became clear that white suffragists did not welcome cooperation. But now that they had a new weapon in their arsenal, they planned to use it to full advantage. In October 1920, the *Owensboro Messenger* reported that around one thousand black women had "flocked to the polls en masse" to register on the first day. "Negro" women, the paper claimed, were not registering for altruistic reasons or even on their own volition. Democratic leaders blamed the Republican Party for injecting the race issue into the election, promising black voters rights, and encouraging hatred.[17]

Relying on a strategy used time and time again to discredit social movements, the paper blamed high black registration numbers on outsiders, notably northern women who had entered Kentucky just to stir up trouble. Supposedly, they had offered black men and women "joy rides" in fancy cars in exchange for registering, a strategy that not only unfairly tilted registration numbers but that also led African Americans to want to climb beyond their social station, the *Messenger* warned. The fact that about fifty black women in one precinct were lined up waiting to register before the polls even opened, as the *Messenger* itself reported, went ignored. White Democrats were sure that black women were going to vote in droves and for all the wrong reasons.[18]

In Louisville, the area of the state where Republicans had always had the most power, Democrats predicted that black women would help their opponents steal the upcoming election. In the past, the Republican machine had been able to manipulate black male votes, and now they stood to do even better. The *Kentucky Irish American* predicted that Republicans in Louisville would be walking to the polls "arm in arm with the colored cooks, washerwomen and other dusky belles."[19]

Fear that voting women would upset the racial order in the 1920 presidential race peaked as election day inched closer. In October, *New York World*, a national Democratic-leaning paper, asserted that "aggressive" black Kentucky voters who were loudly supporting Republican candidates were hurting rather than helping the GOP. Kentuckians who had been on the fence were now vowing to vote for Cox. That, combined with white women's enthusiasm for the League of Nations, would likely be the deciding factors, the paper noted.[20]

Good citizenship was the rallying cry across the country in 1920; but despite claims that it could be taught in a fifteen-week class, not everyone was considered teachable, it turned out. The Democratic party announced that it would send precinct captains to visit the homes of every woman in Lexington to ensure that no votes were squandered, but leaders assured the fearful that they "would not enter the homes of negro women voters." Politically minded African Americans, especially African American women, were not viewed as "engaged" or "intelligent," they were "aggressive" and ready to be manipulated by Republican ward bosses. The electorate had expanded, but the Commonwealth's commitment to giving every citizen a voice remained weak.[21]

Throughout the summer of 1920, Americans watched to see whether ratification would succeed. After Kentucky's win, eleven more states were quickly added to the ratification column. Four had come in mid-February in just a five-day period. NAWSA leaders reviewed the situation in late March. The good news: they just needed one more state to take them over the top. The bad news: the "sure things" and the "more-than-likelys" were gone. Only the "it would take a stroke of luck" and the "never-in-a-million-years" states remained. Never had the states failed to ratify an amendment passed by

Congress. Suffragists dreaded the idea that their amendment might be the first to wither on the vine.[22]

Bad news kept coming in. Connecticut legislators were willing to ratify, but the governor refused to call a session. Carrie Catt was sure that Delaware would come through, but then it didn't. They were running out of states. A good word from Republican candidate Warren G. Harding could have helped, but he refused to intervene, and one could never expect straight talk from him anyway. It was a conspiracy, Catt figured. The two parties must be colluding to stop the count.[23]

But she was not ready to give up yet. Tennessee—situated well below the Mason–Dixon Line—had initially seemed out of the question, but now it was suddenly in play. It was not in the "never-in-a-million-years" category since its women had municipal and presidential suffrage already, but its lawmakers had vowed to oppose ratification and were, so far, succeeding. They, along with leaders in several other former Confederate states, claimed their state constitutions prohibited the governor from calling a ratification convention without the express consent of voters. They could not do anything until the people spoke. The US Supreme Court disagreed, ruling in June 1920 that state law could not interfere with the ratification process. With this decision, Tennessee governor Albert Roberts lost his excuse for foot-dragging. A special session would begin on August 9. More than one thousand suffragists and Antis—including turncoat Laura Clay—would be on hand in Nashville to see history made. All hoped it would be made in their favor.[24]

Tennessee's story of ratification is one that has been often told, its most vivid rendering provided by Elaine Weiss. In her 2018 book, *The Woman's Hour*, she gives a blow-by-blow account of a momentous decision that came down to the wire and of the many forces that made ratification so uncertain. After frustrating suffragists by holding out as undecided, Harry Burn, a twenty-four-year-old freshman legislator from East Tennessee, pleased his dear momma by casting the deciding vote. "I believe in full suffrage as a right; I believe we had a moral and legal right to ratify; and I knew that a mother's advice is always safest for a boy to follow," he later explained.[25]

The Nineteenth Amendment was added to the Constitution on August 18, 1920. And with that, women across the country—Kate Gordon and Laura Clay included—joined the ranks of the enfranchised.

On November 2, 1920, ten million American women, about half of those eligible, went to the polls. Thousands of Kentucky women cast their first votes for president on what reports concluded was a remarkably quiet day. There were a few snags. Richmond election officials underestimated the number of ballots needed and ran out midafternoon, but additional ones soon appeared. Otherwise, things had been routine, a "delightful late fall day." Owensboro correspondents agreed that it had been the quietest election the city had ever seen.[26]

Some women had waited years to vote and relished their opportunity. "Aunt Judy" Perkins, a black woman almost ninety years old, lined up long before the polls opened and thus had the honor of casting the first vote in McCracken County.[27]

Madeline McDowell Breckinridge didn't venture out as early, but she also fulfilled her dream of voting, marking her ballot for Cox and Roosevelt. Several months earlier she had penned an ode to this moment, a parody of "My Old Kentucky Home" that she offered at the NAWSA victory convention:

The sun shines bright in my old Kentucky home,
'Tis winter, the ladies are gay
The corn tops gone, prohibitions in the swing,
The colonel's in eclipse and the women in the ring.
We'll get all our rights with the help of Uncle Sam,
For the way that they come, we don't give a _____;
Weep no more, my lady, Oh, weep no more today,
For we'll vote one vote for the old Kentucky home.
The old Kentucky home, far away.[28]

Since Kentucky's ratification, Breckinridge had been busier than ever. She had helped pass a bill authorizing district tuberculosis hospitals; she had traveled to Europe to participate in the International Women's Suffrage Alliance conference, taking in the sights along the way; and she had traveled the state to promote the League of Nations and Cox. Breckinridge was disappointed when the nation elected Harding, thereby dooming the league, but at least Kentucky had gone Democratic.[29]

When Madge voted that day, she did not know it would be both her first time to do so and her last. On Thanksgiving Day, only three weeks later, forty-eight-year-old Breckinridge died. A servant found her lying on the floor, the victim of a stroke from which she never recovered. Lexington tried to adequately mark her passing, but no gesture seemed grand enough.

The streetcars were stopped for a minute during her funeral and the flag flew at half-staff.[30]

Desha penned a tender tribute to his wife, which appeared in the *Herald* the next day. It was one of dozens of eulogies offered to memorialize the woman who all seemed to agree had been Kentucky's "most useful citizen." "No trip was too long for her to take," her husband recalled, "no task too onerous . . . to help secure for women the instrument she believed would help humanity." She had lived to see her chief aim realized. She had voted, and she would bequeath that right to other women as her legacy. At last, he reported with a mixture of sadness and relief, "Her body is at rest."[31]

Epilogue

Alice Bronston Oldham, one of the three women who resigned from KERA with Laura Clay, wrote to Florence Cantrill on Christmas Day 1920 to congratulate her on the birth of her daughter, Margaret. A new day had dawned in America since women had won the vote, made evident by the enthusiasm bubbling through Oldham's note of congratulations. The sky seemed to be the limit, even for those such as Oldham who had opposed the Nineteenth Amendment. Cantrill's daughter, she predicted, would turn out to be "an astute politician or a celebrated *statesman*." A woman born in 1920 could change the world.[1]

Cantrill shared Oldham's excitement. Several months before, while very pregnant, she had called on women to be "trail blazers in a new path of citizenship." Like their "hardy ancestors who pushed across the Alleghenies" (Cantrill was a proud descendant of the Boones and the Bryans), Kentucky women planned to show the world that they deserved the ballot.[2]

Cantrill decided that she did not need to wait for her daughter to grow to adulthood, when she could be the pathbreaker herself. She became a key player in the Democratic Party, and in 1933, she became the first woman to represent Fayette County in the Kentucky legislature.[3]

Following the amendment's ratification, Laura Clay did not immediately focus on the opportunities now open to women. "Heavy-hearted," she continued to dwell on the damage she believed it would inflict on the nation, as power became increasingly centralized in Washington. While most Kentucky suffragists joined KERA's successor, the Kentucky League of Women Voters (KLWV), Clay refused. It declared itself nonpartisan, a priority of Clay's, but she still worried that it would undermine local control. Three hundred women from all over the state attended the KLWV's inaugural meeting in Lexington in mid-December, but Kentucky's two most revered suffragists were absent. The league would move forward with new leadership. Mary Bronaugh, a lawyer from Hopkinsville, became its first president.[4]

Clay did not agree with how women had won the ballot, but that did not stop her from using it. She continued to faithfully support the

217

Democratic Party and became a member of the Democratic Woman's Club of Kentucky. Writing to her dear friend and NAWSA colleague Harriet Taylor Upton in 1921, she reported that she still loved her Republican friends, despite their political differences. She held no grudges, and neither, it seemed, did her former adversaries.[5]

Clay was in her seventies, but she did not seem to be slowing down. She remained highly active in the Episcopal Church, she championed an unsuccessful effort to remove the word "male" from the election clause in Kentucky's constitution in 1923 (it was defeated by eleven thousand votes), and that same year she agreed to run for the Kentucky Senate. She won the Democratic primary, but her support of pari-mutuel betting machines, which she believed would cut down on corruption and increase tax revenue, spelled her doom. Her Republican opponent accused her of being a threat to family values.[6]

That year was a big year for women in Kentucky politics. Clay did not win her contest, but others found success. It was a foregone conclusion that a woman would be elected secretary of state in 1923, considering the only candidates in the race were female. Emma Guy Cromwell, former state librarian from the Pennyrile, and Mary Elliott Flanery, former correspondent for the *Ashland Daily Independent* and the first woman in Kentucky and in the South to serve in a state legislature, squared off in the Democratic primary. Cromwell, the winner, then faced Republican candidate Eleanor Wickliffe in the general election, again coming out victorious.[7]

Cromwell claimed that as a widow who needed to support herself, she only ran for office out of necessity, but she went on to have a long political career. She followed by serving as state treasurer, a role considered more controversial than her previous posts. It was one thing for a woman to hold positions like librarian and secretary, but taking on the manly responsibility of handling money was another thing entirely. Cromwell defended her qualifications, reminding critics that women usually oversaw their family budgets.[8]

Unfortunately, the flurry of women running for office in 1923 was not the harbinger of things to come. Women have been voting participants—many years their turnout exceeded that of Kentucky men—but they have remained underrepresented among elected officials. Martha Layne Collins's election as governor in 1983 marked a great triumph, but she remained a novelty in state politics. A 2015 study conducted by the Institute for Women's Policy Research ranked Kentucky forty-sixth in terms of women running for office. Women held only four of thirty-eight state senate seats in 2018, and only nineteen out of a hundred seats in the general assembly. Only one of these lawmakers was a woman of color. In 2019, Kentucky still has never had a female US senator and only two of its women have ever held US House seats.[9]

Women have lacked a place at the table in decision-making for far too long, but their votes have made an impact. In 1994, Kentucky governor Paul Patton credited his victory to the state's women. The gender gap in voting first drew attention in the 1980s, and it has continued to matter. In state and national contests, over the last four decades, women have often been the deciding factor.[10]

Kentucky suffragists knew the fight was not over when they cast their first ballots in 1920. The battle continues today. The more we know about woman suffrage's long and complicated story, the more we must commit to preserving what it won and continue to seek what it failed to achieve: an equal voice for all. Casey Cep reminds us that "the right to vote is less a switch than a dial, one that can be turned up or dimmed down." Voting remains a fragile right today, jeopardized by partisan gerrymandering and redistricting, felon restrictions, voter ID requirements, voter roll purges, and overcrowded polling places. Voter apathy serves to erase the voices of millions more Americans, affecting disproportionately the poor and the young in every voting cycle. We must remain vigilant, committed to turning the dial forward.[11]

"I am not ever pained by the fact that the young accept it all as the course of nature, never knowing all it cost," Clay wrote to Alice Stone Blackwell in 1931, reflecting on what suffragists had achieved and the failure of younger women to appreciate their sacrifices. Clay admitted that she had done the same thing in her young ignorance, taking abolition for granted. But then, she found another cause, which demanded her zeal and devotion. "And so it will ever be," Clay continued. "All that those who wrought before need desire is that their spirit of love for the right and willingness to live for it should fall upon those who follow after." That is the charge the suffragists have left to us: to identify injustice, to resist apathy, and to correct it.[12]

> "I have fought the good fight. I have finished my course. I have kept the faith, henceforth—!"
>
> (epitaph of Kentucky suffragist, Caroline Apperson Leech)

Acknowledgments

Working on a book connected to a significant historical anniversary with the strict deadlines it imposes is stressful, but the upside is that when so many people are excited to celebrate a milestone, the process is energetic, collaborative, and especially rewarding. Meeting others around the Commonwealth who are geared up to commemorate the Nineteenth Amendment has been a great joy.

This book has been five years in the making, and every step of the way, it has been a team effort. It all started at a meeting in September 2015 when Genie Potter, Randolph Hollingsworth, Melissa McEuen, and I first discussed the need to plan on a state level for 2020. The brainstorming began then and continued for four years as we and a large group of interested individuals across the state held monthly conference calls to share ideas and to report progress. Randolph Hollingsworth helped the Kentucky Woman Suffrage Project come to life ("project mama" to use Genie's words) and served as the glue. She, with help from Michael Breeding, created the project's website and collected a slew of suffrage-related resources that are housed on H-Kentucky. Marsha Weinstein, Doraine Bailey, and Sylvia Coffey have been particularly active in KWSP and have been helpful to this project.

One of the goals from the start was to develop new scholarship on suffrage. LeeAnn Whites, then director of research at the Filson Historical Society, supported the idea of publishing a special issue of *Ohio Valley History*. Through that effort I met Ann Allen, who has done excellent work on the Louisville movement. Her essay published in the Spring 2020 issue, along with Randolph Hollingsworth's essay on school suffrage, filled important gaps in the story, and I have drawn heavily on their work. Whenever I have needed a sounding board, a sharpened perspective, or just a vote of confidence, Ann and Randolph have provided it. I am grateful to have them as friends and colleagues.

Reconstructing the life stories of women is no easy task; it often takes serious detective work. I have benefited from sleuthing done by dozens of

221

volunteers who contributed to Women and Social Movement's Online Biographical Dictionary of the Woman Suffrage Movement in the United States. Together, volunteers wrote over sixty biographies of Kentucky women, greatly expanding the story of the Commonwealth's role in the fight for the vote. Thank you, everyone!

Working on such a short timeline, I wondered if this project would ever get off the ground. This book would not exist if my UK colleague Jim Albisetti had not encouraged me to seek research leave and if my department chair Karen Petrone had not found a way to make it possible. Erik Myrup and members of the history department cheerfully stepped up to cover my teaching and advising duties. Thank you to the Gheens Foundation for support of this book. I am also grateful to the University of Kentucky for providing two summer research and creativity grants.

I couldn't ask for a better research assistant than Joanna Lile, a history PhD and an expert on Kentucky women. Joanna has worked with the KWSP since 2016. She dug through years of national publications to find mention of Kentucky, she reached out to local and county historical societies all across the state, she provided detailed feedback on the manuscript, and she helped choose images. Her fingerprints are all over this book.

My undergraduate students, including Kristen Thornsberry Dawson, Sean Hjelle, Kelli Lemaster, and Kate Whitfield provided additional research and administrative support. Kate helped bring the project across the finish line with her impeccable attention to detail and her professionalism.

Many local historians and descendants tracked down sources, including C. R. Mitchell from the Knox Historical Museum, Tandy Nash of the Kentucky Gateway Museum, John Rhorer, grandson of Arthur W. Rhorer, Sallie Clay Lanham, great-granddaughter of Mary Barr Clay, Emmalee Krulish of Shaker Village of Pleasant Hill, and Barb Piscopo and George Siss from the Lorain (Ohio) Historical Society. Carol Mattingly generously shared materials about suffrage in Louisville, and Harold Peach shared research on Anderson County. Genie Potter came to the rescue on several occasions to find photos and sources and to sweetly point out some significant omissions.

I am grateful to the staff of the University of Kentucky Special Collections Research Center, with whom I have become friends over the years. Deirdre Scaggs, Jay-Marie Bravent, and Matthew Strandmark provided essential materials and assistance. Digitizing KERA minutes and the Laura Clay papers was a huge task, but researchers will benefit from the effort for years to come.

Thank you to Claudia Knott for writing an excellent dissertation on the Kentucky suffrage movement. Paul Fuller's and Melba Hay's fine biographies of Laura Clay and Madeline McDowell Breckinridge, respectively, were indispensable. Karen Cotton McDaniel's dissertation and email correspondence helped me to understand better African American women's reform work and priorities. Elaine Weiss's entertaining and insightful book about the final push to ratify the Nineteenth Amendment, *The Woman's Hour*, served as a model for this study.

My deep appreciation goes to those who read drafts of the manuscript: Jim Albisetti, Ann Allen, Sean Gladue, Melissa McEuen, Nancy O'Malley, Genie Potter, and Kate Whitfield. Two anonymous readers from the Press were spot on in their suggestions and saved me from embarrassing errors of fact and interpretation.

Thank you to Anne Dean Dotson from University Press of Kentucky, who supported this project from day one and who was always up for a chat over a cup of coffee. Natalie O'Neal, Jewell Boyd, Jackie Wilson, and Ashley Runyon offered excellent ideas on how to market the book. I hope to meet them in person someday, instead of just on Zoom meetings.

Finally, thank you to the people I love best and who inspire my deepest joy. Jim and Cathy Haubenreich continually offered encouragement and assistance. My book club, consisting of Kelli Carmean, Carolyn Dupont, Dee Fizdale, Melissa McEuen, and Dixie Moore, and my parents, sisters, and in-laws all reminded me to pause, relax, and laugh. Without my children— Addison, Eli, and Grayson—my work–life balance would likely skew more to the work side, which I am glad to avoid. They have had to do more cooking and housework with mom working on the book, sometimes simply to survive. One day, I'm sure they will thank me for teaching them self-sufficiency.

Brad Goan, the best life partner possible, deserves the last word. What a blessing it is to live with one of the smartest people around and one of the most selfless. I guarantee that if he had lived one hundred years ago, he would have been a suffragist.

Notes

Introduction

1. Mary Gray Peck, *Carrie Chapman Catt: A Biography* (New York: H. W. Wilson Company, 1944), 329.

2. Elaine Weiss, *The Woman's Hour: The Great Fight to Win the Vote* (New York: Viking, 2018), 261.

3. Grace H. Ruthenburg, "Tennessee in Suffrage Lap," *LC-J*, July 30, 1920, 1.

4. "Rally for State Rights," *Cincinnati Enquirer*, August 8, 1920, 6; "Woman's Party Worker on Way to This State," *Charlotte Observer*, August 9, 1920, 1; and Weiss, *The Woman's Hour*, 43.

5. LC to Miss Gordon, July 31, 1920, LCP, box 3, folder 19; "Rally for State Rights," 6; Weiss, *The Woman's Hour*, 115–16; and Peck, *Carrie Chapman Catt*, 332.

6. *The History of Woman Suffrage*, vol. 4, *1883–1900*, ed. SBA and Ida Husted Harper (Indianapolis, IN: Hollenbeck, 1902), 24; and Weiss, *The Woman's Hour*, 2.

7. Weiss, *The Woman's Hour*, 3; and Jean H. Baker, "Getting Right with Women's Suffrage," *Journal of the Gilded Age and the Progressive Era* 5, no. 1 (January 2006): 15.

8. Ann D. Gordon, "How to Celebrate a Complicated Win for Women," *New York Times*, August 27, 2018.

1. The He-Women Come

1. Anne E. Marshall, *Creating a Confederate Kentucky: The Lost Cause and Civil War Memory in a Border State* (Chapel Hill: University of North Carolina Press, 2013).

2. Marjorie Spruill Wheeler, *New Women of the New South: The Leaders of the Woman Suffrage Movement in the Southern States* (New York: Oxford University Press, 1993), 5.

3. E. Merton Coulter, *The Civil War and Readjustment in Kentucky* (Chapel Hill: University of North Carolina Press, 1926), 406–7.

4. Ibid.

5. "Woman Suffrage in Kentucky—Letter from Mrs. Cutler," *WJ*, February 8, 1873, 44.

6. Eleanor Flexner, *Century of Struggle: The Woman's Rights Movement in the United States*, rev. ed. (Cambridge: Harvard University Press, 1975), 29–30.

225

7. Weiss, *The Woman's Hour*, 52; and Sally G. McMillan, *Lucy Stone: An Unapologetic Life* (Oxford: Oxford University Press, 2015), x.

8. McMillan, *Lucy Stone*, 97.

9. Carol Mattingly, *Appropriate[ing] Dress: Women's Rhetorical Style in Nineteenth-Century America* (Carbondale: Southern Illinois University Press, 2002), 62; "Bloomer Dress—Fugitive Slave Recovered," *Louisville Daily Courier*, May 18, 1852, 2, and "New Bonnet and Ribbon House," *Louisville Daily Courier*, March 18, 1853, 2.

10. *Harriet Taylor Upton's Random Recollections*, ed. Lana Dunn Eisenbraun (Warren, OH: Harriet Taylor Upton Association, 2004).

11. "Public Lectures," *Louisville Daily Courier*, October 31, 1853, 3, and "The Lecture Last Night," *Louisville Daily Courier*, November 3, 1853, 3.

12. "The Lecture Last Night."

13. "Miss Lucy Stone's Lecture," *Louisville Daily Courier*, November 2, 1853, 3; November 15, 1853, 3; November 12, 1853, 3; and November 17, 1853, 3; and *The History of Woman Suffrage: 1876–1885*, vol. 3, eds. ECS, SBA, and Matilda Jocelyn Gage, (Rochester, NY: Susan B. Anthony, 1886), 818.

14. *Louisville Daily Courier*, November 24, 1853, 3.

15. *Louisville Daily Courier*, October 18, 1853, 2.

16. Anna-Lisa Cox, *The Bone and Sinew of the Land: America's Forgotten Black Pioneers & The Struggle for Equality* (New York: PublicAffairs, 2018), 25–26.

17. Allan J. Lichtman, *The Embattled Vote in America: From the Founding to the Present* (Cambridge: Harvard University Press, 2018), 9.

18. Alexander Keyssar, *The Right to Vote: The Contested History of Democracy in the United States* (New York: Basic Books, 2000), 20–24; and Lichtman, *Embattled Vote*, 2.

19. Joan Wells Coward, *Kentucky in the New Republic: The Process of Constitution Making* (Lexington: University Press of Kentucky, 1979); and Lichtman, *Embattled Vote*, 37.

20. Keyssar, *The Right to Vote*, 12–14; Lichtman, *Embattled Vote*, 99–100; and Judith Apter Klinghoffer and Lois Elkis, "The Petticoat Electors," *Journal of the Early Republic* 12, no. 2 (Summer 1992): 160.

21. Linda K. Kerber, *Women of the Republic: Intellect and Ideology in Revolutionary America* (Chapel Hill: University of North Carolina Press, 1980), 9; and Sara Egge, *Woman Suffrage and Citizenship in the Midwest, 1870–1920* (Iowa City: University of Iowa Press, 2018), 1.

22. Kerber, *Women of the Republic*.

23. Barbara Welter, "Cult of True Womanhood, 1820–1860," *American Quarterly* 18, no. 2 (Summer 1966): 151–74; and Sara M. Evans, *Born for Liberty: A History of Women in America* (New York: Free Press, 1991), 69.

24. Evans, *Born for Liberty*, 72–75.

25. Kansas would be the next state to grant school suffrage to women, in 1861. By 1890, seventeen states had school suffrage. Aileen S. Kraditor, *The Ideas of the*

Woman Suffrage Movement, 1890–1920 (New York: W. W. Norton & Company, 1981), 4.

26. *Acts of the General Assembly of the Commonwealth of Kentucky* (Frankfort: A. G. Hodges, State Printer, 1838), 282; Martha Stephenson, "History of Education in Kentucky," *Register of the Kentucky Historical Society* 15, no. 44 (May 1917): 76; and Barksdale Hamlett, *History of Education in Kentucky* (Frankfort: Kentucky Department of Education, 1914), 20.

27. Kathryn A. Nicholas, "Reexamining Women's Nineteenth-Century Political Agency: School Suffrage and Office-Holding," *Journal of Policy History* 30, no. 3 (2018): 458.

28. *The History of Woman Suffrage*, vol. 1, *1848–1861*, ed. ECS, SBA, and Matilda Joselyn Gage (Rochester, NY: SBA, 1887), 640.

29. Suzanne M. Marilley, *Woman Suffrage and the Origins of Liberal Feminism in the United States, 1820–1920* (Cambridge: Harvard University Press, 1996), 22–25.

30. Flexner, *Century of Struggle*, 45–48.

31. Ellen Carol DuBois, *Woman Suffrage and Women's Rights* (New York: New York University Press, 1998), 285–86.

32. *History of Woman Suffrage*, vol. 1, 53.

33. Lisa Tetrault, *The Myth of Seneca Falls: Memory and the Women's Suffrage Movement, 1848–1898* (Chapel Hill: University of North Carolina Press, 2014), 2–3. Tetrault argues that as the suffrage movement became national, Anthony and Stanton recognized that an official history would provide needed unity. They wrote the movement's official history, massaging the story to make themselves the key figures and their goals the movement's main purpose. To this day, many more Americans are familiar with Stanton and Anthony than any other early suffragists. The site of the Seneca Falls convention is the only national park dedicated to women's rights.

34. Ibid., 3. Stanton remembered the two events as linked, but Mott did not. According to Tetrault, Mott's version of the movement's history diverged considerably from the one Stanton and Anthony fashioned in their official account.

35. *History of Woman Suffrage*, vol. 1, 61–62.

36. Flexner, *Century of Struggle*.

37. *History of Woman Suffrage*, vol. 1, 67–68.

38. "Declaration of Sentiments," National Park Service website, https://www .nps.gov/wori/learn/historyculture/declaration-of-sentiments.htm, accessed January 20, 2019; Gerda Lerner, "The Meanings of Seneca Falls, 1848–1998," *Dissent* 45, no. 4 (Fall 1998): 36; and Weiss, *The Woman's Hour*, 48–49.

39. Weiss, *The Woman's Hour*, 49.

40. "Declaration of Sentiments"; *History of Woman Suffrage*, vol. 1, 73.

41. Keyssar, *The Right to Vote*, 177; and Marjorie Spruill Wheeler, ed., *One Woman, One Vote: Rediscovering the Woman Suffrage Movement* (Troutdale, OR: NewSage, 1995), 375.

42. Faye E. Dudden, *Fighting Chance: The Struggle over Woman Suffrage and Black Suffrage in Reconstruction America* (Oxford: Oxford University Press, 2011).

43. Ibid.

44. Historic Glendale, Kentucky, http://www.glendalekentucky.com/index.html, accessed January 31, 2019.

45. "A Kentucky Voice," *Revolution*, December 3, 1868, 346. MBC paraphrased the letter and included it in the Kentucky Report she submitted for the *History of Woman Suffrage*, vol. 3. Clay lists October 1867 as the date of the Glendale Association's creation.

46. "The School Circular . . .," *Owensboro Monitor*, August 19, 1874, 3.

47. Randolph Hollingsworth, "Virginia Penny, Economist and Suffragist," H-Kentucky, https://networks.h-net.org/node/2289/discussions/158064/virginia-penny-economist-and-suffragist, accessed December 9, 2019.

48. "Woman Suffrage and Green Backs," *LC-J*, November 28, 1867, 2; *Louisville Daily Courier*, November 23, 1867, 1; "Woman Suffrage," *Louisville Daily Courier*, November 28, 1867, 1; and Weiss, *The Woman's Hour*, 135.

49. "Another Racy Report from Geo. Francis Traine [*sic*]—Woman's Suffrage—The National Debt," *Owensboro Monitor*, July 3, 1867, 1.

50. "Woman Suffrage in Kentucky—Letter from Mrs. Cutler," *WJ*, February 8, 1873, 4; "A New York Belle . . .," *Stanford Interior Journal*, May 9, 1882, 2; and "Of Northern Girls . . .," *LC-J*, August 17, 1881, 4.

51. "In the Legislature of Massachusetts . . .," *Owensboro Examiner*, March 24, 1876, 4; *Louisville Daily Courier*, November 8, 1867, 1; and Wheeler, *New Women*, 16.

52. J. B. Quinby, "Kentucky Ahead," *WJ*, January 27, 1872, 32.

53. "Women Voting in Kentucky," *Hickman Courier* (reprinted from the *Frankfort Yeoman*), January 27, 1872, 1.

54. Ibid.

55. Henry Cole Quinby, *Genealogical History of the Quinby (Quimby) Family in England and America* (Rutland, VT: Tuttle Company, 1915), 379–81.

56. Quinby, "Kentucky Ahead."

57. "Women Voting in Kentucky."

58. Lichtman, *Embattled Vote*, 16–17; and Egge, *Woman Suffrage and Citizenship*, 9–11.

59. Tetrault, *Myth of Seneca Falls*, 56–73; and DuBois, *Woman Suffrage and Women's Rights*.

60. "The Advocates of Agrarianism, Confiscation, and Repudiation a Little Behind the Age," *Owensboro Monitor*, July 3, 1867; "Female Suffrage," *Louisville Daily Courier*, May 23, 1867, 2; "Scintillations of the Societies," *Ohio County News*, March 30, 1887, 3; and "Bedlamites Still Alive," *Owensboro Monitor*, June 12, 1867, 2.

61. Victoria Woodhull published her ideas in *Woodhull & Claflin's Weekly*, a newspaper that she ran with her sister. She was the first woman to run for president (1872) even though she was technically too young. Tetrault, *Myth of Seneca Falls*,

90; and Joanne E. Passet, *Sex Radicals and the Quest for Women's Equality* (Urbana: University of Illinois Press, 2003), 44.

62. Claudia Knott, "The Woman Suffrage Movement in Kentucky, 1879–1920" (PhD diss., University of Kentucky, 1989), 66.

63. "A Pushing Woman," *Owensboro Messenger*, December 14, 1880, 4.

64. H. T., letter to the editor, *Kentucky Stock Farm*, June 4, 1885, 6; and Keyssar, *The Right to Vote*, 12–14.

65. "In the Legislature of Massachusetts . . .," *Owensboro Examiner*, March 24, 1876, 4.

66. "Woman in Politics," *Stanford Interior Journal*, July 18, 1890, 2.

67. Arthur Krock, *The Editorials of Henry Watterson* (Louisville: Louisville Courier-Journal Company, 1923), 365; and Wheeler, *New Women*, 8.

68. Wheeler, *New Women*, 47, 63.

2. Jars of Clay

1. Knott, "Woman Suffrage Movement," 9.

2. Harold D. Tallant, *Evil Necessity: Slavery and Political Culture in Antebellum Kentucky* (Lexington: UPK, 2003), 116–19; and H. Edward Richardson, *Cassius Marcellus Clay: Firebrand of Freedom* (Lexington: UPK, 1976).

3. Paul E. Fuller, *Laura Clay and the Woman's Rights Movement* (Lexington: UPK, 1975), 1–18.

4. Ibid.; and Clay Lancaster, *Antebellum Architecture of Kentucky* (Lexington: UPK, 1991), 309–11. Prior to renovations, the home had been called Clermont. Changing the name to White Hall reinforced the extreme metamorphosis it underwent.

5. Wheeler, *New Women*, 60; Richardson, *Cassius Marcellus Clay*, 117–18; and Cassius Marcellus Clay, *The Life of Cassius Marcellus Clay: Memoirs, Writings, and Speeches*, vol. 1 (Cincinnati, OH: J. Fletcher Brennan & Co., 1886), 540.

6. "Commencement at Oberlin," *Cleveland Daily Leader*, August 28, 1865, 4; Green Clay to Marguerite, December 1, 1952, provided to the author by Sallie Clay Lanham; and F. H. Mason, *The Twelfth Ohio Cavalry; A Record of Its Organization, and Services in the War of Rebellion, Together with a Complete Roster of the Regiment* (Cleveland: Nevins' Steam Printing House, 1871).

7. Green Clay to Marguerite; and Randolph Hollingsworth, "Biographical Sketch of Mary Barr Clay," BDWSM.

8. George Siss of the Lorain Carnegie Historical Center provided helpful details on Frank Herrick's life in northern Ohio.

9. "Miss Clay's Address," *WJ*, November 12, 1881, 366.

10. Information about the Herrick–Clay marriage is all drawn from Green Clay to Marguerite.

11. Fred A. Engle, "Some of the Clays," August 27, 1969, *Madison's Heritage Online*, http://library-old.eku.edu/blogs/digital/items/show/1067. George Siss notes

that after divorcing Clay, Herrick built a successful political career. He was elected State Senator (R) in 1901 and supported such liberal reforms as a juvenile court bill.

12. Naomi Cahn, "Faithless Wives and Lazy Husbands: Gender Norms in Nineteenth Century Divorce Law," *University of Illinois Law Review* 651 (2002), https://pdfs.semanticscholar.org/4d71/98d01bf4f2bcca2db4b253333850e530 7be5.pdf, accessed January 23, 2019.

13. Carroll Davidson Wright, *A Report on Marriage and Divorce in the United States, 1867 to 1886* (Washington, DC: Government Printing Office, 1891), 113–15, 148.

14. Fuller, *Laura Clay*, 15–16.

15. "Machines," *Kentucky Advocate*, February 6, 1874, 4.

16. Wright, *Report on Marriage and Divorce*, 120; and "Letter from Kentucky," *WJ*, December 6, 1879, 392.

17. *History of Woman Suffrage*, 3: 822; and Paul A. Tenkotte, "Biographical Sketch of Kate Trimble Woolsey," BDWSM.

18. "A Brave Kentucky Woman," *WJ*, March 2, 1889, 72; Mary Clay Herrick, "Kentucky Awakening," *WJ*, June 26, 1875, 205; and W. from Richmond, Kentucky, "Progress in Kentucky," *WJ*, August 14, 1875, 260.

19. "Woman Suffrage in Iowa," *WJ*, September 11, 1875, 293; "Female Suffrage," *St. Louis Post-Dispatch*, May 6, 1879, 1; and "The Woman's Convention," *St. Louis Post-Dispatch*, May 7, 1879, 1. For information on the 1878 attempt to pass a federal suffrage amendment, see Flexner, *Century of Struggle*, 176.

20. "Letter from Kentucky."

21. SBA to MBC, August 21, 1879 and October 17, 1884, CCP, folder 8 (courtesy of Randolph Hollingsworth).

22. SBA to MBC, October 20, 1879, and April 21, 1900, CCP, folder 8 (courtesy of Randolph Hollingsworth).

23. Mary Jane Warfield Clay to Dearest Children (Mary and Laura), March 15, 1880, LCP, box 1, folder 10; and Fuller, *Laura Clay*, 23.

24. Lucy Stone to MBC, August 6, 1887, CCP, folder 9 (courtesy of Randolph Hollingsworth).

25. "The Equal Suffrage Association—Gov. Begole an Officer," *Detroit Free Press*, May 22, 1884, 4; and "Mrs. Mary B. Clay . . .," *Wichita New Republic*, June 19, 1884, 8.

26. "Planks from the W. S. Platform," *Lincoln (Kansas) Beacon*, July 15, 1880, 1.

27. Lucy Stone, "The Louisville Meetings," *WJ*, November 5, 1881, 356; "The Women," *LC-J*, October 26, 1881, 1; and "The Suffragists," *LC-J*, October 27, 1881, 2.

28. "Woman Suffrage," *Chicago Tribune*, June 2, 1880, 9; and "Miss Clay's Address," *WJ*, November 12, 1881, 366. No evidence suggests that Sallie Clay Bennett was too scared to give her speech. Any number of scenarios could explain her absence. Parker Pillsbury was called to the platform in her place. It appears that she addressed the delegates later in the convention.

29. "Miss Clay's Address."

30. "Resolutions and Officers," *WJ*, November 5, 1881, 356; "Officers," *WJ*, October 20, 1883, 331; and NWSA, *Report of the Sixteenth Annual Washington Convention*, ed. ECS and SBA (Rochester, NY: Charles Mann, 1884), 33.

31. Constitution of the Kentucky Woman Suffrage Association, LCP, box 15, folder 11; and "The Women," *LC-J*, October 28, 1881, 6.

32. National reports of this inaugural meeting incorrectly list Mary B. Clay as president. She is not even listed as a signer of the organization's first constitution. See Stone, "The Louisville Meetings."

33. Fuller, *Laura Clay*, 22; Mrs. Jennie C. Morton to Miss Laura, December 18, 1903, LCP, box 2, folder 23; and MBC, "Kentucky," *WJ*, December 6, 1884, 393.

34. Fuller, *Laura Clay*, 25; and J. C. S. Blackburn to LC, February 20, 1884, LCP, box 1, folder 2.

35. Fuller, *Laura Clay*, 27; SBA to MBC, October 29, 1880, Lucy Stone to MBC, February 10, 1884, and SBA to MBC, October 17, 1884, CCP, folder 8 (courtesy of Randolph Hollingsworth).

36. Alumni Survey Database, Bentley Historical Library, University of Michigan, accessed January 24, 2019, https://bentley.umich.edu/legacy-support/um/voices/voices_search.php?id=522; and Sally Lanham Clay sketch of MBC, in author's possession.

37. "What Women Are Doing," *Portis (KS) Whisperer*, November 2, 1882, 4; MBC, "Kentucky," *History of Woman Suffrage*, 3: 820; "Land, Stock and Crop," *Stanford Interior Journal*, April 1, 1884, 3; and "Our Neighbors—Madison," *Kentucky Advocate*, July 13, 1888, 1.

38. Knott, "Woman Suffrage Movement," 54.

39. Ibid., 40.

40. Wheeler, *New Women*, 60; Fuller, *Laura Clay*, 174; and "Reunions at Old Yale," *New York Times*, June 29, 1887, 5.

41. Fuller, *Laura Clay*, 31; H. B. B. [Henry Browne Blackwell], "Suffrage Meetings in Kentucky," *WJ*, May 19, 1888, 158; Melinda Senters, "Biographical Sketch of Henrietta Earle 'Ettie' Bronston Chenault," BDWSM; and *Minutes of the Kentucky Equal Rights Association, November 19th, 20th, & 21st, 1889, Court House, Lexington, Kentucky, with Reports and Constitution* (Lexington: Will S. Marshall Jr., 1890), UKSCRC (hereafter 1889 Minutes).

42. Trillia Newbell, "It's Good to Be a Jar of Clay," *Desiring God*, July 25, 2013, https://www.desiringgod.org/articles/its-good-to-be-a-jar-of-clay, accessed February 11, 2019.

3. To Frankfort

1. "Home, Sweet Home," *LC-J*, January 5, 1890, 7; and "The Road Problem," *LC-J*, January 27, 1890, 4.

2. "Home, Sweet Home"; "Fifty-Three New Ones," *LC-J*, April 30, 1890, 8; and *Acts of the General Assembly of the Commonwealth of Kentucky*, vol. 1 (Frankfort: Capital Office, 1890).

3. Knott, "Woman Suffrage Movement," 139; "Powwows," *Cincinnati Enquirer*, February 17, 1895, 17; and Eugenia B. Farmer, "Kentucky Notes," *WJ*, October 17, 1891, 332.

4. "Mrs. Josephine K. Henry," *Blue Grass Blade*, February 23, 1908, 2; "Pioneer Woman Leader Is Dead," *LC-J*, January 8, 1928, 5; and Aloma Williams Dew, "Biographical Sketch of Josephine K. Henry," BDWSM.

5. "Light Wanted in Kentucky," *WJ*, March 24, 1888, 96.

6. Knott, "Woman Suffrage Movement," 138.

7. "Frappe New York Women," *Weekly Wisconsin*, October 27, 1894, 3; and KERA, 1889 Minutes, 22.

8. Leslie Greaves Radloff, "Biographical Sketch of Eugenia B. Farmer," BDWSM.

9. Fuller, *Laura Clay*, 46.

10. "Women Are Bicycle Mad," *LC-J*, July 1, 1894, 11.

11. KERA constitution, appended to 1889 Minutes.

12. "Report of Superintendent of Legislative and Petition Work," in KERA, *Minutes of the Third Annual Convention Held at the Court House, Richmond, Kentucky, 1890* (Cincinnati: Robt. T. Morris, 1890), 13, UKSCRC (hereafter 1890 Minutes).

13. Wheeler, *New Women*, 79; A.S.B. [Alice Stone Blackwell], "A Wail from Kentucky," *WJ*, March 26, 1892, 102.

14. "Married Women's Rights," *LC-J*, January 12, 1890, 16; Annie E. Pearce to Miss Clay, March 30, 1893, LCP, box 1, folder 7; and Ellen Battelle Dietrick, "How Kentucky Laws Affect Women," *WJ*, April 27, 1889, 130.

15. "Kentucky and Women," *Springfield Leader and Press*, August 2, 1891, 8.

16. Mrs. Josephine K. Henry, "Property Rights of Kentucky Wives," *WJ*, April 27, 1889, 131.

17. "Report of Superintendent of Legislative and Petition Work," KERA, 1889 Minutes, 29–30.

18. "Fair Arguers," *LC-J*, January 11, 1890, 5.

19. "Fifty-Three New Ones," and "Closed for Repairs," *LC-J*, May 28, 1890, 8.

20. "Report of Superintendent of Legislative and Petition Work," KERA, 1890 Minutes, 13.

21. Quoted in Terry L. Birdwhistell and Deirdre A. Scaggs, *Our Rightful Place: A History of Women at the University of Kentucky, 1880–1945* (Lexington: UPK, 2020), 16.

22. Ibid.

23. Kolan Thomas Morelock, *Taking the Town: Collegiate and Community Culture in the Bluegrass, 1880–1917* (Lexington: UPK, 2009), 81.

24. KERA, 1890 Minutes, 16; Fuller, *Laura Clay*, 48–49; and "Centre History," Centre College, https://www.centre.edu/centre-facts/centre-history/, accessed February 23, 2019.

25. Birdwhistell & Scaggs, *Our Rightful Place*; "State Correspondence: Kentucky," *WJ*, May 2, 1902, 144; "What the Kentucky Equal Rights Association Has Done and What it Proposes to Do," 1913, MMBP, box 6, folder 48; and Fuller, *Laura Clay*, 89.

26. J.K.H., "The Constitutional Convention of Kentucky," *WJ*, March 14, 1891, 86; and Thomas D. Clark, *A History of Kentucky* (Ashland, KY: The Jesse Stuart Foundation, 1992), 430–31. The first vote to rewrite the third constitution failed in 1873. The matter was reconsidered every two years thereafter. Finally, the measure passed in 1887 and again in 1889.

27. Lowell H. Harrison and James C. Klotter, *A New History of Kentucky* (Lexington: UPK, 1997), 264–65; and Fuller, *Laura Clay*, 43.

28. JKH, "The Woman Question in Kentucky," *WJ*, May 10, 1890, 152; "Report of Frankfort Committee," in KERA, *Minutes of the Fourth Annual Convention, Held at the Liederkranz Hall, 1891* (Cincinnati: Robt. T. Morris, 1891), 9, UKSCRC (hereafter 1891 Minutes); Knott, "Woman Suffrage Movement," 142; and Harrison and Klotter, *New History*. Yellow became a symbolic color of the suffrage movement in the 1860s after Stanton and others campaigned in Kansas, known as the "Sunflower State." Suffragists saw it as an appropriate choice because it suggested a "golden dawn of equal suffrage" was breaking. See "Why the Yellow?" *WC*, June 16, 1917, 47.

29. Mary B. Clay's petition to the Constitutional Convention, *Official Report of the Proceedings and Debates in the Convention*, vol. 1 (Frankfort, KY: E. P. Johnson, printer to the Convention, 1890), 335; KERA, 1890 Minutes, 4, and 1891 Minutes, 9–10; and Robert M. Ireland, *The Kentucky State Constitution*, 2nd ed. (Oxford: Oxford University Press, 2012), 133.

30. Fuller, *Laura Clay*, 45.

31. Henry, "Constitutional Convention," 86.

32. Knott, "Woman Suffrage Movement," 61, 119. The Clay women attended the Episcopal Church, but Knott argues that Kentucky Episcopalians were "decidedly evangelical."

33. KERA, *Minutes of the Fifth Annual Convention, Held at the Court House, Richmond, KY, 1892* (Cincinnati: Robt. T. Morris, 1892), UKSCRC (hereafter 1892 Minutes), 6; Knott, "Woman Suffrage Movement," 42, 119; Rachel Wolters, "Biographical Sketch of Sarah Hardin Sawyer," BDWSM; and KERA, 1889 Minutes, 3, 36–37, 39.

34. Knott, "Woman Suffrage Movement," 112–13, 126.

35. KERA, 1891 Minutes, 5. Membership estimate was calculated based on the dues paid (ten cents per member) by locals to the state association, as noted in the treasurer's report.

36. KERA, 1891 Minutes, 12; and "Woman Suffragists Meet," *LC-J*, December 9, 1891, 4.

37. "Our State," *Danville Kentucky Advocate*, October 29, 1891, 1; and "Frederick W. Henry," *Chicago Tribune*, October 19, 1891, 3.

38. KERA, 1891 Minutes, 4–5.

39. Paul A. Tenkotte, "Our Rich History: Eugenia B. Farmer Was a Suffragist, an Early Proponent of Equal Rights in Northern Kentucky," *Northern Kentucky Tribune*, May 2, 2016; and Miss Laura Clay to JKH, October 27, 1891, LCP, box 1, folder 6.

40. Ireland, *Kentucky State Constitution*, 154; and "Report of Frankfort Committee," KERA, 1892 Minutes, 9–10.

41. Kentucky's 1838 original school suffrage provision did not specify race, but an 1870 amendment to the common schools policy narrowed school suffrage to only "qualified white voters." See Randolph Hollingsworth, "Kentucky Legislature Limits 1838 School Suffrage Law to White Widows," H-Kentucky, December 29, 2018, https://networks.h-net.org/node/2289/discussions/3414167/kentucky-legislature-limits-1838-school-suffrage-law-white-widows, accessed November 19, 2019. Women probably had a greater say in school or other municipal matters than we might expect. See Nicholas, "School Suffrage and Office-Holding," 457. Nicholas shows that nationally, rural school elections were often conducted in a "happy-go-lucky style" through voice voting that allowed women full participation in elections held separately from the general elections.

42. Nicholas, "School Suffrage and Office-Holding," 471–72; and Ellen Battelle Dietrick, "School Suffrage in Kentucky," *WJ*, April 27, 1889, 132.

43. MBC, "Kentucky," *WJ*, December 6, 1884, 393; and MBC, "Kentucky," *History of Woman Suffrage*, 3:820.

44. "Madison," *Danville Kentucky Advocate*, August 13, 1886, 1. Mrs. Million was not unusual. In many cases, a husband's death propelled women into office-holding.

45. Ibid.; "In and About," *LC-J*, April 21, 1887, 4; "Madison," *Danville Kentucky Advocate*, September 3, 1886, 7; "A Lady School Commissioner," *Hazel Green Herald*, September 1, 1886, 2; LC, "Kentucky," *History of Woman Suffrage*, 4:675; and "The Mystic Tie," *Owensboro Twice-A-Week-Messenger*, October 13, 1897, 4.

46. Fuller, *Laura Clay*, 36; "Moral Lepers," *LC-J*, July 22, 1890, 5; Ireland, *Kentucky State Constitution*, 120; and JKH, "The Constitutional Convention of Kentucky," 86.

47. "The Lady Fainted," *Owensboro Twice-A-Week Messenger*, July 10, 1890, 3.

48. "Dr. Brooks," *Stanford Interior-Journal*, July 18, 1890, 3; "News Paragraphs," *Richmond Climax*, August 27, 1890, 3; "In Hotel Corridors," *Washington, D. C. Evening Star*, February 15, 1894, 6; A.S.B., "The Kentucky Election," *WJ*, August 23, 1890, 269; and *Louisville Post* editorial, reprinted in the *Owensboro Messenger-Inquirer*, August 18, 1890, 2.

49. KERA, *Minutes of the Seventh Annual Convention, Held at Merrick Lodge, Lexington, KY, 1894* (n.p., 1894), UKSCRC (hereafter 1894 Minutes); "What the Kentucky Equal Rights Association Has Done and the Work for the Future," 1894, LCP, box 18, folder 7; and *Owensboro Twice-a-Week Messenger*, March 15, 1894, 4.

50. *History of Woman Suffrage*, 4:670; and "Letter from Mrs. Henry," *WJ*, February 23, 1895, 59.

4. Woman Triumphant

1. "Bivouac of the Dead," *Owensboro Messenger*, May 31, 1894, 1; Anne E. Marshall, *Creating a Confederate Kentucky*, 82–83; and "Memorial Day," Library of Congress, Today in History Series, https://www.loc.gov/item/today-in-history/may-30/, accessed March 13, 2019.

2. Ida Withers Harrison, *Memoirs of William Temple Withers by His Daughter* (Boston: Christopher Publishing House, 1924), 36, 39–40.

3. Robert Peter, MD, *History of Fayette County, Kentucky: With an Outline Sketch of the Blue Grass Region*, ed. William Henry Perrin (Chicago: O. L. Baskin & Co., 1882), 822–24.

4. Harrison, *Memoirs of William Temple Withers*, 71, 76–77, 105, 133.

5. "Apoplectic Stroke Fatal to Col. A. M. Harrison," *LC-J*, May 25, 1916, 4; and G. Melvin Herndon, "The Confederate States Naval Academy," *Virginia Magazine of History and Biography* 69, no. 3 (July 1961): 300–323.

6. "Mad Women," *LC-J*, May 23, 1894, 3.

7. Ibid.; and "All Torn Up," *Maysville Evening Bulletin*, May 25, 1894, 3.

8. "Attention Confederates," *Mt. Sterling Advocate*, June 6, 1893, 1.

9. "Damaging Evidence," *Owensboro Twice-A-Week Messenger*, March 22, 1894, 2; and Patricia Miller, *Bringing Down the Colonel: A Sex Scandal of the Gilded Age, and the "Powerless" Woman Who Took on Washington* (New York: Farrar, Straus, and Giroux, 2018).

10. James C. Klotter, "Sex, Scandal, and Suffrage in the Gilded Age," *Historian* 42, no. 2 (February 1, 1980): 231.

11. Ibid.

12. Elizabeth De Wolfe, "More Than a Congressman's Mistress: Ambition and Scandal in the Life of Madeleine Pollard," *Register of the Kentucky Historical Society* 115, no. 3 (Summer 2017); and "Personal Mention," *Danville Kentucky Advocate*, June 22, 1893, 3.

13. De Wolfe, "More Than a Congressman's Mistress."

14. "Jerry Has His Inning," *Owensboro Twice-A-Week Messenger*, April 5, 1894, 5; and "Says She Seduced Him," *Owensboro Messenger*, March 22, 1894, 1.

15. "Verdict $15,000," *Owensboro Twice A Week Messenger*, April 19, 1894, 2; Klotter, "Sex, Scandal, and Suffrage," 235; and "The Wages of Sin," *Pittsburgh Press*, April 15, 1894, 1.

16. "Madeline Gets $15000," *Danville Kentucky Advocate*, April 16, 1894, 2; *Stanford Interior Journal*, April 27, 1894, 2; and "A Campaign of Education," *Owensboro Twice-A-Week Messenger*, reprinted from the *New York Sun*, April 26, 1894, 3.

17. Melba Porter Hay, *Madeline McDowell Breckinridge and the Battle for a New South* (Lexington: UPK, 2009), 32–34; and "All Met to Condemn Breckinridge," *New York Times*, May 15, 1894, 5.

18. Wheeler, *New Women*, 6–7.

19. Randolph Hollingsworth, *Lexington: Queen of the Bluegrass* (Charleston, SC: Arcadia, 2004), 128–29.

20. Ibid; and https://westegg.com/inflation/.

21. Issa Desha Breckinridge and Mary Desha, *"The Work Shall Praise the Master": A Memorial to Joel T. Hart, the Kentucky Sculptor from the Women of the Bluegrass* (n.p., 1884), 22, 25.

22. Ibid., 26–30.

23. "A Mother and Her Sons," *Hickman Courier*, June 4, 1885, 4; "Brief Notes, *LC-J*, August 12, 1885, 3; and "Triumph of Chastity," *LC-J*, May 4, 1884, 12.

24. "In and About Kentucky," *LC-J*, December 19, 1887, 4; "Rude Fellows of the Baser Sort," *Danville Kentucky Advocate*, April 2, 1886, 3; and "Not Cultured," reprinted in *Danville Kentucky Advocate*, December 11, 1888, 2.

25. "In and About Kentucky," *LC-J*, January 12, 1889, 4; and "In Lexington," *LC-J*, April 21, 1886, 7.

26. Ida Withers Harrison, https://www.findagrave.com/memorial/84227245 /ida-harrison, accessed March 24, 2019.

27. "A Year's Work," *Maysville Evening Bulletin*, August 19, 1892, 2; Ida Withers Harrison, *Forty Years of Service: A History of the Woman's Christian Board of Missions, 1874–1914* (n.p., 1915); and Debra B. Hull, "Christian Woman's Board of Missions," *The Encyclopedia of the Stone-Campbell Movement*, ed. Douglas A. Foster, Paul M. Blowers, Anthony L. Dunnavant, and D. Newell Williams (Grand Rapids, MI: William B. Eerdmans, 2004), 201.

28. "Women's Clubs," *LC-J*, March 27, 1895, 20. For a history of the woman's club movement, see Karen J. Blair, *The Clubwoman as Feminist: True Womanhood Redefined, 1868–1914* (New York: Holmes & Meier, 1980).

29. "To Fight It Out," *LC-J*, May 5, 1894, 1.

30. "Is Denounced," *LC-J*, May 15, 1894, 1; and "All Met to Condemn Breckinridge," 5.

31. "War on Breckinridge," *San Francisco Call*, May 12, 1894, 1.

32. Maryjean Wall, *Madam Belle: Sex, Money, and Influence in a Southern Brothel* (Lexington: UPK, 2014), 6.

33. G. W. Craddock to W. C. P. Breckinridge, August 15, 1893, box 787, BFP, LOC, quoted in De Wolfe, "More Than a Congressman's Mistress," 319; and Kentucky Secretary of State, "George Washington Craddock," http://apps.sos.ky .gov/secdesk/sosinfo/default.aspx?id=43, accessed March 24, 2019.

34. "Boycotting Breckinridge," *Atlanta Constitution*, May 12, 1894, 1; and "Each Claims It," *LC-J*, September 9, 1894, 10.

35. "The Ladies Indignant," *Newark (OH) Advocate*, May 25, 1894, 1; "Confederate Graves Decorated," *Cincinnati Enquirer*, May 27, 1894, 2; *Asheville Citizen-Times*, May 25, 1894, 2; and *Austin American-Statesman*, May 29, 1894, 2.

36. "In the Ashland District," *Indianapolis News*, September 15, 1884, 1; and "They Were Answered," *LC-J*, September 16, 1894, 4. Harrison did not hold a

grudge against Confederate war heroes. Later, she became an active member of the Daughters of Confederacy. "At Richmond," *LC-J*, November 19, 1898, 6.

37. Klotter, "Sex, Scandal, and Suffrage," 241; "The Sun Still Shines on the Old Kentucky Home," and "Women's Noble Work," *LC-J*, September 16, 1894, 3, 4; and "Pastor Ceased Praying," *Boston Globe*, September 17, 1894, 1.

38. "Local Lines," *Boston Globe*, September 18, 1894, 5; and "Women in Politics," *Caldwell (KS) News*, September 27, 1894, 1.

39. Klotter, "Sex, Scandal, and Suffrage," 240; and "Woman's Column," *Winfield (KS) Industrial Free Press*, June 21, 1894, 6.

40. Mrs. Josephine K. Henry, "An Appeal from the Kentucky Equal Rights Association to the General Assembly of Kentucky" (Kentucky Equal Rights Association, 1893), LCP, box 21, folder 2; and *Minutes of the Sixth Annual Convention of the Kentucky Equal Rights Association, October 17th, 18th, and 19th, 1893, Fifth Street Christian Church, Newport, KY* (n.p., 1893), 7, UKSCRC (hereafter 1893 Minutes). KERA finally got the age of consent raised to sixteen in 1906.

41. Anne E. Marshall, "Kentucky's Separate Coach Law and African American Response, 1892–1900," *Register of the Kentucky Historical Society* 98, no. 3 (Summer 2000): 241.

42. Kentucky tried to disfranchise black men by adding a literacy qualification in 1904, but the measure failed in the legislature. See "Kentucky General Assembly," *Danville Kentucky Advocate*, February 3, 1904, 1.

43. George C. Wright, *A History of Blacks in Kentucky: In Pursuit of Equality, 1890–1980*, vol. 2 (Frankfort: Kentucky Historical Society, 1992), 1.

44. Marshall, "Kentucky's Separate Coach Law."

45. Wright, *History of Blacks in Kentucky*," 69–72.

46. "Only a Few Kicked," *LC-J*, October 3, 1893, 6; *LC-J*, December 21, 1892, 4; and Wright, *History of Blacks in Kentucky*, 71.

47. *The B. O. Gaines History of Scott County*, vol. 2 (1890): 390, "Justice's Quick Work," *LC-J*, September 12, 1889, 2.

48. Erin Wiggins Gilliam, "A Beacon of Hope: The African American Baptist Church and the Origins of Black Higher Learning Institutions in Kentucky" (PhD diss., University of Kentucky, 2018), 145; "Two Separate Coach Law Suits," *LC-J*, October 19, 1893, 2; "Items on the Wing," *Cincinnati Enquirer*, October 7, 1893 and September 29, 1894, 10. By 1900, Redd was living back in Georgetown with her husband. 1900 US Census, ancestry.com.

49. Marshall, "Kentucky's Separate Coach Law," 245–46; and "The Separate Coach Law," *LC-J*, October 9, 1893, 3.

50. "*Quinn, & c. v. Louisville & Nashville R. R. Co.*," *Kentucky Law Reporter* 17, no. 14 (January 15, 1896): 811–12.

51. Ibid., 813; *Maysville Public Ledger*, November 4, 1895, 4; and "Circuit Court Proceedings," *Elizabethtown News*, March 27, 1896, reprinted in *Bits and Pieces of Hardin County History* XXVV, no. 1 (Spring 2011): 8, http://www

.hardinkyhistoricalsociety.org/uplimg/Spring%202011_1.pdf, accessed February 3, 2019.

52. "Separate Coach Law," *Kentucky Encyclopedia*, ed. John E. Kleber (Lexington: UPK, 1992), 809–10.

53. JKH, "The New Woman of the New South," *Arena* 2, no. 3 (February 1895): 356–57.

54. Harrison, *Forty Years of Service*, 113; and "Woman's Club Election," *Maysville Public Ledger*, December 3, 1895, 2.

55. Mary Hume and Jennifer Walton-Hanley, "Biographical Sketch of Ida Withers Harrison," BDWSM; *Minutes of the Eighth Annual Convention of the Kentucky Equal Rights Association, December 10th, 11th, and 12th, 1895, Court-House of, Richmond, KY* (n.p., 1895), 4, 15, UKSCRC (hereafter 1895 Minutes); and KERA, *Journals of the Ninth Annual Convention, Held at Guild Hall, Trinity Church, Covington, KY, October 14 and 15, 1897, and the Tenth Annual Convention, Held at Court House, Richmond, KY, December 1, 1898* (London, KY: Mountain Echo, [1899]), 41, UKSCRC, (hereafter 1897 and 1898 Minutes).

56. "Hart's Masterpiece," *Hopkinsville Kentuckian*, May 18, 1897, 1; and *Bourbon News*, June 22, 1897, 5.

5. How Do You Spell Equality?

1. JKH, "Pith and Point," *WJ*, July 16, 1892, 228.

2. Kentucky Department of Libraries and Archives, "Kentucky's State Seal," https://web.archive.org/web/20070607194805/http://www.kdla.ky.gov/resources/kyseal.htm, accessed April 4, 2019; and Michael Smith, "The Story of Our State Seal," *LC-J*, June 20, 2007, A11.

3. *LC-J*, February 4, 1893, 6; *LC-J*, February 12, 1893, 5; and *St. Louis Dispatch*, February 11, 1893, 4.

4. KERA, 1894 Minutes, 12.

5. KERA, 1895 Minutes, 15; "Women at Work," *Lexington Leader*, January 23, 1895, 6; and "Editorial Notes," *WJ*, September 21, 1895, 297.

6. *Lexington Leader*, September 26, 1895; and "Reports of Local Associations," KERA, 1895 Minutes, 16–18.

7. "Women at the Polls in Lexington Last Fall," *LC-J*, May 17, 1896; Knott, "Woman Suffrage Movement," 215–16; and KERA, 1895 Minutes, 16.

8. KERA, 1894 Minutes, 7; "What Women are Doing," *Los Angeles Times*, February 24, 1895, 2; KERA, 1895 Minutes, 6, 22; and Knott, "Woman Suffrage Movement," 211.

9. KERA, 1895 Minutes, 15; and Randolph Hollingsworth, "African American Voters in Lexington's School Suffrage Times, 1895–1902: Race Matters in the History of the Kentucky Woman Suffrage Movement," *Ohio Valley History* 20, no. 1 (Spring 2020): 37.

10. E. B. Jackson, "Colored Women Declare Themselves for the Women's Ticket," *Lexington Leader*, October 18, 1895, 4. For more information on Belle Jackson, see *The Kentucky African American Encyclopedia*, ed. Gerald L. Smith, Karen Cotton McDaniel, and John A. Hardin (Lexington: UPK, 2015), 269, 539.

11. KERA, 1895 Minutes, 15–16; *Lexington Press-Transcript*, November 6, 1895, quoted in Knott, "Woman Suffrage Movement," 218; and *Proceedings of the Twenty-Seventh Annual Convention of the National-American Woman Suffrage Association, Held in Atlanta, GA., January 31st to February 5th, 1895*, ed. Harriet Taylor Upton (Warren, OH: Wm. Ritezel & Co, 1902), 129 (hereafter 1895 Proceedings).

12. Other symposium participants included Miss Mary Anderson of Frankfort, Mrs. Lizzie Morris, Miss Mary V. Cook, Miss Bena Coleman of Louisville, and Mrs. I. C. Cluke of Lancaster. *Danville Kentucky Advocate*, July 8, 1887, 5.

13. Mary E. Britton, "Woman's Suffrage: A Potent Agency in Public Reforms," *American Catholic Tribune*, July 22, 1887, 1.

14. Lauretta Flynn Byars, "Mary Elizabeth Britton," in *Notable Black American Women: Book 2*, ed. Jessie Carney Smith (New York: Gale Research, 1996), 55–57.

15. "Miss Mary E. Britton (MEB)," in *The Afro-American Press and Its Editors*, ed. Irvine Garland Penn (Springfield, MA: Willey & Co., 1891), 415–19; "'MEB' Talks to the Point," *Cleveland Gazette*, October 1, 1887, 4, NewsBank; and M. A. Majors, "Mrs. Mary E. Britton (MEB)," in *Noted Negro Women: Their Triumphs and Activities* (Chicago: Donohue and Henneberry, 1893), 214–15.

16. Evelyn Brooks Higginbotham, *Righteous Discontent: The Women's Movement in the Black Baptist Church, 1880–1920* (Cambridge: Harvard University Press, 1993), 11; and Gilliam, "'A Beacon of Hope.'"

17. Karen Cotton McDaniel provides a useful definition of respectability in "Local Women: The Public Lives of Black Middle Class Women in Kentucky before the 'Modern Civil Rights Movement'" (PhD diss., University of Kentucky, 2013), 83. Higginbotham refers to the "Female Talented Tenth" in *Righteous Discontent*, 20. W. E. B. DuBois borrowed these instructions and included them in *Efforts for Social Betterment among Negro Americans* (Atlanta: Atlanta University Press, 1909), 23–24.

18. McDaniel, "Local Women"; and Rosalyn Terborg-Penn, "African-American Women and the Woman Suffrage Movement," in Wheeler, *One Woman, One Vote*, 137.

19. Higginbotham, *Righteous Discontent*, 2, 60; and Gilliam, "'A Beacon of Hope,'" 133.

20. "State Teachers' Association, Colored," *Richmond Climax*, July 11, 1888, 3; "Colored State Teachers," *LC-J*, July 7, 1886, 3; McDaniel, "Local Women," 85; and "Miss Lucy Wilmot Smith," *Women of Distinction: Remarkable in Works and*

Invincible in Character, ed. Lawson Andrew Scruggs (Raleigh, NC: L. A. Scruggs, 1892).

21. Higginbotham, *Righteous Discontent*, 126. Smith wrote for *Our Women and Children*, a Baptist publication. This is where the quote appears. She may have written more about suffrage, but it appears the short-lived publication is no longer extant. See "Miss Lucy Wilmot Smith," in *The Afro-American Press and Its Editors*, ed. Penn., 380.

22. "Mary V. Cook, 1868–1945," in *Women's Work: An Anthology of African-American Women's Historical Writings from Antebellum America to the Harlem Renaissance*, ed. Laurie F. Maffly-Kipp and Kathryn Lofton (New York: Oxford University Press, 2010), 67–81; and "Afro-American Women in Journalism," in *Afro-American Press*, ed. Penn, 372–73.

23. Byars, "Mary Elizabeth Britton"; and Rosalyn Terborg-Penn, *African American Women in the Struggle for the Vote, 1850–1920* (Bloomington: Indiana University Press, 1998), 54.

24. Weiss, *The Woman's Hour*, 134–37.

25. Susan Look Avery, "Justice to the Negro," 1903, LCP, box 18, folder 3; and JKH, "An Appeal from the Kentucky Equal Rights Association."

26. Sara Hunter Graham, *Woman Suffrage and the New Democracy* (New Haven: Yale University Press, 1996), 6, 21.

27. LC to Mrs. McCulloch, December 13, 1907, LCP, box 7, folder 22; SBA to William Lloyd and Ella Garrison, January 29, 1904, Garrison Family Papers, MS 60, folder 26, quoted in Tricia Franzen, *Anna Howard Shaw: The Work of Woman Suffrage* (Urbana: University of Illinois Press, 2014), 100; and LC to Mrs. Farmer, August 5, 1907, LCP, box 5, folder 9.

28. "Laura Clay on Charles Sumner," *WJ*, January 14, 1893, 16.

29. Kraditor, *The Ideas of the Woman Suffrage Movement*, 163–64; and Keyssar, *The Right to Vote*, 78–79, 142–44.

30. [LC], "The Race Question Again," *Lexington Gazette*, 1890, Scrapbook, LCP, box 22, folder 2.

31. "The Woman's Convention," *Washington D. C. Evening Star*, February 15, 1890, 5.

32. ECS, "Address to the Founding Convention of the National American Woman Suffrage Association, February 1890," in *Elizabeth Cady Stanton/Susan B. Anthony: Correspondence, Writings, and Speeches*, ed. Ellen Carol DuBois (New York: Schocken Books, 1981), 226.

33. Terborg-Penn, *African American Women*, 66.

34. Graham, *Woman Suffrage and the New Democracy*, 7.

35. SBA to Miss Laura C. Clay, May 24, 1897, LCP, box 2, folder 1.

36. Elna C. Green, *Southern Strategies: Southern Women and the Woman Suffrage Question* (Chapel Hill: University of North Carolina Press, 1997), 8; and Fuller, *Laura Clay*, 57–61, 80.

37. Michael Perman, *Struggle for Mastery: Disfranchisement in the South, 1888–1908* (Chapel Hill: University of North Carolina Press, 2001), 116.

38. LC to Mr. Blackwell, October 14, 1907, LCP, box 7, folder 21; LC to Mr. Blackwell, January 29, 1908, LCP, box 7, folder 23; and LC to Mrs. McCulloch, December 7, 1907, LCP, box 7, folder 22.

39. Perman, *Struggle for Mastery*, 78–79.

40. H.B.B., "Woman Suffrage in Kentucky," *WJ*, April 27, 1889, 132; and Henry Blackwell, "A Solution of the Southern Question," *Woman Suffrage Leaflet*, October 15, 1890, 1, http://www.everydaylife.amdigital.co.uk.ezproxy.uky.edu /Documents/Images/WomanSuffrageLeafletScatteredIssues/13.

41. "Novel, to Say the Least," *Cincinnati Enquirer*, October 21, 1893, 9.

42. *Proceedings of the Thirty-First Annual Convention of the National-American Woman Suffrage Association at the St. Cecilia Club House, Grand Rapids, Mich., April 27, 28, 29, 30, and May 1, 2, 3, 1899* (Warren, OH: Press of Perry, [n.d.]), 58–61. Clay later attempted to correct the record, claiming that she had been misquoted as saying that it was a disgrace for black women and white women to ride together on trains. She noted that she had opposed the Kentucky Separate Coach Bill and thought it unjust. See "Miss Clay on the Race Question," *Chicago Inter Ocean*, May 9, 1899, 3.

43. Green, *Southern Strategies*, 89; Kraditor, *The Ideas of the Woman Suffrage Movement*, 165–66; and Franzen, *Anna Howard Shaw*, 91.

44. JKH, "Kentucky Notes," *WJ*, April 9, 1898, 119.

45. Fuller, *Laura Clay*, 47–48; "Woman," *LC-J*, June 28, 1896, 16; "Lancaster, Garrard County," *Stanford Interior Journal*, December 15, 1893, 1; and JKH, "The Art Craze vs. Equal Rights," *WJ*, January 11, 1890, 15.

46. Henry, "New Woman of the New South," 353; "Letter from Mrs. Henry," *WJ*, February 23, 1895, 59.

47. "All Sorts," *Free Thinkers' Magazine* 12, no. 1 (1894): 70. Maryjean Wall provides a description of Moore in *Madam Belle*, 60.

48. Kathi Kern, *Mrs. Stanton's Bible* (Ithaca: Cornell University Press, 2001), 2.

49. SBA to Mary Stafford Anthony, January 13, 1895, quoted in Kern, *Mrs. Stanton's Bible*, 185; and "The Woman's Bible," *Greenville Daily News*, November 23, 1895, LCP, box 18, folder 18.

50. Fuller, *Laura Clay*, 78; and Knott, "Woman Suffrage Movement," 135.

51. JKH to Miss Laura, January 19, 1899, LCP, box 6, folder 19; and Knott, "Woman Suffrage Movement," 137.

52. Kern, *Mrs. Stanton's Bible*, 181–84; and Fuller, *Laura Clay*, 75. The following Kentucky delegates voted for the resolution: Sallie Clay Bennett, Laura Clay, Sarah H. Sawyer, Amanthus Shipp, Mrs. M. R. Stockwell. Only Mary Wood voted against. Josephine Henry did not attend. *Proceedings of the Twenty-Eighth Annual Convention of the National-American Woman Suffrage Association, Held in Washington, D. C., January 23–28, 1896* (n.p.), 94.

53. Kern, *Mrs. Stanton's Bible*, 198–200.

54. Henry gives her take on the events leading up to her ejection in JKH to Miss Laura, January 19, 1899, LCP, box 6, folder 19. See also KERA, 1898 Minutes, 29–30.

55. KERA, 1898 Minutes, 29–30; "Mrs. Margaret Anderson Watts," *A Woman of the Century: Biographic Sketches of Leading American Women*, ed. Frances Willard and Mary Livermore (Buffalo: Charles Wells Moulton, 1893); Alexis Doerr, "Biographical Sketch of Margaret A. Watts," BDWSM; "Secular League Officers," *Washington, D. C. Evening Star*, May 6, 1901, 2; and JKH to Mrs. Farmer, February 10, 1904, LCP, box 7, folder 1.

56. JKH to LC, January 19, 1899; and Knott, "Woman Suffrage Movement," 144–50, 160. Henry continued to write about free thought and atheism for the rest of her life. She was often asked to eulogize the state's agnostics who were unfortunate enough to confront the afterlife they did not endorse. See "Colonel John L. Logan," *Columbus (IN) Republic*, October 15, 1897, 5. Henry was briefly involved in the National Legislative League, a competing national suffrage organization formed by those ousted from NAWSA, but her suffrage work effectively ended in 1898. She ran for president in 1900 as the "prohibition and agnostic candidate." Her promises to pursue wide-ranging reforms including abolishing Thanksgiving made her election prospects unlikely. See "Mrs. Josephine K. Henry," *Richmond Climax*, October 20, 1897, 5.

6. Rescission

1. "Frankfort Committee Report," in KERA, 1898 Minutes, 33–34; and Louise Jones, "Biographical Sketch of Mary Reddig Cramer," BDWSM.

2. "Report of the Plan of Work Committee," in KERA, 1898 Minutes, 33.

3. LC to Reah Whitehead, December 19, 1908, LCP, box 8, folder 4; and "What the Kentucky Equal Rights Association Has Done and the Work for the Future," 1894 version, LCP, box 18, folder 7.

4. JKH, "Kentucky Notes," *WJ*, April 9, 1898, 119.

5. "President's Report," in *Minutes of the Fifteenth Annual Convention of the Kentucky Equal Rights Association, Held at Rooms of the Lexington Woman's Club of Central Ky., November 17–18, 1904* (Newport, KY: Davies Print, 1905), UKSCRC, 2 (hereafter 1904 Minutes).

6. James C. Klotter, *William Goebel: The Politics of Wrath* (Lexington: UPK, 1977), 52; and Yvonne Honeycutt Baldwin, *Cora Wilson Stewart and Kentucky's Moonlight Schools: Fighting for Literacy in America* (Lexington: UPK, 2006), 94.

7. Klotter, *William Goebel;* and "Vile and Wicked Stain on the Escutcheon of Kentucky," *Washington Post*, reprinted in *LC-J*, January 31, 1900, 5.

8. *Proceedings of the Thirty-Second Annual Convention of the National American Woman Suffrage Association, Held at the Church of Our Father, Cor. Thirteenth and L Sts., N. W. Washington, D. C., February 8, 9, 10, 12, 13, and 14, 1900*, ed.

Rachel Foster Avery (Philadelphia: Press of Alfred J. Ferris, [n.d.]), 49; *Minutes of the Eleventh Annual Convention of the Kentucky Equal Rights Association, December 11th and 12th, Held at Merrick Lodge, Lexington, Ky. [1899]*, 4, 5 (hereafter 1899 Minutes); and *History of Woman Suffrage*, 4:207.

9. Knott, "Woman Suffrage Movement," 224.

10. "Appeal to Women," *Lexington Leader*, October 3, 1899, 4; and "Women Register," *Lexington Leader*, October 4, 1899, 5.

11. [Unknown author], "Women, Politics, and School Suffrage in Kentucky, 1895–1912," 13, MPHF, box 3, folder 10; and "School Suffrage in Kentucky," *WJ*, March 22, 1902, 96, reprinted from *Boston Transcript*.

12. Hollingsworth, "African American Voters." Lexington women still had it out for Russell in the nineteen-teens. Dr. Mary Britton wrote an open letter to the *Lexington Leader* to urge his removal as head of the city's black schools in 1912. He in turn sued her. By all accounts, Russell had an abrasive manner and often played favorites. Later, as president of Kentucky State, he was often involved in disputes with students and faculty. See Wright, *History of Blacks in Kentucky*, 130.

13. "Sharp Fight," *Lexington Leader*, November 4, 1900. The *Lexington Leader* piece includes reprints of several editorials.

14. Ibid.

15. "Women, Politics, and School Suffrage," 18; and "Like a Cyclone," *Lexington Leader*, November 7, 1900.

16. Quoted in Hollingsworth, "African American Voters," 40.

17. Fuller, *Laura Clay*, 89; "The Worst in History," *Lexington Leader*, November 6, 1901, 1; and Hollingsworth, "African American Voters," 40–41, 44. According to Hollingsworth, the loss of voters between registration and voting day in 1899 was 30 percent. It was only 7 percent in 1897.

18. Knott, "Woman Suffrage Movement," 227; and "A Voice from the Other Side," *Lexington Leader*, January 27, 1902.

19. James Duane Bolin, *Bossism and Reform in a Southern City: Lexington, Kentucky, 1880–1940* (Lexington: UPK, 2000), 36, 78.

20. "Against Woman Suffrage," *LC-J*, January 22, 1902, 1; and "School Suffrage in Kentucky."

21. *Minutes of the Thirteenth Annual Convention of the Kentucky Equal Rights Association, Held at Trinity Church, Covington, Ky., October 17–18, 1901 [+1902]* (Lexington, 1903), 11 (hereafter 1901 and 1902 Minutes); "Women Up in Arms," *LC-J*, January 6, 1902, 2; and "Vigorous," *LC-J*, February 6, 1902, 2.

22. J. Embry Allen to Mrs. Eugenia D. Potts, January 25, 1902, LCP, box 6, folder 21. For more information on Potts, see Randolph Hollingsworth, "Eugenia S. Potts, 1839–1912, Suffragist and Lost Cause Advocate," H-Kentucky, https://networks.h-net.org/node/2289/discussions/5518338/eugenia-s-dunlap-potts-1839-1912-suffragist-and-lost-cause, accessed December 9, 2019.

23. Clay understood that educational qualifications could be manipulated by corrupt election officers. To protect against this, she advocated for use of the

Australian ballot, a ballot that included no party symbols identifiable by illiterate voters. See LC to Miss Mary Winsor, January 1, 1912, LCP, box 10, folder 15.

24. "Voice from the Other Side," *Lexington Leader,* January 27, 1902; Knott, "Woman Suffrage Movement," 227–28, 235, 239; and Ann Allen, "Woman Suffrage and Progressive Reform in Louisville, 1908–1920," *Ohio Valley History* 20, no. 1 (Spring 2020): 67.

25. J. Embry Allen to Mrs. Potts, January 30, 1902, LCP, box 6, folder 21.

26. "School Suffrage in Kentucky"; and "Statement of the Executive Committee for the Retention of School Suffrage," in KERA, 1901 Minutes, 15.

27. LC to Mrs. Ida Husted Harper, April 3, 1902, LCP, box 3, folder 20.

28. Bolin, *Bossism and Reform*, 18.

29. Ibid., 55.

30. Ibid., 40, 52.

31. "Editorial Notes," *WJ*, March 22, 1902, 89.

32. Mary Atkinson Cunningham to Miss [Anna] Miller, February 6, 1902, LCP, box 6, folder 21.

33. JKH to Dear Miss Laura, November 10, 1898, LCP, box 6, folder 19; and JKH, "Kentucky," *WJ*, April 5, 1902, 112.

34. Olympia Brown, "Work Only for Full Suffrage," *WJ*, May 10, 1902, 149.

35. Graham, *Woman Suffrage and the New Democracy*, 21; and KERA, 1904 Minutes, 2. KERA never explained how it would determine literacy, although in 1905 leaders suggested that it should be measured by ability to read the US Constitution. See *Minutes of the Sixteenth Annual Convention of the Kentucky Equal Rights Association, Held at the Spiritual Temple, Newport, Kentucky, November 10, 1905* (Newport, KY: Davies, n.d.), 1, UKSCRC (hereafter 1905 Minutes).

7. All Women Cannot Be Heroes

1. 1890 US Census, ancestry.com; KERA, 1889 Minutes, 2–8.

2. KERA, 1893 Minutes, 2; and *Minutes of the Fourteenth Annual Convention of the Kentucky Equal Rights Association, Held at Guild Hall, Trinity Episcopal Church, Covington, Ky., November 11–12, 1903* (Newport, KY; Davies, 1904), 11, UKSCRC (hereafter 1903 Minutes).

3. Ella Porter, "Is It Ruining Our Girls?" *WJ*, April 27, 1889, 132–33; Weiss, *The Woman's Hour*, 33; S. J. Millsop to Miss Clay, January 5, 1889, LCP, box 6, folder 11.

4. Mary B. Clay, "Kentucky," *WJ*, December 6, 1884, 393.

5. Eleanor T. Little to LC, March 6, 1911, LCP, box 10, folder 1; W. S. McLaughlin to Miss Clay, July 28, 1911, LCP, box 10, folder 6; and Margaret W. Castleman to Miss Clay, September 19, 1911, LCP, box 10, folder 10.

6. Laura R. White to Miss Clay, November 30, 1909, LCP, box 8, folder 16; and Emma Roebuck to Miss Clay, January 11, 1910, LCP, box 9, folder 3.

7. "State Convention, Kentucky W. C. T. U.," *Earlington Bee*, October 9, 1902, 7, and August 24, 1893, 3.

8. Thomas H. Appleton Jr., "'Like Banquo's Ghost': The Emergence of the Prohibition Issue in Kentucky Politics" (PhD diss., University of Kentucky, 1981), 54; Mrs. Agnes L. Eifort to Miss Clay, November 4, 1904, LCP, box 7, folder 2; L. C. Obenchain to Miss Clay, January 15, 1909, LCP, box 8, folder 5; Wheeler, *New Women*, 11; and Hay, *Madeline McDowell Breckinridge*, 142.

9. "Women Leave Hall," *Owensboro Messenger*, May 7, 1903, 1; and Randolph Hollingsworth, "Biographical Sketch of Frances R. Estill Beauchamp," BDWSM.

10. LC to Brutus [Clay], March 31, 1905, LCP, box 1, folder 4. She ended up purchasing a typewriter the following year after a company offered her a discount in exchange for advertising space in KERA's quarterly newsletter.

11. Parts of this chapter also appear in Melanie Beals Goan, "The 'Argument of Numbers': Laura Clay and the Failure of the Kentucky Plan," *Ohio Valley History* 20, no. 1 (Spring 2020): 9–29.

12. "Aunt Susan and Her Girls," *Omaha Daily Bee*, May 30, 1901, http://nebnewspapers.unl.edu/lccn/sn99021999/1901–05–30/ed-1/seq-4.pdf, accessed November 28, 2018.

13. Dubois, ed., *Elizabeth Cady Stanton/Susan B. Anthony*, 178; *History of Woman Suffrage*, 4:xxx.

14. NAWSA, 1895 Proceedings, 22–24, 47, 41; and Graham, *Woman Suffrage and the New Democracy*, 7.

15. *Proceedings of the Thirtieth Annual Convention of the National American Woman Suffrage Association and the Celebration of the Fiftieth Anniversary of the First Woman's Rights Convention at the Columbia Theater, Twelfth and F. Streets, Washington, D. C., February 13, 14, 15, 16, 17, 18, 19, 1898*, ed. Rachel Foster Avery (Philadelphia: Press of Alfred J. Ferris, n.d.), 55 (hereafter 1898 Proceedings); *Proceedings of the Thirty-Fourth Annual Convention of the National American Woman Suffrage Association, Held at Washington, D. C., February 14th, 15th, 16th, 17th, 18th, 1902*, ed. Alice Stone Blackwell and Harriet Taylor Upton (n.p.), 1902, 26, 31, 43, 118 (hereafter 1902 Proceedings); and *Proceedings of the Thirty-Seventh Annual Convention of the National-American Woman Suffrage Association, Held at Portland, Oregon, June 28th to July 5th, Inclusive, 1905* (Warren, OH: Tribune Company, n.d.), 41.

16. KERA, "Report of Treasurer," 1901 Minutes, 8–9; and 1895 Minutes, 21.

17. NAWSA, 1902 Proceedings, 45; Constitution appended to KERA, 1889 Minutes, 50; and KERA, 1904 Minutes, 2.

18. Anne Firor Scott and Alexander MacKay Scott, "Do a Majority of Women . . . Want the Ballot?" in *One Half the People: The Fight for Woman Suffrage* (Urbana: University of Illinois Press, 1982), 106–11.

19. Kentucky E. R. A. Newsletter, May 1903, LCP, box 15, folder 7.

20. NAWSA, "Report on Increase of Membership," *Proceedings of the Thirty-Eighth Annual Convention of the National-American Woman Suffrage Association, Held Baltimore, MD., February 7th to 13th inclusive, 1906* (Warren, OH: Wm. Ritezel & Co., n.d.), 41, 42.

21. LC to May Hamilton, August 5, 1907, LCP, box 7, folder 20; and KERA, 1903 Minutes, 4–5.

22. *Proceedings of the Thirty-Third Annual Convention of the National American Woman Suffrage Association, Held at First Baptist Church, Corner of 10th Street and Harmon Place, Minneapolis, Minn., May 30 and 31, June 1, 2, 3, 4, and 5, 1901*, ed. Alice Stone Blackwell (Warren, OH: Press of Frank W. Perry, n.d.), 48–51; and NAWSA, 1902 Proceedings, 44–45.

23. Lynn E. Niedermeier, *Eliza Calvert Hall: Kentucky Author and Suffragist* (Lexington: UPK, 2007); KERA, 1903 Minutes, 13; L. C. Obenchain to Miss Clay, June 3, 1904, LCP, box 7, folder 1; and L. C. Obenchain to LC, August 1, 1906, LCP, box 7, folder 11.

24. L. C. Obenchain to Miss Clay, December 11, 1906, LCP, box 7, folder 16; and LC to Mrs. Obenchain, October 1, 1906, LCP, box 7, folder 13.

25. Kentucky E. R. A. Newsletter, May 1903; and Virginia Franceway to Miss Clay, November 4, 1904, LCP, box 7, folder 2.

26. Perle Penfield to LC, May 5, 1909, LCP, box 8, folder 12; Graham, *Woman Suffrage and the New Democracy*, 7–8.

27. NAWSA, 1898 Proceedings, 95; KERA, "Report of Emma Smith DeVoe," 1897 Minutes, 22–23. Because Kentucky had Miss Clay, one of the national stars of the suffrage movement, leaders often assumed that it did not need as many resources. Clay may have reinforced this idea that she could handle things without assistance. Kentucky also seemed less strategically important than other states where constitutional campaigns had more promise of success.

28. Lisa Lindell, "A Woman of Her Time: Dr. Frances Woods and the Intersection of War, Expansionism and Equal Rights," *Women's History Magazine* 75 (Summer 2014): 11–19, https://openprairie.sdstate.edu/cgi/viewcontent.cgi?article=1025&context=library_pubs, accessed April 30, 2019; KERA, 1901 Minutes, 6; "Report of Dr. Woods' Organizing Tour," 1904 Minutes, 22; and Frances Woods to Miss Clay, November 9, 1904, LCP, box 7, folder 2.

29. Frances Woods to Miss Clay, November 22, 1904 and October 21, 1904, LCP, box 7, folder 2; and Frances Woods, "Some Kentucky Comments," *WJ*, December 17, 1904, 406.

30. "Report of Dr. Woods' Organizing Tour," 1904 KERA Minutes, 22; and LC to Miss Rosalie G. Jones, September 3, 1913, LCP, box 11, folder 17.

31. Frances Woods to Miss Clay, November 2, 1904, LCP, box 7, folder 2.

32. KERA, 1905 Minutes, 10, 15.

33. KERA, 1894 Minutes, 9; *Minutes of the Twenty-Sixth Annual Convention of the Kentucky Equal Rights Association, Held at Lexington, Kentucky, November 8, 9 and 10, 1915*, (n.p.), 3, 11, UKSCRC (hereafter 1915 Minutes); and KERA, 1904 Minutes, 12.

34. Mary J. Coggeshall to LC, August 4, 1907, LCP, box 7, folder 20; LC to Mrs. Franceway, September 28, 1907, LCP, box 7, folder 21.

35. Virginia Franceway to LC, February 14, 1909, LCP, box 8, folder 7; "Mrs. James Franceway Dies in Madisonville," *LC-J*, February 10, 1907, 29; and 1910 US Census, ancestry.com.

36. Holly J. McCammon, "Stirring Up Suffrage Sentiment: The Formation of the State Woman Suffrage Organizations, 1866–1914," *Social Forces* 80, no. 2 (December 2001): 449–80; and Graham, *Woman Suffrage and the New Democracy*, 8.

37. KERA, 1901 Minutes, 5.

38. Kelli Lemaster and Melanie Beals Goan, "Biographical Sketch of Laura Rogers White," BDWSM.

39. "Report of Local Associations" in *Minutes of the Seventeenth Annual Convention of the Kentucky Equal Rights Association, Held at Ashland, KY, November 21st and 22nd, 1906* (Newport, KY: The Newport Printing Co., n.d.), 14, UKSCRC (hereafter 1906 Minutes); *Reports of the Twenty-First and Twenty-Second Annual Meetings of the Kentucky Equal Rights Association, Held at Covington, November 14–15–16, 1910* (Newport, KY: Newport Printing Co., n.d.), 6, UKSCRC (hereafter 1910 Minutes).

40. "Report of Local Associations" KERA, 1906 Minutes, 14; and Agnes L. Eifort to Miss Clay, May 30, 1905, LCP, box 7, folder 5.

41. LC to Laura [R. White], October 17, 1906, LCP, box 7, folder 13.

42. *Report of the Eighteenth Annual Convention of the Kentucky Equal Rights Association, Held at Richmond, KY, November 14th and 15th, 1907* (Newport, KY: Newport Printing Co., n.d.), 9, UKSCRC (hereafter 1907 Minutes); and LC to Miss Averill, January 16, 1909, LCP, box 8, folder 6.

43. NAWSA, "Report of Committee on Increase of Membership," *Proceedings of the Thirty-Ninth Annual Convention of the National American Woman Suffrage Association, Held at Chicago, Ill., February 14–19 (inclusive), 1907* (n.p.), 55–56; and "Woman's Party," *Lexington Leader*, February 19, 1907, 1.

44. See NAWSA convention proceedings for 1902–1908. The drop in 1907 was likely due to Clay being out of the state so much, assisting Oklahoma suffragists with their state campaign.

45. LC to Mrs. Franceway, January 7, [1909], LCP, box 8, folder 5; "Taft's Troubles Have Begun," *Owensboro Messenger*, November 6, 1908, 1; NAWSA, "The Report of the National Committee on Petition to Congress," *Forty-Second Annual Report of the National-American Woman Suffrage Association, Given at the Convention Held at Washington, D. C., April 14 to 19 (inclusive)* (New York: Headquarters, [1910]), 34–37 (hereafter, 1910 Proceedings); and President, Ky. ERA to Miss Sallie Edmonds, January 11, 1909, LCP, box 8, folder 5.

46. LC to Mrs. S. M. Hubbard, January 8, 1909, LCP, box 8, folder 5; and LC to Mrs. Anna K. Potts, October 30, 1909, LCP, box 8, folder 15.

47. LC to Mrs. Mae R. Patterson, January 7, [1909], LCP, box 7, folder 23.

48. Mary M. Mitchell to Mrs. Obenchain, January 22, 1909, LCP, box 8, folder 7.

49. LC to Mrs. S. M. Hubbard, January 8, 1909, Emma Hast to Miss LC, January 11, 1909, and LC to Mrs. Emma M. Roebuck, January 15, 1909, LCP, box 8, folder 5.

50. Emma M. Roebuck to Miss Clay, January 17, 1909, LCP, box 8, folder 6. For biographical information on Roebuck, see Jennifer Hootman, "Biographical Sketch of Emma Massman Roebuck," BDWSM.

51. Laura R. White to LC, January 25, 1909, LCP, box 8, folder 6; Laura R. White to Miss Clay, February 8, 1909, LCP, box 8, folder 7; and Mary Reed [Clay's stenographer] to Miss Clay, February 25, 1909, LCP, box 8, folder 8.

52. Virginia Franceway to Miss Clay, February 14, 1909, LCP, box 8, folder 7.

53. LC to Mrs. Emma M. Roebuck, January 19, 1909, LCP, box 8, folder 6; and Fuller, *Laura Clay*. Clay was in Oregon from mid-1905 to mid-1906 and in Arizona in early 1909.

54. "Kentucky," in NAWSA, 1910 Proceedings, 113–14; and correspondence in LCP, box 9.

55. "Report of the National Committee on Petition to Congress" in 1910 Proceedings, 19–24; KERA, 1910 Minutes, 16–17; *The History of Woman Suffrage*, vol. 5, *1900–1920*, ed. Ida Husted Harper (National American Woman Suffrage Association, 1922), 275, and 1910 Census, ancestry.com.

56. *Report of the Nineteenth Annual Convention of the Kentucky Equal Rights Association, Held at Richmond, KY, November 17th and 18th, 1908* (Newport, KY: Newport Printing Co., n.d.), 3, UKSCRC (hereafter 1908 Minutes).

8. Louisville Awakens

1. LC to Mrs. White, January 3, 1911, LCP, box 9, folder 20; LC to Mrs. Gamble, February 22, 1911, LCP, box 9, folder 21.

2. National Register of Historic Places nomination form for Seelbach Hotel, July 17, 1975, https://npgallery.nps.gov/GetAsset/2ccf1b04–0e1d-4961-bc74 -a8e643459916, accessed May 17, 2019.

3. LC to Mrs. Dennett, September 2, 1911, LCP, box 10, folder 9; "Excursions," *WJ*, September 16, 1911, 293; and KERA, 1911 Minutes, 29–30. For a useful discussion of Kentucky's paradoxical public image, see James C. Nicholson, *The Kentucky Derby: How the Run for the Roses Became America's Premier Sporting Event* (Lexington: UPK, 2012).

4. LC to Mrs. Roebuck, January 14, 1910, LCP, box 9, folder 3; Louisville reports in KERA minutes, 1908–1912; and LC to Miss Robinson, January 11, 1909, LCP, box 8, folder 5.

5. "Louisville, Kentucky," Wikipedia, https://en.wikipedia.org/wiki/Louisville, _Kentucky, accessed May 11, 2019; and Carol Guethlein, "Women in Louisville: Moving toward Equal Rights," *Filson Club Quarterly* 55, no. 2 (April 1981): 152–53.

6. Ann Allen, "A Suffragist Dynasty: Susan Look Avery (1817–1915); Lydia Avery Coonley Ward (1845–1924); Helen Avery Robinson (1855–1943); Kate

Shindler Jewett Avery (1856–1926)," H-Kentucky, https://networks.h-net.org/node/2289/discussions/1413924/suffragist-dynasty-susan-look-avery-1817–1915-lydia-avery-coonley, accessed May 4, 2020.

7. Susan Look Avery to Miss Clay, October 21, 1903, LCP, box 6, folder 21.

8. LERA Minute Book, transcribed and included with LeeAnn Whites and Andrew Fialka, *The Woman Suffrage Movement and Progressive Reform in Louisville, Kentucky, 1889–1920*, https://www.arcgis.com/apps/MapJournal/index.html?appid=63ca790d23e94978b15247b78113e868, published April 2019, accessed December 8, 2019; KERA, 1890 Minutes, 2; "Work in the Missionary Field," *LC-J*, April 5, 1888, 8; and "Ramabai Circle," *LC-J*, February 25, 1891, 2.

9. Ann Allen, "Biographical Sketch of Caroline Apperson Leech," BDWSM; and "Caroline Apperson Leech," *A Dictionary of Prominent Women of Louisville and Lexington*, ed. Bess A. Ray (Louisville: Louisville Free Public Library, 1940), 148–49, UKSCRC.

10. "Many Marriages Unhappy," *LC-J*, October 4, 1892, 8; and "Type-Writers and Bicycles," *LC-J*, January 1, 1891, 30.

11. LERA Minute Book, April 13, 1889.

12. See LERA Minute Book, 1889–1892, but especially November 1, 1889, May 1890, and January 8, 1892.

13. Susan Look Avery to Miss Clay, October 21, 1903, LCP, box 6, folder 21; and Allen, "Woman Suffrage and Progressive Reform," 55.

14. Allen, "A Suffragist Dynasty"; and Chicago Woman's Club, *Annals of the Chicago Woman's Club for the First Forty Years of Its Existence, 1876–1916* (Chicago: Chicago Woman's Club, 1916).

15. Mrs. George C. Avery and Mrs. C. P. Barnes to Madam, March 21, 1900, LCP, box 6, folder 20; "Proceeding of the Mass Meeting of the Women of Louisville, held Tuesday, February Sixth, 1900," LCP, box 2, folder 18; "Women," *LC-J*, February 7, 1900, 3; and "Out with Polygamy," *LC-J*, October 27, 1901, 12.

16. Allen, "A Suffragist Dynasty"; KERA, 1898 Minutes, 40; "Reports of Associations for 1902," KERA, 1901 Minutes, 21; and LC to Mrs. Roebuck, November 2, 1906, LCP, box 4, folder 3.

17. "Reports of Local Associations," KERA, 1905 Minutes, 16; and "Reports of Local Associations" KERA, 1908 Minutes, 18. The National asked state and local suffrage organizations to adopt uniform names, all ending with "Woman Suffrage Association." Clay left the matter to the discretion of locals. The state organization retained its existing name.

18. "The Girl Orator," *Stanford Interior Journal*, August 27, 1886, 3; *Stanford Interior Journal*, October 12, 1886, 1; *Danville Kentucky Advocate*, March 4, 1887, 3; and "Temperance," *Stanford Interior Journal*, May 5, 1896, 3.

19. "Civic Department," *LC-J*, February 23, 1908, 15; "Immoral Wages," *LC-J*, November 13, 1909, 2; and Ann Allen, "Biographical Sketch of Lucy Adams (Mrs. Charles S.) Nield," BDWSM.

20. "Woman's Suffrage Association of Louisville," *Report of the Twentieth Annual Convention of the Kentucky Equal Rights Association, Held at the Public Library Assembly Room, Louisville, KY., November 11th and 12th, 1909* (Newport, KY: Newport Printing Co., n.d.), 17–18, UKSCRC (hereafter 1909 Minutes); "Emma W. Hast," Google Patents, https://patents.google.com/?inventor=Emma+W+Hast, accessed April 25, 2019; and "Virginia Pollard Robinson," Virginia Commonwealth University Social Welfare History Project, https://socialwelfare.library.vcu.edu/eras/great-depression/robinson-virginia-pollard/, accessed April 25, 2019.

21. "Will Do Research Work," *LC-J*, March 29, 1912, 5.

22. L. C. Obenchain to LC, August 1, 1906, LCP, box 7, folder 11; New List of Mrs. Obenchain and Lida Calvert Obenchain to Miss Clay, March 11, 1909, LCP, box 8, folder 10; and Krock, *Editorials of Henry Watterson*, 358.

23. Lida Calvert Obenchain to Miss Clay, March 11, 1909, LCP, box 8, folder 10; and LC to [Member of the Executive Committee], [March 29, 1910], LCP, box 9, folder 7.

24. "Louisville Society Woman Working for Woman Suffrage," *Owensboro Messenger*, May 9, 1909, 14.

25. Virginia P. Robinson to Miss Clay, November 13, 1909, LCP, box 8, folder 16.

26. KERA minutes, 1903–1909.

27. "Report of Officers," KERA, 1909 Minutes, 2; and "Large Concourse at Dr. Roark's Funeral," *LC-J*, April 17, 1909, 3. In 2015, the EKU Board of Regents voted to name Roark officially as the institution's second president. See "Regents Designate Mary Roark as Eastern's Second President," https://www.eku.edu/news/regents-designate-mary-roark-easterns-2nd-president, accessed May 14, 2019.

28. "Programme," *LC-J*, November 10, 1909, 3. Judah was scheduled to speak, but it appears that she did not. The KERA meeting minutes and a follow up piece in the *Courier-Journal* note that a representative of the Outdoor Art League offered greetings but mention no appearance by Judah. See KERA, 1909 Minutes, 3; and "Equal Suffrage for the Women," *LC-J*, November 12, 1909, 2. Judah went on to serve as KERA's treasurer for most of the decade. See Allen, "Woman Suffrage and Progressive Reform"; and Randolph Hollingsworth, "Biographical Sketch of Rebecca Rosenthal Judah," BDWSM.

29. KERA, 1909 Minutes, 3, 6.

30. "Consumers League to Call Meeting," *LC-J*, May 12, 1901, 12; and "'The Battles with the Slums,'" *LC-J*, January 26, 1902, 15.

31. Ruth Sapinsky, "A Kentucky Settlement," *Wellesley College News* (1910), 2–10, quoted in Allen, "Woman Suffrage and Progressive Reform," 60.

32. "S. Thruston Ballad, Ill for a Year, Is Dead," *LC-J*, January 19, 1926, 1, 4; and S. Thruston Ballard, "Eight-Hour Shifts in the Milling Industry," *American Labor Legislation Review*, 4 (1914): 117–19.

33. Mrs. Mary C. Roark to LC, April 15, 1908, LCP, box 8, folder 1; LC to Mrs. Roark, October 25, 1909, LCP, box 8, folder 15; and "Immoral Wages," *LC-J*, November 13, 1909, 2.

34. KERA, 1901 Minutes, 13; "Suffragists to Meet," *LC-J*, February 21, 1911, 10; and Allen, "Woman Suffrage and Progressive Reform."

35. Caroline A. Leech to Miss Laura, September 11, 1908, LCP, box 8, folder 3; Ann Allen, "Biographical Sketch of Caroline Apperson Leech," BDWSM; "Woman's Suffragette Association Revived," *LC-J*, November 24, 1908, 6; "A Suffragette Here," *Winchester News*, October 20, 1908, 6; "Mrs. Snowden to Speak at the Woman's Club," *LC-J*, November 11, 1909, 8; and KERA, 1910 and 1911 Minutes, 13, 34.

36. LC to Miss Henry, September 29, 1911, LCP, box 10, folder 11.

37. Thank you to Ann Allen for helping me sharpen my thinking on this point.

38. "Miss Laura Clay May Be President of Suffragists," *Lexington Leader*, October 23, 1911, 12; "Agree on '300' Limit," *LC-J*, October 22, 1911, 31; LC to Mrs. Roebuck, May 25, 1911, LCP, box 10, folder 2; and Franzen, *Anna Howard Shaw*, 118–23.

39. "Suffragists in National Meeting," *Lexington Leader*, October 21, 1911, 4; Catherine Waugh McCullough to Miss Clay, June 10, 1911, LCP, box 10, folder 3; Jessie Ashley, "National Headquarters Letter," *WJ*, November 11, 1911, 356; Martha Gruening, "Universal v. Limited Suffrage," *WJ*, May 20, 1911, 158; and LC to Editor of *WJ* and LC to Miss Blackwell, June 19, 1911, LCP, box 2, folder 6.

40. LC to Mrs. McCulloch and Mrs. Stewart, July 3, 1911, LCP, box 10, folder 5.

41. "Suffragists to Meet Here," *LC-J*, October 15, 1911, 19; and "Mrs. Belmont Can't Attend," *LC-J*, October 19, 1911, 1.

42. CCC to Mary Gray Peck, December 13, 1911, and December 26, 1911, CCC Papers, quoted in Franzen, *Anna Howard Shaw*, 136.

43. Guethlein, "Women in Louisville," 170; and *Forty-Third Annual Report of the National-American Woman Suffrage Association, Given at the Convention Held at Louisville, KY., October 19 to 25, Inclusive* (New York: Headquarters, [1911]), 186–89 (hereafter 1911 Proceedings).

44. NAWSA, 1911 Proceedings, 186–89; Telegram from Nisba Breckinridge to Miss Laura Clay, [n.d.], LC to Miss Sophonisba, November 1, 1911, LCP, box 10, folder 13.

45. "Mrs. Pankhurst Makes Defense," *LC-J*, October 25, 1911, 2; "Election Not Pleasing to Kentucky Women," *LC-J*, October 26, 1911, 2; and Catherine Waugh McCulloch to Miss Clay, October 25, 1911, LCP, box 10, folder 12.

46. "Philadelphia Suffragist Says 'Rope People In,'" *LC-J*, October 22, 1911, 31; Ann Allen, "Biographical Sketch of Jennie Angell Mengel," BDWSM; and "Pledges for Children," *LC-J*, October 25, 1911, 2.

47. "Mrs. Pankhurst at Convention," *LC-J*, October 22, 1911, 31; and "Mrs. Pankhurst Makes Defense," *LC-J*, October 25, 1911, 1.

48. LC to Virginia P. Robinson, November 17, 1911, LCP, box 10, folder 13.

9. Meeting New Work with New Methods

1. LC to Mrs. Roebuck, August 27, 1912, LCP, box 11, folder 5.

2. "Miss Clay Will Not Be President," *Lexington Leader*, October 23, 1912, 1.

3. KERA, 1911 Minutes, 20, 22; and "Name Officers of State Body," *LC-J*, October 26, 1911, 2. The failed motion is not noted in the official KERA minutes, only in news coverage. The term of office had first been set at two years, but it was soon changed to three. The position of treasurer was later exempted from term limits.

4. KERA Minutes, 1889–1910; and N. S. McLaughlin to LC, [June 2, 1908], LCP, box 8, folder 2.

5. LC to Miss Robinson, November 17, 1911, LCP, box 10, folder 13; and "Miss Clay Will Not Be President."

6. LC to Rev. Olympia Brown, June 22, 1915, LCP, box 12, folder 7.

7. LC to Mrs. Jefferson Myers, LCP, box 9, folder 20. For a discussion of the thrill of campaigns see *Harriet Taylor Upton's Random Recollections*, ed. Eisenbrun, 146.

8. Helen Bynum, *Spitting Blood: The History of Tuberculosis* (Oxford: Oxford University Press, 2012).

9. Hay, *Madeline McDowell Breckinridge*, 44–45, 103; and "She Is Dead," *Lexington Herald*, November 23, 1920, copy located in Maude Ward Lafferty papers, scrapbook no. 2, UKSCRC.

10. Sophonisba Preston Breckinridge, *Madeline McDowell Breckinridge: A Leader in the New South* (Chicago: University of Chicago Press, 1921), viii; and Lindsey Apple, "Madeline McDowell Breckinridge (1872–1920): A Sense of Mission," in *Kentucky Women: Their Lives and Times*, ed. Melissa A. McEuen and Thomas H. Appleton Jr. (Athens: University of Georgia Press, 2015), 226.

11. Hay, *Madeline McDowell Breckinridge*.

12. "Model School for Lexington," *Lexington Leader*, May 30, 1909, MMBP, box 3, folder 21.

13. Breckinridge, *Madeline McDowell Breckinridge*, 217–18.

14. "Fair Lobbyists," *LC-J*, January 23, 1908, 3; and N. S. McLaughlin to Miss Clay, March 7, 1908, LCP, box 8, folder 1.

15. "A Triumph of Prejudice," *Lexington Leader*, February 28, 1910, 4; Nancy K. Forderhase, "The Clear Call of Thoroughbred Women: The Kentucky Federation of Women's Clubs and the Crusade for Educational Reform," *Register of the Kentucky Historical Society* 83, no. 1 (Winter 1985); and "Liquor Interests," *Lexington Herald*, May 27, 1910, 11, MPHF, box 2, folder 68.

16. "Dealt Fairly by Opponents," *Breckinridge News* (Cloverport, KY), January 10, 1912, 3; Hay, *Madeline McDowell Breckinridge*, 148; and Bolin, *Bossism and Reform*, 58.

17. "School Suffrage," *Barbourville Mountain Advocate*, June 21, 1912, 4; and "Women Organize to Urge the Suffrage Movement," *LC-J*, September 29, 1912, 10.

18. Allen, "Suffrage and Progressive Reform."

19. KERA, 1911 Minutes, 22.

20. "Plan of Work Committee," *Report of the Twenty-Third Annual Convention of the Kentucky Equal Rights Association, Held at Lexington, Kentucky in the Arts Club Building, October 24th and 25th, 1912* (n.p.), 5, UKSCRC (hereafter 1912 Minutes).

21. "Miss Clay Will Not Be President"; KERA Minutes, 1912–1919; and Fuller, *Laura Clay*, 136, 141.

22. See correspondence between Clay and Breckinridge in LCP, box 12.

23. MMB, "Some Reasons for Granting School Suffrage to Kentucky Women," May 1910, MMBP, box 6, folder 48; and Florence Taylor to Mrs. Breckinridge, October 20, 1914, MMBP, box 1, folder 9.

24. One example of these press plates is "Stand Up and Be Counted Right Now," which ran in the *Clay City Times* (November 27, 1913) and *Danville Advocate-Messenger* (November 21, 1913). See also "Report of the Kentucky Equal Rights Association for the Year 1912–13," *Report of the Twenty-Fourth Annual Convention of the Kentucky Equal Rights Association, Held at Louisville, Kentucky, November 20, 21 and 22, 1913* (Louisville: Westerfield-Bonte Co., [1914]), 8, UKSCRC (hereafter 1913 Minutes).

25. LC and MMB to Mrs. Dennett, February 4, 1913, LCP, box 11, folder 12; and Wynelle Deese, *Lexington, Kentucky: Changes in the Early Twentieth Century* (Charleston, SC: Arcadia, 1998), chap. 1.

26. KERA, 1906 Minutes, 4; and Treasurer's Report, KERA, 1912 Minutes, 11.

27. Treasurer's Report, KERA, 1913 Minutes, 18; and Expenses of the Kentucky Equal Rights Association for month of August 1914, LCP, box 15, folder 9.

28. "Stand Up and Be Counted Right Now."

29. Weiss, *The Woman's Hour*, 58, 192. Alva Belmont, in fact, supported the Kentucky suffrage movement, donating $200 to help with a state campaign in 1913. She noted that Kentucky's pioneer blood ran through her veins (she was a descendent of General Robert Desha), thus giving her a special interest in its suffrage efforts. See "Mrs. Belmont on Kentucky's Work," *WJ*, December 27, 1913, 410.

30. "In Memoriam," *Register of the Kentucky Historical Society* 3, no. 7 (January 1905): 85–87; and Catherine Waugh McCulloch to Miss Clay, April 1905, LCP, box 7, folder 5. KERA paid tribute to Bruce after she died, but never mentioned the money she left. See Kentucky E. R. A. newsletter, October 1904, LCP, box 15, folder 7. The Clay women's contributions to KERA and NAWSA were considerable, coming in small amounts frequently given. See KERA minutes and NAWSA convention proceedings for a sense of their generosity. Also see receipts in LCP, box 15, folder 1. For conversion of 1904 to 2018 dollars, see https://westegg.com /inflation/infl.cgi.

31. KERA, 1913 Minutes, 20; and S. M. Hubbard to Miss Clay, November 12, 1912, LCP, box 11, folder 8. For more on Hubbard, see Jennifer Walton-Hanley, "Biographical Sketch of Sallie McConnell Hubbard," BDWSM; and "Wealthy Fulton County Man Expires," *LC-J*, October 1, 1901, 2.

32. Knott, "Woman Suffrage Movement," 174–81; and Allen, "Woman Suffrage and Progressive Reform."

33. KERA, 1913 Minutes; "Kentucky Equal Rights Ass'n Meets in Louisville This Week," *Danville Advocate-Messenger*, November 21, 1913, 2; and "Full Ballot," *LC-J*, November 23, 1913, 2.

34. Mrs. Desha Breckinridge, "A New Hope," National Conference of Charities and Correction, [1914], MMBP, box 6, folder 48.

35. MMB to Mr. J. B. Head, April 28, 1916, BFP, copy located in MPHF, box 2, folder 126; and KERA, 1911 Minutes, 30.

36. Hay, *Madeline McDowell Breckinridge*, 123.

37. Ibid., 161, 181; and "Full Ballot," *LC-J*, November 23, 1913, 2.

38. LC to Miss Annie Haney, February 14, 1911, LCP, box 9, folder 21.

39. Weiss, *The Woman's Hour*, 62; and "Follow Flag," *LC-J*, October 18, 1911, 8.

40. N. S. McLaughlin to LC, May 8, 1908, and LC to Mrs. McLaughlin, June 9, 1908, LCP, box 8, folder 2; Mrs. Giltner to LC, April 18, 1908, and LC to Mrs. Giltner, April 22, 1908, LCP, box 8, folder 1; and NAWSA, 1911 Proceedings, 28.

41. Fuller, *Laura Clay*, 132–33; and KERA, 1913 Minutes, 19.

42. J. D. Zahniser and Amelia R. Fry, *Alice Paul: Claiming Power* (Oxford: Oxford University Press, 2014), 134.

43. "Kentucky Women Asked to Take Part in Suffrage Parade at Capital and Help to Bolster the Cause," unidentified newspaper, [1913], Laura White Papers, Kentucky Historical Society; and "Suffragists," *Richmond Climax*, February 21, 1913, 3. For background on the growing popularity of suffrage parades, see Michael McGerr, "Political Style and Women's Power,1830–1930," *Journal of American History* 77, no. 3 (December 1990): 864–85.

44. Zahniser and Fry, *Alice Paul*, 148; "Mice to Rout Suffragettes," *Paducah Sun-Democrat*, February 3, 1913, 7; and "Mob Breaks Up Pageant," *LC-J*, March 1, 1913, 1.

45. "Ardent Suffragists," *Cincinnati Enquirer*, March 1, 1913, 10; and "Would Sue Government," *Washington Herald*, March 11, 1913, 2. See also Rachel Wolters, "Biographical Sketch of Mary Light Ogle," and Paul A. Tenkotte, "Biographical Sketch of Jessica (Jessie) Riddell Firth," BDWSM.

46. Heather Qaddura and Jennifer Walton-Hanley, "Biographical Sketch of Alice Barbee Castleman," BDWSM; and "Suffrage Women Plan 'Parade in Perry Parade,'" *LC-J*, September 21, 1913, 22.

47. "Suffragists Win Applause All Along Line of March," *Louisville Herald*, October 3, 1913. Thank you to Carol Mattingly for providing this helpful source.

48. KERA, 1913 Minutes, 8.

49. LC to Mr. W. P. Marsh, July 24, 1915, LCP, box 12, folder 8.

50. M. M'D. Breckinridge, "The Women of Kentucky versus the Honorable Harry G. Meyers of Covington, Now of the Legislature," *Lexington Herald* [n.d.], MMBP, box 6, folder 8.

51. Quoted in Hay, *Madeline McDowell Breckinridge*, 116.

10. The Pink Tea Stage

1. Mary Holland Kinkaid to LC, June 17, 1911, LCP, box 10, folder 3; and Mary Holland Kinkaid, "The Feminine Charms of the Woman Militant," *Good Housekeeping*, February 1912, 146–55.

2. LC to Mrs. M. H. Kinkaid, July 25, 1911, LCP, box 10, folder 6.

3. Breckinridge, *Madeline McDowell Breckinridge*, 202–3.

4. "Program Features of State Federation," *Paducah Sun-Democrat*, June 3, 1913, 5; Hebe Hamilton, "What Kentucky Women Owe the Clay Women," *Paducah News-Democrat*, June 7, 1913, 3; "Favors Giving Women Ballot," *LC-J*, June 14, 1913, 7; Alben W. Barkley interview with Sidney Shalett, August 4, 1953, Louie B. Nunn Center for Oral History, University of Kentucky Libraries.

5. "W. C. T. U. Is against the Use of Tobacco," *Owensboro Messenger*, October 9, 1914, 6; and "Suffrage is Endorsed by Bakers' Association," *Owensboro Messenger*, September 8, 1912, 4.

6. By 1915, 106 of Kentucky's 120 counties were dry. See Bolin, *Bossism & Reform*, 61. See also Graham, *Woman Suffrage and the New Democracy*, 73; and Wheeler, *One Woman, One Vote*, 375.

7. "President's Report," *Report of the Twenty-Fifth Annual Convention of the Kentucky Equal Rights Association, Held at Owensboro, Kentucky, November 6, 7 and 8, 1914* (Louisville: C. T. Dearing Co., [1915]), 11, UKSCRC (hereafter 1914 Minutes).

8. "In Readiness for Meeting of Ky Suffragists," *Owensboro Messenger*, November 1, 1914, 14; and "Equal Suffrage Plan Discussed," *Louisville Evening Post*, [January 1913], Laura White Papers, Kentucky Historical Society.

9. LC to Mrs. Obenchain, May 6, 1913, LCP, box 11, folder 15; and KERA, 1913 Minutes, 6.

10. LC to Mrs. Lizzie Tucker, May 12, 1913, LCP, box 11, folder 15; and "Denounces Her English Cousins," *Owensboro Messenger*, April 26, 1913, 1.

11. "Denounces Her English Cousins"; and LC to Mrs. Obenchain, April 9, 1913, LCP, box 11, folder 14.

12. KERA, 1913 Minutes, 9.

13. KERA, 1910 Minutes, 8.

14. "Need More Men in Suffrage Movement," *LC-J*, January 18, 1913, 7.

15. "Equal Suffrage Plan Discussed"; and KERA, 1913 Minutes, 18.

16. James C. Klotter, *The Breckinridges of Kentucky, 1760–1981* (Lexington: UPK, 1986), 215.

17. "The Most Momentous Question of Modern Times," *LC-J*, April 22, 1913, 6; Wheeler, *New Women*, 49; and Desha Breckinridge, May 8, 1913 editorial, "In Which Army Will You Enlist?" *Lexington Herald*, Linda Neville Papers, UKSCRC, box 204, folder 17.

18. Ida Porter Boyer to Miss Clay, June 3, 1915, LCP, box 2, folder 14; and "Suffrage is Endorsed by Bakers' Association."

19. Mrs. Desha Breckinridge to Mrs. Geo. H. Rudy, October 3, 1914, LCP, box 11, folder 23; KERA, 1915 Minutes, 9, 13, 22; and "Lexington," *LC-J*, February 7, 1915, 22.

20. "Report of the Kentucky Equal Rights Association for the Year 1912–13," KERA, 1913 Minutes, 8.

21. Ibid., 9.

22. See for example, "An Appeal to Legislators," *Danville Advocate-Messenger*, December 2, 1913, 3.

23. "Women Are Coming," *Paducah Sun-Democrat*, January 7, 1914, 1; "Report of Legislative Work," KERA, 1914 Minutes, 15; and "Solons in Seats," *Paducah Sun-Democrat*, January 12, 1914, 3.

24. "Swarm of Bills Descends Upon House Members," *Paducah Sun-Democrat*, January 13, 1914, 1.

25. "Capitol Filled with Women," *Cincinnati Enquirer*, January 16, 1914, 4.

26. "Suffrage May Suffer Delay," *LC-J*, January 16, 1914, 4; and Hay, *Madeline McDowell Breckinridge*, 173.

27. Hay, *Madeline McDowell Breckinridge*, 169, 174, 177.

28. "Suffrage for Women," *Owensboro Messenger*, January 15, 1895, 1; and *Owensboro Examiner*, January 16, 1895, 4. The Owensboro club was still listed among KERA locals in 1897, but it sent no dues and no report. See KERA, 1897 Minutes.

29. LC to Miss J. F. W. Johnson, August 10, 1906, LCP, box 7, folder 11; and "First Address in Owensboro," *Owensboro Messenger*, March 29, 1913, 3.

30. KERA, 1913 Minutes, 25; "Campaign," *Owensboro Messenger*, February 22, 1913, 2; and "Much Good Is Accomplished," *Owensboro Messenger*, May 25, 1913, 11.

31. "At Utica," *Owensboro Messenger*, July 2, 1913, 4; "Personal Notes from Hawesville," *Owensboro Messenger*, April 26, 1914, 22; 1910 US census, ancestry. com; and "Ohio County Teachers," August 24, 1913, 2.

32. "In Readiness for Meeting of Ky Suffragists," *Owensboro Messenger*, November 1, 1914, 14; Whitney Raines and Jennifer Hanley, "Biographical Sketch of Julia Duke Henning," BDWSM; and Graham, *Woman Suffrage and the New Democracy*, 83.

33. Sara Egge, "How Midwestern Suffragists Used Anti-Immigrant Fervor to Help Gain the Vote," Zocalo Public Square, September 17, 2018, http://www .zocalopublicsquare.org/2018/09/17/midwestern-suffragists-used-anti-immigrant -fervor-help-gain-vote/ideas/essay/, accessed April 3, 2019; and Egge, *Woman Suffrage and Citizenship*, 2.

34. "Woman Suffrage," *Owensboro Messenger*, October 14, 1902, 4.

35. Hopkinsville report, KERA, 1915 Minutes, 20–21.

36. "Woman's Club," *Maysville Public Ledger*, April 15, 1912, 4; and "Suffrage," *Maysville Public Ledger*, July 23, 1912, 3.

37. "Report of Mason County Woman Suffrage Association," KERA, 1913 Minutes, 25–26.

38. "'Maid of Winchester,'" *Hopkinsville Kentuckian*, April 2, 1908, 5; Tandy Nash, "Biographical Sketch of Alice Lloyd," BDWSM; and "Attention Suffragists," *Maysville Public Ledger*, October 26, 1916, 1.

39. "Woman Suffrage Meeting Today," *Maysville Public Ledger*, May 4, 1914, 1; and "Report of Local Leagues," KERA, 1914 Minutes, 23.

40. "Report of the Bell County League for Woman Suffrage," KERA, 1913 Minutes, 26–27; and Harold G. Peach Jr., "Lee Davis Maddox Campbell, The First Female Superintendent of Anderson County Schools," unpublished essay in possession of the author.

41. "In Readiness for Meeting of Ky Suffragists," *Owensboro Messenger*, November 1, 1914, 14.

42. "President's Report," KERA, 1914 Minutes, 11.

43. "Reports of Organizers: Lily Ray Glenn," and "Reports of Organizers: Mrs. Charles. E. Firth," KERA, 1914 Minutes, 20–21.

44. Mrs. Desha Breckinridge to Board Member, July 21, 1915, LCP, box 2, folder 19.

45. "Report of Congressional Chairman," KERA, 1914 Minutes, 15–16; and "President's Report, 1914–1915," KERA, 1915 Minutes, 13.

46. MMB to Madam President [LC], January 1, 1915, LCP, box 2, folder 19.

11. Working for Peace

1. "Suffrage Parade Is Biggest Ever Held in Kentucky," *Lexington Herald*, May 7, 1916, 1, 3, H-Kentucky, transcribed by Randolph Hollingsworth, July 4, 2017, https://networks.h-net.org/node/2289/discussions/185737/suffrage-parade -biggest-ever-held-kentucky-lexington-herald-may-7, accessed June 13, 2019.

2. *Lexington City Directory, 1916–1917* (Columbus, OH: R. L. Polk & Co.), UKSCRC; National Register of Historic Places nomination form for Fayette National Bank Building, January 4, 1980, https://npgallery.nps.gov/NRHP /GetAsset/NRHP/80001513_text, accessed June 25, 2019; also see ads in *Kentucky Kernel* 8, no. 29 (April 20, 1916). Union Station stood at the corner of what is now East Main and Martin Luther King Boulevard, where the Fayette County Clerk's office is now located. See "Lexington's Union Station, 1944," *Kentucky Photo Archive*, posted on September 22, 2016, http://www.kyphotoarchive.com/2016/09 /22/lexingtons-union-station-1944/, accessed June 25, 2019.

3. *Maysville Public Ledger*, July 9, 1909, 1; and "Suffrage Parade Is Biggest."

4. "Suffrage Parade Is Biggest."

5. Breckinridge, *Madeline McDowell Breckinridge*, 223–25.

6. Hay, *Madeline McDowell Breckinridge*, 198–99; "Report of Campaign Chairman," *Report of the Twenty-Seventh Annual Convention of the Kentucky Equal Rights Association, Held at Louisville, Kentucky, November 15 and 16, 1916* (n.p.),

15, UKSCRC (hereafter 1916 Minutes); and Louise T. Jones, "Biographical Sketch of Elizabeth Chenault Bennett Smith Gagliardini," BDWSM.

7. "In Readiness for Meeting of Ky Suffragists," *Owensboro Messenger*, November 1, 1914, 14; "Report of Congressional Chairman," KERA, 1914 Minutes, 15–16; and LC to Mrs. C. C. Trent, June 16, 1915, LCP, box 12, folder 6.

8. David J. Bettez, *Kentucky and the Great War: World War I on the Home Front* (Lexington: UPK, 2016), 5; and "Judge Barker Makes Plea for Equal Rights," *Owensboro Messenger*, November 7, 1914, 6.

9. "Resolutions," KERA, 1914 Minutes, 9; and Laura R. White, "Report of Peace and Arbitration Committee," KERA, 1914 Minutes, 18–19.

10. "Louisville Women Join Cry for Termination of War," *LC-J*, April 8, 1915, 2; "Equal Rights Meeting," *LC-J*, May 24, 1915, 3; and KERA, 1915 Minutes, 5.

11. MMB, "An Open Letter to Governor McCreary," *Maysville Public Ledger*, November 17, 1915, 4.

12. *Paducah News-Democrat*, June 1, 1916, 1; *Danville Kentucky Advocate*, June 15, 1916, 3; "Thousands See Militia March as Band Plays," *Owensboro Messenger-Inquirer*, June 25, 1916, 1; and "CRIME: Moody and Billings," *Time* 16, no. 2 (July 14, 1930).

13. Robert Booth Fowler, "Carrie Chapman Catt, Strategist," in *One Woman, One Vote*, 295–300.

14. "Suffrage Help in War," *Washington Post*, February 26, 1917, 4.

15. Weiss, *The Woman's Hour*, 92; and Zahniser and Fry, *Alice Paul*.

16. Matthew Costello, "Picketing the White House," *White House Historical Association*, April 14, 2017, https://www.whitehousehistory.org/picketing-the-white -house, accessed June 27, 2019; and "World Must Be Made Safe for Democracy," *WJ*, April 7, 1917, 80.

17. Randolph Hollingsworth, "Biographical Sketch of Christine Duncan Bradley South," BDWSM; and *Report of the Twenty-Eight and Twenty-Ninth Annual Conventions of the Kentucky Equal Rights Association, Held at Lexington, Kentucky, November 30 and December 1, 1917, and Louisville, Kentucky, March 11th and 12th, 1919* (n.p.), 5, UKSCWC (hereafter 1919 Minutes).

18. Lynn Dumenil, *The Second Line of Defense: American Women and World War I* (Chapel Hill: University of North Carolina Press, 2017); FERA meeting minutes, December 18, 1917, UKSCRC; and "Report of the Franklin County Equal Rights League," KERA, 1919 Minutes, 60.

19. Bettez, *Kentucky and the Great War*, 38–41.

20. Ibid., 90; and KERA, 1917 and 1919 Minutes, 17, 58, 60.

21. Bettez, *Kentucky and the Great War*, 44; and "Report of the Louisville Woman's Suffrage Association," KERA, 1919 Minutes, 63; and "Women's Wit in War Work," *WC*, May 11, 1918, 474.

22. Bettez, *Kentucky and the Great War*, 139; and Dumenil, *Second Line of Defense*, 99–100.

23. Carol Mattingly, "Biographical Sketch of Patty Blackburn Semple," BDWSM; and Bettez, *Kentucky and the Great War*, 146, 186.

24. KERA, 1917 Minutes, 23; and Guethlein, "Women in Louisville," 176.

25. Christine Bradley South to Miss Laura Clay, March 29, 1917, LCP, box 12, folder 21; LC to Mrs. South, April 3, 1917, LCP, box 12, folder 22.

26. Dumenil, *Second Line of Defense*, 97–98; and "Report of the Franklin County Equal Rights League," KERA, 1919 Minutes, 60.

27. KERA, 1917 Minutes, 19, 25; Bettez, *Kentucky and the Great War*, 42–44; and "Just Cause for Pride," Florence McDowell Shelby Cantrill and Mary Brinker Bryan papers, box 7, folder 8, UKSCRC.

28. KERA, 1917 Minutes, 24.

29. Graham, *Woman Suffrage and the New Democracy*, 104; KERA, 1917 Minutes, 5; and "Laura Clay Ambulance," *Maysville Public Ledger*, April 16, 1918, 3.

30. KERA, 1917 Minutes, 5–6, 12, 18.

31. "Anxiety for Louisvillians on Vacation in Europe," *LC-J*, August 1, 1914, 5.

32. "Visiting Woman Killed by Auto on Fourth," *LC-J*, June 8, 1917, 2; and "Asks Heavy Damages for Mother's Death," *Owensboro Messenger*, August 5, 1917, 7. Callahan was found not guilty in the criminal trial and was not held liable in the civil suit.

33. Emily Bingham, *Irrepressible: The Jazz Age Life of Henrietta Bingham* (New York: Farrar, Straus and Giroux, 2016), 106; and "The New Woman's Party Plan—'Trail the Administration,'" *Suffragist*, August 18, 1917, 8.

34. "Woman's Party Office Opened at Seelbach," *LC-J*, August 5, 1917, 28; Hay, *Madeline McDowell Breckinridge*, 163; and Wheeler, *New Women*, 76.

35. "Dixie Drive," *Richmond Kentucky Register*, March 23, 1917, 1; Julia D. Henning, "Does Not Favor Militancy," *LC-J*, March 21, 1917, 4; and Christine Bradley South, "An Appeal for Justice," *Danville Advocate-Messenger*, March 30, 1917, 3.

36. Ann Allen, "Biographical Sketch of Cornelia Alexander Beach," BDWSM.

37. Zahniser and Fry, *Alice Paul*, 254–97; and Allen, "Cornelia Alexander Beach."

38. "Local Woman Is Taken by Police as 'Suff' Picket," *LC-J*, August 29, 1917, 1.

39. Ibid.; "The National Woman's Party in 1917," *Suffragist*, January 5, 1918; and Allen, "Cornelia Alexander Beach."

40. Dumenil, *Second Line of Defense*, 3.

41. Bettez, *Kentucky and the Great War*, 112.

42. KERA, 1917 Minutes, 6–7; FERA meeting minutes, April 30, 1918; and Bettez, *Kentucky and the Great War*, 149.

43. "Miss Clay Talks in Bay State," *WJ*, March 10, 1917, 57.

44. Bettez, *Kentucky and the Great War*, 31, 175; and L. P. Fant, "Suffragists Make an American," *WC*, September 21, 1918, 337.

45. Peck, *Carrie Chapman Catt*, 305.

46. "Women and Democracy," *Owensboro Messenger*, June 20, 1918, 4.

12. Ignis Fatuus

1. "Our Ollie," *Asheville Citizen-Times*, June 30, 1918, 4; *Kansas Observer*, August 1918, 7; "Ollie James Crosses the Great Divide," *Stanford Interior Journal*, August 30, 1918, 4; and "Senator James," *Crittenden Record-Press*, March 14, 1918, 6.

2. "Senator Ollie James Ill with Tonsillitis," *Washington Herald*, April 20, 1918, 1; and "Still Confined to Bed in Baltimore Hospital," *Washington, D. C. Evening Star*, May 8, 1918, 22.

3. "Speeches and Remarks Opposed to Woman Suffrage during the Second Session of the Sixty-Third Congress," *The Handbook of the National American Woman Suffrage Association and Proceedings of the Forty-Sixth Annual Convention, Held at Nashville, Tenn., November 12 to 17, Inclusive, 1914* (New York: Headquarters, [1914]), 146; "Suffragists Are Hopeful after Defeat," *Wilmington (DE) Evening Journal*, March 20, 1914, 2; "Negro Vote Is Used as Argument against Granting Suffrage," *Oregon Daily Journal*, March 3, 1914, 1; and "Ollie Murray James," *Kentucky Encyclopedia*, 463.

4. Hay, *Madeline McDowell Breckinridge*, 194–96.

5. "Senator James Very Ill," *Brooklyn Citizen*, July 28, 1918, 3; "World's Eyes on U. S. Suffrage Action," *Owensboro Messenger-Inquirer*, June 25, 1918, 2; and "Postponement," *Owensboro Twice-a-Week Messenger*, July 3, 1918, 7.

6. "Senator James Passes Over," *LC-J*, August 29, 1918, 1.

7. Maud Wood Park, "Congressional Work for the Nineteenth Amendment," in Scott and Scott, *One Half the People*, 147.

8. "Ollie James Crosses the Great Divide," and "Courier-Journal becomes Suffragette," *Stanford Interior Journal*, August 30, 1918, 4.

9. "A Great Paper Won to Suffrage," *WC*, September 7, 1918, 288–89.

10. "Hearing before the Select Committee on Woman Suffrage of the United States Senate," March 27, 1908, MMBP, box 4, folder 35; LC to Mrs. Roebuck, January 1, 1909, LCP, box 8, folder 5; and Fuller, *Laura Clay*, 157.

11. LC to Rev. Anna Howard Shaw, April 2, 1909, LCP, box 8, folder 11; and LC to Mrs. McCulloch November 14, 1913, LCP, box 11, folder 18.

12. Elna C. Green, "The Rest of the Story: Kate Gordon and the Opposition to the Nineteenth Amendment in the South," *Louisiana History* 33, no. 2 (Spring 1992).

13. [KG] to Miss Clay, September 30, 1913, LCP, box 11, folder 17; and Fuller, *Laura Clay*, 140.

14. LC to Mrs. Harrison, November 30, 1914, LCP, box 12, folder 1; LC to Mrs. J. H. Douglas, February 19, 1912, LCP, box 10, folder 17; Green, *Southern Strategies*, 132–33; and LC to Mrs. McCulloch November 14, 1913, LCP, box 11, folder 18.

15. Elliot Jaspin, *Buried in the Bitter Waters: The Hidden History of Racial Cleansing in America* (New York: Basic Books, 2007).

16. "Kentucky," *WJ*, January 5, 1907, 4; LC to Mrs. McCulloch, December 13, 1907, LCP, box 7, folder 22; and "Laura Clay on Charles Sumner," *WJ*, January 14, 1893, 16.

17. 1910 US Census, ancestry.com.

18. Flexner, *Century of Struggle*, 275–77; and Graham, *Woman Suffrage and the New Democracy*, 8–9.

19. LC to Mrs. Breckinridge, April 21, 1915, LCP, box 12, folder 5; and LC to Rev. Olympia Brown, June 22, 1915, LCP, box 12, folder 7.

20. Kimberly A. Hamilton, "How Racism Almost Killed Women's Right to Vote," *Washington Post*, June 4, 2019; and "Beware! The Negro and the New Social Order," [1920], Josephine A. Pearson Papers, Tennessee Virtual Archive, https://teva.contentdm.oclc.org/digital/collection/p15138c01127/id/63/rec/24; and Graham, *Woman Suffrage and the New Democracy*, 124–26.

21. Graham, *Woman Suffrage and the New Democracy*, 85.

22. Antoinette Funk to Miss Clay, November 11, 1915, LCP, box 12, folder 9; Fuller, *Laura Clay*, 142–44; LC to Miss Grim, February 4, 1914, LCP, box 11, folder 19; Mary Jane Smith, "Laura Clay (1849–1941): States' Rights and Southern Suffrage Reform," in McEuen and Appleton, *Kentucky Women*, 134; and KERA minutes, 1895 to 1916.

23. Fuller, *Laura Clay*, 144.

24. Graham, *Woman Suffrage and the New Democracy*, 83.

25. "Report of Congressional Chairman," KERA, 1916 Minutes, 15.

26. "Mrs. Catt Here for Meetings," *LC-J*, March 27, 1916, 10.

27. Allen, "Suffrage and Progressive Reform."

28. "Says Women Held in Fear," *LC-J*, March 29, 1916, 5.

29. CCC, *Woman Suffrage by Federal Constitutional Amendment* (New York: National Woman Suffrage Publishing Co., 1917), 7, 98; and *Woman Voter* 7, no. 1 (January 1916): 8.

30. "Report of Congressional Committee," KERA, 1914 Minutes, 14–15; and Jaime Chapman and Jennifer Hanley, "Biographical Sketch of Josephine Fowler Post," BDWSM.

31. Peck, *Carrie Chapman Catt*, 257; and Christina A. Lunardini and Thomas J. Knock, "Woodrow Wilson and Woman Suffrage: A New Look," *Political Science Quarterly* 95, no. 4 (Winter 1980–1981): 662.

32. Graham, *Woman Suffrage and the New Democracy*, 86–90.

33. Smith, "Laura Clay (1849–1941)," 133–34.

34. Peck, *Carrie Chapman Catt*, 257.

35. "Platform," 1916 Minutes, 6.

36. KERA, "Report of Congressional Chairman," 1916 Minutes, 14–15; and KERA, "Report of the Louisville Woman's Suffrage Association," 1919 Minutes, 62.

37. LC to Mrs. W. M. Stoner, January 27, 1917 and LC to Mrs. McCulloch, January 24, 1917, LCP, box 12, folder 19; and Green, "The Rest of the Story," 183.

38. Fuller, *Laura Clay*, 147.

39. Graham, *Woman Suffrage and the New Democracy*, 110–11; Tracy Campbell, "James Campbell Cantrill," *Kentucky Encyclopedia*, 160; Hay, *Madeline McDowell Breckinridge*, 221; and "Report of Congressional Committee," KERA, 1919 Minutes, 50–51.

40. Keyssar, *The Right to Vote*, 214; "Miss Laura Clay Plans Retirement," *Lexington Leader*, April 28, 1912; "Cantrill May Run against Beckham," *Owensboro Messenger*, February 25, 1919, 2; and "Southerners," *Owensboro Messenger*, January 10, 1918, 8.

41. LC to Mrs. McCulloch, November 30, 1916, LCP, box 12, folder 17.

42. LC to KG, March 17, 1919, LCP, box 3, folder 17; and KERA, 1917 Minutes, 7.

43. Knott, "Woman Suffrage Movement," 267; KERA, 1916 Minutes, 6–9; and "President's Report," KERA, 1919 Minutes, 45.

44. KERA, 1919 Minutes, 45–47; Christine B. South to LC, January 16, 1918, LCP, box 12, folder 25; and CCC to Miss Clay, January 12, 1918, LCP, box 2, folder 24.

45. "President's Report," KERA, 1919 Minutes, 45–47; and MMB to Mrs. South, January 3, 1918, LCP, box 12, folder 25.

46. Hay, *Madeline McDowell Breckinridge*, 210–11; LC to Sallie Clay Bennett, January 14, 1918, quoted in Fuller, *Laura Clay*, 149; and LC to CCC, January 16, 1918, LCP, box 2, folder 24.

47. *New Orleans Item*, November 10, 1913, quoted in Green, "The Rest of the Story," 178; KG to Miss Clay, January 21, 1918 and LC to Miss Gordon, March 18, 1918, LCP, box 3, folder 15.

48. Knott, "Woman Suffrage Movement," 284, 295.

49. "War Lecture," *Paducah Sun-Democrat*, June 3, 1918, 5; "Mrs. Catt Addresses Suffrage Mass Meeting," *LC-J*, June 4, 1918, 5; and LC to Miss Gordon, June 4, 1918, LCP, box 3, folder 15.

50. Desha Breckinridge to LC, June 7, 1918, LCP, box 13, folder 3.

51. KG to Miss Clay, July 20, 1918, LCP, box 3, folder 16; LC to Mrs. South, April 13, 1918, LCP, box 13, folder 3; and LC to Mrs. Upton, May 9, 1919, LCP, box 6, folder 7.

52. KERA Executive Board Minutes, October 5, 1918, LCP, box 15, folder 8; LC to Mrs. South, October 9, 1918 and Christine Bradley South to Miss Laura, October 24, 1918, LCP, box 13, folder 4.

53. "Speech of Chief Justice John C. Anderson before Alabama Legislature July 16, 1919," MMBP, box 6, folder 44; "Woman Suffrage: Speech of Hon. George Sutherland, in the Senate of the United States," July 20, 1916, MMBP, box 5, folder 42; and "Miss Clay Gives Suffrage Views," *Lexington Herald*, June 9, 1919.

54. "Socialism, Bolshevism, Feminism, Negro Rule, and States Rights," February 1919, MMBP, box 6, folder 43.

55. KERA, 1919 Minutes, 34, 38.

56. "Suffrage Is a Certainty Next Session," *LC-J*, March 12, 1919, 1.

57. KERA, 1919 Minutes, 39.

58. Hay, *Madeline McDowell Breckinridge*, 212; and MMB, "A Mother's Sphere," May 1917, MMBP, box 5, folder 42.

59. MMB to Board Member, May 1, 1919, BFP, copy located in MPHF, box 3, folder 20; and Esta Tovstiadi, "Biographical Sketch of Jessie Leigh Hutchinson," BDWSM. For more information on Desha's affair, see Hay, *Madeline McDowell Breckinridge*, 209.

60. LC to Miss Gordon, May 28, 1919, LCP, box 3, folder 17.

61. *History of Woman Suffrage*, 5:646; and Hay, *Madeline McDowell Breckinridge*, 221.

62. LC to Miss Gordon, April 26, 1919, LCP, box 3, folder 17; and LC to Miss Gordon, June 9, 1919, LCP, box 3, folder 18.

63. "Veteran Suffrage Worker Withdraws from Association," *Paducah News-Democrat*, June 5, 1919, 9; and LC to Mrs. H. G. Foster, June 5, 1919, appended to Fayette Equal Rights Association Records, UKSCRC.

13. Twenty-Four

1. CCC to Mrs. Desha Breckinridge, June 27, 1919, BFP, copy located in MPHF, box 3, folder 21; and CCC to Mrs. Desha Breckenridge [*sic*], July 2, 1919, BFP, MPHF, box 3, folder 19.

2. "Miss Lloyd Will Meet Miss Clay in Debate at Louisville," *Maysville Public Ledger*, September 2, 1919, 1; and "Women Want to Vote Next Year," *LC-J*, June 9, 1919, 3.

3. Madge Breckinridge to Dunster [Foster], February 7, 1919, PDGFP, box 64, folder 4; Hay, *Madeline McDowell Breckinridge*, 220; and "Fayette Suffragists Reelect Miss Clay," *LC-J*, January 15, 1919, 3

4. "Local Suffragists Were 'On the Job,'" *Richmond Daily Register*, May 16, 1919, 1.

5. LC to KG, April 15, 1920, LCP, box 3, folder 17; Green, "The Rest of the Story," 183; and LC to KG, June 9, 1919, LCP, box 3, folder 18.

6. "Open Letter to the Public," [June 11, 1919], signed by Alice Bronston Oldham, Laura Clay, Dunster Gibson Foster, Elizabeth Burgess McQuaid, PDGFP, box 64, folder 3.

7. LC to KG, June 9, 1919 and June 13, 1919, LCP, box 3, folder 18; and Citizens Committee meeting minutes, [June 12, 1919], LCP, box 15, folder 4.

8. Mary Scrugham to MMB, n.d., BFP, MPHF, box 3, folder 102.

9. *History of Kentucky*, vol. 4, ed. Judge Charles Kerr (Chicago: American Historical Society, 1922): 377–79; Mrs. Harrison G. Foster to Governor Burnquist, June 19, 1919, PDGFP, box 161, folder 15; and Molly Morris, "Women Feeling Sure of Suffrage Help," *Chicago Daily News*, June 12, 1916, PDGFP, box 64, folder 5.

10. Hay, *Madeline McDowell Breckinridge*, 220; and "Women Want Suffrage Submitted to the People," *LC-J*, June 13, 1919, 7.

11. "In Interest of State Suffrage," *Wilmore Enterprise*, August 28, 1919, PDGFP, box 64, folder 5; MMB to Mrs. Catt, December 15, 1919, BFP, MPHF, box 3, folder 12; and Mary Scrugham to MMB, n.d., BFP, MPHF, box 3, folder 102.

12. "Miss Clay Gives Suffrage Views," *Lexington Herald*, June 9, 1919; and "Women Win Out on Fight to Get O. K. on U. S. Vote," *LC-J*, September 5, 1919, 3.

13. Scott and Scott, *One Half the People*, 45; LC to KG, June 13, 1919 and April 15, 1920, LCP, box 3, folder 19; and J. H. Callan to Miss Laura Clay, June 20, 1919, LCP, box 13, folder 9.

14. Mrs. Harrison G. Foster to Governor Burnquist, June 19, 1919, PDGFP, box 161, folder 15; "Prominent Advocates of Woman Suffrage Visit Paris," *Bourbon News*, August 15, 1919, 1; and Alice Bronston Oldham to Miss Laura [Clay], August 5, [1919], LCP, box 13, folder 11.

15. "Most of Kentucky's Congressmen Favor Ratification of Suffrage," *LC-J*, July 5, 1919, 4; *Tennesseean*, July 6, 1919, 14; and CCC to Mrs. Desha Breckenridge, July 2, 1919, BFP, MPHF, box 3, folder 19.

16. Heather Kuzma, "Biographical Sketch of Mary Scrugham," BDWSM; "Mountains Organized by Suffrage Leaders," *LC-J*, July 12, 1919, 5; and "Kentucky," *WC*, November 15, 1919, 489.

17. Breckinridge, *Madeline McDowell Breckinridge*, 235.

18. LC to James D. Black, June 21, 1919, LCP, box 13, folder 9; *Woman Patriot*, July 26, 1919, 3; and "Citizens Committee's Fourteen Points against the Susan B. Anthony Federal Amendment," PDGFP, box 64, folder 3.

19. "Miss Clay Won't Go as Delegate," *Richmond Daily Register*, September 3, 1919, 1; "This Week in Ratification," *WC*, September 13, 1919, 361; and "Statement of Principles Adopted by Democrats for State Campaign," *Owensboro Messenger*, September 6, 1919, 4.

20. "Women Win Out in Fight to Get O. K. on U. S. Vote," *LC-J*, September 5, 1919, 3.

21. Alice Lloyd to LC, October 22, 1919, quoted in Fuller, *Laura Clay*, 157; and Harriet Taylor Upton to Miss Laura Clay, May 21, 1919, LCP, box 6, folder 7.

22. Hay, *Madeline McDowell Breckinridge*, 222; and "Miss Lloyd Will Meet Miss Clay in Debate at Louisville," *Maysville Public Ledger*, September 2, 1919, 1.

23. "Debate before the Woman's Club of Central Kentucky," October 18, 1919, PDGFP, box 64, folder 4.

24. Ibid.

25. Mrs. Desha Breckinridge, "Suffrage by Amendment versus the States Rights Route," *LC-J*, January 4, 1920, 20.

26. Ibid.

27. Breckinridge, *Madeline McDowell Breckinridge*, 218–19.

28. MMB, "A Mother's Sphere" (National Woman Suffrage Publishing Company, Inc., May 1917), MMB papers, box 5, folder 42.

29. MMB to Mrs. Catt, December 15, 1919, BFP, MPHF, box 3, folder 12; and MMB to Mrs. Catt, December 20, 1919, BFP, MPHF, box 3, folder 13.

30. Scott and Scott, *One Half the People*, 45.

31. Mrs. Desha Breckinridge, "The Suffrage Victory in Kentucky," *Lexington Herald Magazine*, March 14, 1920, PDGFP, box 64, folder 5; and MMB to Mrs. Catt, December 20, 1919, BFP, MPHF, box 3, folder 13.

32. "Riotous Scenes in Front of White House," *Owensboro Messenger*, January 2, 1919, 1; "Wilson Burned in Effigy: Sixty-Five Women Are Arrested," *LC-J*, February 10, 1919, 4; and "Kentucky Suffragettes Sound Wilson's Praise," *Owensboro Messenger*, March 12, 1919, 1.

33. MMB to Mrs. Catt, December 20, 1919, BFP, MPHF, box 3, folder 13.

34. "Kentucky," *The History of Woman Suffrage*, vol. 6, *1900–1920*, ed. Ida Husted Harper, 214, "Governor Morrow to Establish Precedents," *Bourbon News*, January 2, 1920, 2.

35. *Biennial Message of Governor Edwin P. Morrow before the General Assembly of Kentucky* (Frankfort: s.n., 1920).

36. Breckinridge, *Madeline McDowell Breckinridge*, 231–32.

37. "Overwhelming Vote Given in Both Houses," *Lexington Herald*, January 7, 1920, 1, 3; and "Organization News," *WC*, January 24, 1920, 764.

38. "State Steps into the Suffrage Line," *Owensboro Messenger-Inquirer*, January 7, 1920, 2; and Hay, *Madeline McDowell Breckinridge*, 227.

14. An Instrument to Help Humanity

1. Breckinridge, *Madeline McDowell Breckinridge*, 235–36; and MMB to CCC, December 20, 1919, LOC, MPHF, box 3, folder 13.

2. "Women Voters' League Formed," *LC-J*, January 8, 1920, 5.

3. Ibid.

4. CCC to Mrs. Desha Breckenridge [*sic*], December 11, 1919, BFP, MPHF, box 3, folder 18.

5. LC to Mrs. Breckinridge, [March 17, 1920], BFP, MPHF, box 3, folder 95; and "Kentucky," *History of Woman Suffrage*, 6:207–15.

6. "Debate before the Woman's Club of Central Kentucky"; LC to A. O. Stanley, May 29, 1919, LCP, box 13, folder 8; and LC to J. M. Carey, August 11, 1919, LCP, box 13, folder 11.

7. "Miss Laura Clay Wins Big Point in House," *Richmond Daily Register*, February 11, 1920, 1; LC to Miss Gordon, February 20, 1920, LCP, box 3, folder 19; MMB to Mrs. Catt, February 7, 1920, BFP, MPHF, box 3, folder 40; and "Organization News," *WC*, February 7 1920, 820.

8. "G. O. P. Planning Strong Fight," *Danville Advocate-Messenger*, March 4, 1920, 1; "1920 Suffrage Victory Year," *LC-J*, December 26, 1920, 25; "Organization News," *WC*, January 24, 1920, 764; and "Women Greeted to Both Parties," *LC-J*, January 7, 1920, 3.

9. "Autobiography," appended to "Negro Woman Sits as Delegate in Kentucky Republican Convention," reprinted from *New York Age*, March 13, 1920, 1, Women's

Suffrage in Tennessee Digital Collection, Tennessee Virtual Archive, https://cdm15138.contentdm.oclc.org/digital/collection/p15138c01127/id/900/rec/1; and Terborg-Penn, *African American Women*, 150.

10. "160 Women to Be Delegates," *Buffalo Evening News*, May 25, 1920, 4.

11. "Women Exult in Power in Party," *LC-J*, June 27, 1920, 1; and "Half a Vote," *WC*, May 15, 1920, 1254.

12. "To the Manhood of the Democratic Party," *San Francisco Examiner*, July 1, 1920, 11; and "First of Sex to Get Vote as President," *LC-J*, July 6, 1920, 3.

13. "Democratic Speaking at Ruddles Mills," *Bourbon News*, October 22, 1920, 1; "Kentucky Woman Actual Head," *St. Louis Post-Dispatch*, June 7, 1920, 3; "Mrs. Christine Bradley South," *Wausau Daily Herald*, August 28, 1920, 3; and "Big Crowds Hear Speakers in Eastern Kentucky," *Maysville Public Ledger*, September 23, 1920, 4.

14. "Citizenship Class Meets at City Hall," *Owensboro Messenger*, March 13, 1920, 2; "I See in *The Courier-Journal*," April 3, 1920, 4; and "Citizenship School," *WC*, February 7, 1920, 824.

15. "Women's Citizenship Classes," *Crisis* 21, no. 1 (November 1920): 23; and "Race Issue Looms Large as Negroes Present Demands," *Owensboro Messenger*, October 24, 1920, 13.

16. "The Balance of Power," *Owensboro Messenger*, September 22, 1920, 6.

17. "4832 Democrats, 4269 Republicans March Up to Polls," *Owensboro Messenger*, October 6, 1920, 1, 9.

18. Ibid.

19. "Beckham," *Kentucky Irish American*, August 21, 1920, 1.

20. "Democrats Look to Women to Give Kentucky Victory," *Owensboro Messenger*, October 21, 1920, 3.

21. "Women in Fayette Are Enthusiastic," [*Lexington Herald*, September 1920], copy found in the Florence McDowell Shelby Cantrill and Mary Brinker Bryan Papers, box 7, folder 8, UKSCRC.

22. "Suffragists Get Ready to Fight for Amendment," *Danville Advocate-Messenger* (reprinted from *Louisville Times*), December 27, 1919, 1.

23. Weiss, *The Woman's Hour*, 94–99.

24. Ibid., 30, 68.

25. Ibid., 315.

26. Keyssar, *The Right to Vote*, 218; Weiss, *The Woman's Hour*, 325; "Election Passes Off Quietly," *Richmond Daily Register*, November 2, 1920, 1; and "Quietest Election in History of Daviess County," *Owensboro Messenger*, November 3, 1920, 3.

27. "Town Gossip," *Paducah Sun-Democrat*, November 4, 1920, 9.

28. "My Old Kentucky Home" parody is quoted in Hay, *Madeline McDowell Breckinridge*, 229.

29. Ibid., 231–35.

30. Ibid., 235–36; and Breckinridge, *Madeline McDowell Breckinridge*, 242.

31. "She Is Dead," *Lexington Herald*, November 28, 1920, copy located in Maude Ward Lafferty papers, scrapbook no. 2, UKSCRC; and Breckinridge, *Madeline McDowell Breckinridge*, viii.

Epilogue

1. Alice Bronston Oldham to Florence Cantrill, December 25, 1920, Cantrill/Bryan Papers, box 5, folder 1.

2. "Women in Fayette Are Enthusiastic," [*Lexington Herald*, September 1920], Cantrill/Bryan Papers, box 7, folder 8;

3. Tracy A. Campbell, "Florence McDowell (Shelby) Cantrill," *Kentucky Encyclopedia*, 160.

4. "Miss Clay Disapproves Action of Legislature," *Nashville Tennessean*, August 24, 1920, 7; "Women Voters of State to Organize at Meeting Today," *Danville Advocate-Messenger*, December 15, 1920, 1; Smith, "Laura Clay (1849–1941)," 135; and Sara Wilson and Jennifer Walton-Hanley, "Biographical Sketch of Mary Edmunds Bronaugh," BDWSM.

5. Fuller, *Laura Clay*, 162–63; and LC to Mrs. Upton, November 18, 1921, LCP, box 6, folder 7.

6. Wheeler, *New Women*, 182; and John M. Murphy, "Laura Clay, 1849–1941: A Southern Voice for Woman's Rights," *Women Public Speakers in the United States, 1800–1925: A Bio-critical Sourcebook*, ed. Karlyn Kohrs Campbell (Westport, CT: Greenwood, 1993), 106–7. The word "male" remained in Kentucky's constitution until it was amended to lower the voting age from twenty-one to eighteen in 1955. See Ireland, *The Kentucky State Constitution*, 133–34.

7. Rebecca S. Hanly, "Emma Guy Cromwell and Mary Elliot Flanery: Pioneers for Women in Kentucky Politics," *Register of the Kentucky Historical Society* 99 (Summer 2001).

8. Ibid.

9. Penny M. Miller, "Staking Their Claim: The Impact of Kentucky Women in the Political Process," *Kentucky Law Journal* 84, no. 4 (1995–1996): 1165; Ashley Lopez, "Kentucky Earns 'D' Grade for Political Participation among Women, Study Says," WFPL, May 26, 2015, https://wfpl.org/kentucky-earns-d-grade-for-political-participation-among-women-study-says/; and "Women Need More Seats at Kentucky's Legislative Table," *LC-J*, August 24, 2018.

10. Miller, "Staking Their Claim," 1168.

11. Lichtman, *Embattled Vote*, 3–7; and Casey Cep, "The Imperfect, Unfinished Work of Woman Suffrage," *New Yorker*, July 8 and 15, 2019, https://www.newyorker.com/magazine/2019/07/08/the-imperfect-unfinished-work-of-womens-suffrage.

12. LC to Alice Stone Blackwell, June 9, 1931, NAWSA Papers, reel 5, quoted in Graham, *Woman Suffrage and the New Democracy*, 163–64.

Further Reading

To understand the national suffrage scene:

Weiss, Elaine. *The Woman's Hour: The Great Fight to Win the Vote.* New York: Viking, 2018.

DuBois, Ellen Carol. *Suffrage: Women's Long Battle for the Vote.* New York: Simon & Schuster, 2020.

Terborg-Penn, Rosalyn. *African American Women in the Struggle for the Vote, 1850–1920.* Bloomington: Indiana University Press, 1998.

Tetrault, Lisa. *The Myth of Seneca Falls: Memory and the Women's Suffrage Movement, 1848–1898.* Chapel Hill: University of North Carolina Press, 2014.

To better understand the Kentucky movement:

Fuller, Paul E. *Laura Clay and the Woman's Rights Movement.* Lexington: UPK, 1975.

Hay, Melba Porter. *Madeline McDowell Breckinridge and the Battle for a New South.* Lexington: UPK, 2009.

McEuen, Melissa A., and Thomas H. Appleton Jr., eds. *Kentucky Women: Their Lives and Times.* Athens: University of Georgia Press, 2015.

Niedermeier, Lynn E. *Eliza Calvert Hall: Kentucky Author and Suffragist.* Lexington: UPK, 2007.

To learn about suffrage in your own community:

Kentucky Equal Rights Association Annual Minutes, digitized at https://exploreuk.uky.edu/

Kentucky Woman Suffrage Project, H-Kentucky, https://networks.h-net.org/KyWomanSuffrage

Kentucky Woman Suffrage Project, http://www.kentuckywomansuffrageproject.org/

Abbreviations

AWSA	American Woman Suffrage Association
BDWSM	Biographical Database of NAWSA Suffragists, 1890–1920, *Women and Social Movements in the United States*, Alexander Street Press, https://documents.alexanderstreet.com/c/1009677121
BFP	Breckinridge Family Papers, Library of Congress Manuscript Division, Washington, DC
CCC	Carrie Chapman Catt
CCP	Cassius Marcellus Clay Papers, Filson Historical Society, Louisville, Kentucky
ECS	Elizabeth Cady Stanton
JKH	Josephine K. Henry
KERA	Kentucky Equal Rights Association
KG	Kate Gordon
LC	Laura Clay
LC-J	*Louisville Courier-Journal*
LCP	Laura Clay Papers, Special Collections Research Center, Margaret I. King Library, University of Kentucky, Lexington, Kentucky
LERA	Louisville Equal Rights Association
LOC	Library of Congress
MBC	Mary Barr Clay
MMB	Madeline McDowell Breckinridge
MMBP	Madeline McDowell Breckinridge Papers, Special Collections Research Center, Margaret I. King Library, University of Kentucky, Lexington, Kentucky
MPHF	Melba Porter Hay Research Files, Special Collections Research Center, Margaret I. King Library, University of Kentucky, Lexington, Kentucky
NAWSA	National American Woman Suffrage Association
NWP	National Woman's Party

NWSA   National Woman Suffrage Association
PDGFP   Pettit, Duncan, Gibson Family Papers, Special Collections
          Research Center, Margaret I. King Library, University of
          Kentucky, Lexington, Kentucky
SBA   Susan B. Anthony
UKSCRC   Special Collections Research Center, Margaret I. King
          Library, University of Kentucky, Lexington, Kentucky
UPK   University Press of Kentucky
WC   *Woman Citizen*
WJ   *Woman's Journal*

Index